BARRON'S HOW TO PREPARE FOR THE GRE ADVANCED PSYCHOLOGY TEST

UPDATE

This is a new, exclusive feature of Barron's test preparation series. When changes are made in the GRE examination, we will furnish you with information on these changes. It is our attempt to provide you with the most up-to-date information available and to offer you the most complete preparation for the examination.

GRE National Test Dates

REGISTRATION DEADLINE	TESTING DATES
September 17, 1981	October 17, 1981*
November 6, 1981	December 12, 1981
December 31, 1981	February 6, 1982
March 19, 1982	April 24, 1982*
May 7, 1982	June 12, 1982†

IN NEW YORK STATE: Only the following Advanced Tests are offered: Biology, Chemistry, Education, Engineering, Literature in English, and Psychology.

*IN NEW YORK STATE: Six Advanced Tests only will be offered on this date. The Aptitude Test will *not* be offered.

†IN NEW YORK STATE: No GRE tests will be offered on this date.
  IN OTHER STATES: The Aptitude Test only will be offered on this date.

© Copyright 1980 Barron's Educational Series, Inc.      0-8120-0530-9

BARRON'S HOW TO PREPARE FOR THE GRADUATE RECORD EXAMINATION— ADVANCED PSYCHOLOGY TEST

by
Dr. Edward L. Palmer
Associate Professor of Psychology
Davidson College
Davidson, North Carolina

Woodbury, New York • London • Toronto
Barron's Educational Series, Inc.

© Copyright 1978 by Barron's Educational Series, Inc.

All rights reserved.
No part of this book may be reproduced
in any form, by photostat, microfilm, xerography,
or any other means, or incorporated into any
information retrieval system, electronic or
mechanical, without the written permission
of the copyright owner.

All inquiries should be addressed to:
Barron's Educational Series, Inc.
113 Crossways Park Drive
Woodbury, New York 11797

Library of Congress Catalog Card No. 77-12747

International Standard Book No. 0-8120-0530-9

Library of Congress Cataloging in Publication Data
Palmer, Edward L.
  Barron's how to prepare for the graduate record
examination advanced psychology test.
  1. Psychology — Examinations, questions, etc.
2. Graduate record examination.   I. Title.   II. Title:
How to prepare for the graduate record examination
advanced psychology test.
BF78.P34   150'.7'6   77-12747
ISBN 0-8120-0530-9

PRINTED IN THE UNITED STATES OF AMERICA

Contents

	Acknowledgments	vi
	Preface	vii
Chapter 1	**The Advanced Psychology Test**	1
	Purpose	1
	Application Procedure	1
	Format of the Test	1
	Test-taking Strategy	2
	Scoring	2
	Preparing for the Test	2
Chapter 2	**Advanced Psychology Review**	5
	About the Review	5
	Physiological and Comparative Psychology	6
	Sensation and Perception	8
	Learning	14
	Cognition and Complex Human Learning	15
	Developmental Psychology	19
	Motivation and Emotion	22
	Social Psychology	24
	Personality	37
	Psychopathology	42
	Clinical Psychology	44
	Methodology	49
	Applied Psychology	57
	Sources for Further Reading	61
Chapter 3	**Sample Tests**	65
	How to Use the Sample Tests	65
	Test 1	69
	Test 1: Answer Comments	93
	Evaluating Your Score	103
	Test 2	107
	Test 2: Answer Comments	131
	Evaluating Your Score	140
	Test 3	145
	Test 3: Answer Comments	170
	Evaluating Your Score	179
	Test 4	183
	Test 4: Answer Comments	208
	Evaluating Your Score	217
	Test 5	221
	Test 5: Answer Comments	245
	Evaluating Your Score	254

Acknowledgments

I want to express deep appreciation to my immediate family — Ruth-Ann, Eddie, and Jennifer. They knew my pressures, gave generous support, and made our brief times together very special. In addition, the patient secretarial help of Mrs. Sara Penland, Mrs. Jane Biggerstaff, and Ms. Nancy Arnette made it all possible.

Preface

There is no substitute for study in preparing for any examination. *Barron's How to Prepare for the Graduate Record Examination Advanced Psychology Test* is a study guide, designed to aid you in your test preparation by providing general information on testing purposes and procedures, establishing the areas in psychology on which you should concentrate for best results, and enabling you to become more familiar with the actual test by offering five sample tests with answers to check your progress.

The first chapter gives general information about the test including an explanation of its purpose, directions on how to apply, the format of the test, test-taking strategy, and how the test is scored. There is also a section on test preparation and how to make best use of this book.

Chapter 2, a comprehensive review of the main areas covered on the test, includes discussions of physiological and comparative psychology, sensation and perception, learning, cognition and complex human learning, developmental psychology, motivation and emotion, social psychology, personality, psychopathology, clinical psychology, methodology, and applied psychology. This review, along with the sources for further reading appearing at the end of the chapter, should serve as the basis for your study. By using this information as a starting point, you will be able to touch on all the major areas of psychology, concentrating on those topics you are least familiar with.

The third chapter consists of five sample tests, modeled after the actual GRE Advanced Psychology Test, with answers and answer explanations. By simulating the conditions of the real test as you take these sample tests, you can judge how well you will do.

Used properly, *Barron's How to Prepare for the Graduate Record Examination Advanced Psychology Test* can be very helpful to you in your test preparation. If at the conclusion of your review you have developed confidence in your ability to do well on this test, it will have served its purpose well.

CHAPTER ONE
The Advanced Psychology Test

Purpose

The Graduate Record Examination (GRE) Advanced Psychology Test, administered by the Educational Testing Service (ETS), is used by graduate admissions committees to assess and select applicants for graduate programs in psychology, and to determine the recipients of scholarships, fellowships, and various other academic awards.

Due to the large number of applicants for graduate study in psychology, it is often difficult for graduate schools to compare the qualifications of all the candidates for admission to their psychology programs. The Advanced Psychology Test, taken by nearly all applicants, serves as a common denominator. While it seldom is the sole criterion for an admission or rejection, the Advanced Psychology Test is an important factor in the admissions decision. When considered along with information such as each candidate's undergraduate program and grade average, it can give the graduate school a good idea of the individual's capabilities and chances for success in graduate study.

Application Procedure

Students interested in taking the Advanced Psychology Test should send for the *GRE Information Bulletin*, published by ETS. The *Bulletin* contains information about application deadlines, exam dates, fee schedules, and testing locations, along with the necessary test registration forms. It can be obtained by writing:

Graduate Record Examinations
Box 955
Princeton, New Jersey 08540

The Advanced Psychology Test is usually given in October, December, January, April, and June. Since the competition for places in graduate psychology programs is intense, you would be wise to take the examination as early as possible to ensure that your scores are reported to the schools of your choice in plenty of time to receive full consideration.

Format of the Test

The Advanced Psychology Test is a multiple-choice examination consisting of 200 questions, each with five possible answer choices. Some questions will involve the interpretation of graphs, diagrams, and reading passages; others will require you to directly recall information gathered from your psychology courses. The test runs for 170 minutes, and as there are no separately timed sections, you may set your own pace as you work through the questions.

Test-Taking Strategy

It is important to remember that the Advanced Psychology Test has been designed in such a way that even those students who achieve the highest scores will not answer every question correctly. The questions you may find difficult are not worth any more points than those that come easily to you, so make sure that you answer all the questions you are sure about before going back to tackle the harder ones.

Guessing

"Should I guess?" is one of the most common questions asked by students taking standardized tests. In the scoring of the GRE Advanced Psychology Test, correct answers count one point, incorrect answers are minus ¼ point, and unanswered questions neither add to nor detract from the total score:

correct answers − ¼ # incorrect answers = total score

Since each question has five possible answers, statistically you have a one in five chance of correctly answering a question in which you cannot eliminate even one of the possible answers. The more choices you can eliminate, of course, the better are the odds of your guessing the right answer. So, since you only lose ¼ point for a wrong answer, guessing will very likely work to your benefit if you can eliminate at least one possible choice. On the other hand, it is very unlikely that guessing will prove detrimental to your total score as long as you refrain from guessing indiscriminately.

Scoring

Each student who takes the Advanced Psychology Test will receive 3 scaled scores: a total score for the entire test, an Experimental Psychology subscore, and a Social Psychology subscore. The Total Score will range from 200 to 990, with a score of approximately 530 constituting an average performance. The subscores are reported on a scale of 20 to 99, with a score of approximately 53 constituting the mean. The scores are reported on a scaled basis to enable the ETS and graduate admissions committees to directly compare performances across different administrations of the test. The scale acts as a yardstick by which all scores on the Advanced Psychology Test can be compared, regardless of the test date or the form of the test taken. Score interpretation information is contained in the booklet *A Description of the Advanced Psychology Test*, which is sent by the ETS to all test applicants. Be sure to retain this booklet so that you may accurately interpret your scores when you receive them.

Preparing for the Test

Psychology is a very broad subject, as you are already aware. This breadth gives the field interest, but at the same time means that preparation for a test such as the Advanced

Psychology Test will require you to refamiliarize yourself with a wide range of material and concepts. There is no way to determine exactly how much test coverage will be given to each of the areas within the discipline. Proportionate area coverage will vary slightly from one examination to the next, although the areas being tested will remain constant. In a recent administration, the percentages of material devoted to the respective area concentrations were as follows:

Physiological and comparative psychology	13.6%
Developmental psychology	12.2%
Learning and motivation	12.2%
Sensation and perception	12.2%
Clinical psychology and psychopathology	10.8%
Personality and social psychology	10.8%
Cognition and complex human learning	10.0%
Applied psychology	9.1%
Methodology	9.1%

Each of the above topic areas contains a central core of material that will demand your competence. Also, since psychology is an active research field, major current studies will be of prominent interest to the psychologists who construct the GRE questions. A comprehensive introductory psychology textbook can provide an excellent starting point for your psychology review. Titles in this category are John Darley, Sam Glucksberg, Leon Kamin, and Ronald Kinchla's *Psychology* (Englewood Cliffs, New Jersey: Prentice-Hall, 1981), Henry Gleitman's *Psychology* (New York: Norton, 1981), Philip Zimbardo's *Psychology and Life* (Glenview, Illinois: Scott, Foresman, 1979), Clifford Morgan and Richard King's *Introduction to Psychology* (New York: McGraw-Hill, 1979), and Ernest R. Hilgard, Richard C. Atkinson, and Rita L. Atkinson's *Introduction to Psychology* (New York: Harcourt Brace Jovanovich, Inc., 1979).

How to Use This Book

Barron's How to Prepare for the GRE Advanced Psychology Test has been designed to help you review for the Advanced Psychology Test, while you are at the same time familiarizing yourself with the test format and the types of questions used on the test. Chapter 2 of this book contains a comprehensive review of the basic areas of knowledge covered by the test. Chapter 3 consists of five model tests, including answers and explanations for each of the questions. These tests simulate the actual Advanced Psychology Test in both number of questions, type of questions, and time allotted. By studying the material in Chapter 2 and testing your knowledge on the five practice examinations, you will develop a familiarity with the Advanced Psychology Test which will bolster your confidence when taking the test and, most important of all, let you earn the highest score you can.

It should be stressed here that *How to Prepare for the GRE Advanced Psychology Test* is *not* intended to take the place of an extensive review of your college psychology courses. For an examination such as the Advanced Psychology Test, where specific knowledge is tested, it would be impossible to cover all the pertinent review material in a book of this size. *You* must decide what you need to concentrate on most heavily and how much time you will need to adequately complete your review. This book can help by showing you where your weaknesses lie. By taking one of the practice exams at an early point in your review schedule, you will be able to see which areas give you the most trouble and then devote extra time to strengthening your knowledge of those particular areas.

Here are a few suggestions to help you get the most from this book:

- Don't try to cram your review into a few short evenings — give yourself enough time.
- Utilize as many review sources as you feel are necessary.
- Try to simulate the actual exam as you take each practice test (170 minutes per test, no looking at notes or other study aids).

- Learn from your mistakes. The answers and explanations included in this book are geared toward pointing out your weaknesses so that you may strengthen them.

By using this book throughout your review, in conjunction with other review materials, we feel that you will be well on your way to achieving a better score on the GRE Advanced Psychology Test.

CHAPTER TWO
Advanced Psychology Review

About the Review

This section presents a review of the major subject areas contained in the Advanced Psychology Test and is designed to provide you with the basis for your exam preparation.

Start by reading through the entire section, spending more time in the areas you might not be as familiar with. After you have finished, take a sample test. Evaluate your score to determine which areas need more review. Then return to these sections for additional work. Use the *Sources for Further Reading* at the end of the review to find other books dealing with the topics you want to spend more time on.

The subject areas covered by the Advanced Psychology Test and included in this review are:

- Physiological and comparative psychology
- Sensation and perception
- Learning
- Cognition and complex human learning
- Developmental psychology
- Motivation and emotion
- Social psychology
- Personality
- Psychopathology
- Clinical psychology
- Methodology
- Applied psychology

Topics are arranged in a continuum starting with the basic elements of behavior and brain function (physiological aspects of psychology) and moving toward a consideration of the whole person (clinical, social, and applied psychology). This arrangement enables you to see the basic interrelationship of all aspects of psychology and points up the need for an overall comprehension of the entire subject area in order to understand the value of each topic. At the onset of your review you will find that you are more familiar with some of the areas than with others; our mutual goal is to have all of them sounding very familiar to you by the time you take the Advanced Psychology Test.

A standardized test such as this will not necessarily correspond with the emphasis that you encountered during your studies in the field of psychology. Therefore, if you were trained in the "whole-person-centered" approach you will now need to concentrate on the physiological, basic experimental, and methodological sides of psychology. If, on the other hand, you are thoroughly grounded in experimental design, statistics, and the animal laboratory, you will have to work on the personality, clinical, and developmental aspects of the field. Finally, if you have received a balanced education, a general review to sharpen the knowledge you already have will be your best approach.

During your review, keep in mind that for each subject area you will be expected to exhibit a mastery of basic principles and concepts (theories and laws, if the area has any), names of persons associated with the better-known concepts and research, and primary research findings. By concentrating on these aspects in each review area, you will soon gain a clearer understanding both of the individual areas and of the science of psychology as a whole.

Physiological and Comparative Psychology

When you have completed this section of the review, you should be quite familiar with such names as Delgado, Olds, Penfield, and Krech, and definitions relating to parts of the brain, the glands, and the nervous system should be as familiar as your best friend's favorite meal. Much is happening in physiological and comparative psychology today, and it is impossible to be in on the excitement unless you know the playing field and the game rules. Mastery of key names and definitions will prepare you to share the action and perhaps even contribute to it — as well as tell the Educational Testing Service that you know what it's all about.

Physiological Psychology

The brain, as "mission control" in the central nervous system, works very closely with muscles and glands. Thus, the function and contribution of each to the total picture is critically important. To familiarize you with "mission control," any of the comprehensive introductory textbooks mentioned earlier would be helpful. With so much material to cover, it would be easy to get bogged down in a mountain of names, functions, and small details. You will not, of course, be expected to have a Ph.D.'s competence in physiology in order to pass the Advanced Psychology Test, but you should understand the basics and the function of physiology within behavior.

To guide this aspect of your review, I shall list some terms and concepts with which you should be familiar. Then, I shall ask several questions designed to help you either confirm your knowledge or head for more review.

- Neuron
- Distinction between central nervous system and peripheral nervous system
- Distinction between receptors and effectors (and corresponding words such as sensory, afferent fibers and motor, efferent fibers)
- Dendrite, axon, synapse
- Autonomic nervous system (and its subdivisions into sympathetic and parasympathetic)
- Brain hemispheres and the four lobes within each — frontal, temporal, parietal, and occipital — with knowledge of what general behavioral functions each area encompasses
- Distinction between cortex and subcortex
- Terms such as fissure of Rolando, fissure of Sylvius, thalamus, hypothalamus, reticular formation, limbic system, hippocampus, neurotransmitters, acetylcholine, epinephrine, norepinephrine, serotonin, thyroxin, blood-brain barrier
- Distinction among striated (voluntary), smooth (visceral), and heart muscles
- Location and function of endocrine glands — pineal, anterior and posterior pituitary, thyroid, parathyroid, thymus, adrenal medulla and adrenal cortex, and ovaries/testes

You need not spend time and energy on terms such as brachial plexus, ventral nerve root, and the like. Your time is limited, and your goal is basic understanding.

Research activity associated with the area you have been studying includes such abbreviations as ESB and EMG. The first abbreviation stands for electrical stimulation of the brain, an area in which Olds has been very active at the animal level while Delgado has come to prominence at the human level. Olds has investigated pleasure centers in the hypothalamus, finding that a rat will happily send electric current to these centers hour after hour. In the human spectrum, Delgado raises the possibility of helping people avert depression or aggressive behavior, for instance, by teaching them to recognize signals that accompany the onset of these problems and to stimulate their own brains via implanted electrodes. The possibilities are fascinating and thought-provoking, and your familiarity with such work is essential.

Other brain-stimulation researchers have examined behavioral effects in such areas as the control of feeding and drinking, sexual behavior, and emotion-based responses. Through ESB, Hoebel has produced eating behavior in completely satiated animals; similar drinking behavior has been produced by Miller, et al. Fisher has been able to obtain mating and maternal sexual behaviors in male animals, while Delgado has convincingly demonstrated that the dominant animal in a colony can become quite submissive under certain conditions. Additional names that will be important to you in this area include Valenstein (brain stimulation and psychosurgery), Sperry Gazzaniga (split-brain operations) and Magoun (reticular formation).

EMG refers to the electromyograph, an instrument designed to enable a person to monitor such bodily functions as his or her own blood pressure or heart rate. Neal Miller and his associates have had surprising success with experiments in this area; their findings indicate that individuals can control functions previously thought entirely involuntary. You may know the area as "bio-feedback," and you should definitely be familiar with it when you take the GRE.

To continue your review, you should now refer to one of the recent introductory textbooks mentioned above and delve into some of the readings recommended there. In the general area, a classic article that you may find helpful is W. Penfield's "The Interpretive Cortex" (*Science*, 1959, pp. 1719–25). General sources that you will find valuable for tuning in to current developments include *Annual Editions: Readings in Psychology* (Guilford, Ct.: Dushkin Publishing) and the monthly issues of *Psychology Today*. Indeed, such sources will be helpful to you throughout your work in the various topic areas covered in this book. *Scientific American* may be an equally valuable source — especially the issue featuring brain research (September, 1979) now available as a paperback book *(The Brain)* from Freeman Publishing.

Another brain-related area with which you will need to be familiar involves brain waves. With the development of the electroencephalograph (EEG), a whole new area of research work unfolded. The EEG revealed distinctions among brain waves and their relationship to general bodily activity. The EEG capability also set the stage for sleep research, which is in current prominence. Basic knowledge you will need in this area includes an understanding of:

- Alpha, beta, delta, and theta waves (the types of activity and the general wave frequency associated with each)
- Stages of sleep (their sequence and frequency)
- Dreams (their relationship to sleep stages, their frequency, and bodily functioning, such as REM, that accompanies them)

Again, the appropriate section of one of the basic textbooks mentioned will be helpful to you in obtaining an initial grasp of the above information.

A closely related area involves such questions as the effect of drugs upon sleep patterns. A general understanding of the terms *stimulant* and *depressant*, and a familiarity with the major names appearing in each category would be helpful. Many introductory works now devote an entire chapter to "altered states of consciousness," including a discussion of the effects of "mind-expanding" drugs. Because it reflects prominent current interest and concern, this area can be expected to be covered on the GRE.

Virtually no aspect of our behavior can be divorced from its neuroanatomy and physiology, and this fact becomes especially apparent in the area of learning and memory. A knowledge of neurotransmitters and their function in memory trace will be critically important. Lindsay and Norman's chapter entitled "Neural Basis of Memory" can provide an excellent introductory orientation to this area.

Equally important to your thorough review of physiology will be some knowledge in the following areas:

- Relationships between hormonal secretions and behavior
- The neuroendocrine system
- The physiology and neuroanatomy of sexual behavior

In addition, a basic understanding of the physiology of sense organs will prepare you for your upcoming review of sensation and perception.

Comparative Psychology

Comparative psychology centers upon the evolution of behavior. Dewsbury and Rethlingshafer indicate its panoramic definition to be "the systematic study of everything every species does or is capable of doing." Through reasonable limitations upon the number of organisms studied, however, it has become "a broad, but manageable, science of behavior." Within this basic definitional framework, researchers attempt to describe and explain species differences and similarities with regard to all aspects of behavior including communication, sexual and aggressive patterns, learning, social, fixed-action patterns, and so on. An investigator could approach these tasks by grouping muscle-contraction patterns observed, but most researchers in the area prefer a second option — describing behaviors in terms of effects on the environment.

The field had its historic moorings and primary foundation within classical European ethology. Given impetus and direction through the pioneering work of Tinbergen, Lorenz, and von Frisch, ethology focused upon instinctive behavior and its observation within the natural habitat of the species. Comparative psychologists in the American tradition have placed their major emphasis upon observing animal behavior under controlled laboratory conditions. Lashley pioneered post-World War II research in this tradition and has inspired Hebb and other gifted students to follow his impressive lead. Ethology has had major influence upon the laboratory approach, and communication between those involved in these orientations is frequent and constructive.

As outlined by Tinbergen, the four areas of study in animal behavior are development, mechanisms, function, and evolution. Development is concerned with genetic determinants of behavior and their interaction with environmental determinants. Mechanisms deals with the interaction between behavior and physiological systems, while function places emphasis upon the adaptive and survival capacities of a species. Evolution provides the unifying central theme and cohesive focus for all aspects of the field.

Dewsbury and Rethlingshafer's *Comparative Psychology: A Modern Survey* (New York: McGraw-Hill, 1973) will give you a general orientation to this area. Its contributors will introduce you to the topics mentioned at the outset, and you can become familiar with such terms as species, species-typical behavior, fixed-action patterns, imprinting, releasers, and the like. But before you delve too deeply into adrenogenital hermaphroditism, pause to remember that your goal continues to be general, basic understanding.

Sensation and Perception

Sensation is a first cousin to the physiological and comparative areas just discussed; perception, on the other hand, adds learning to sensory phenomena. Taken together, sensation and perception constitute both an important combination of areas in their own right and a viable bridge to the discussions of learning in the next section.

Sensation

Because sensation is, in effect, an extension of the physiological aspects of psychology, an understanding of the basic terms and concepts in the preceding section will be essential to you now. The physiology of sense organs provides building blocks and mortar for subsequent understanding of thresholds and general psychophysical concepts. The building blocks consist of knowledge of neural pathways and the ways in which sensory information is processed within them.

Let us use the eye, a thoroughly researched sense organ, to demonstrate the area and some of its basic concepts. The comment that visual sensation results from light striking the retina, prompting nerve impulses that travel to the brain, is deceptively simple. Central to the process is the receptor cell, a specialized cell that is excited by external stimuli and transforms them into a neural output. Receptor cells are distinct from neural cells (bipolar or ganglion), which serve to combine neural signals. In the case of the eye, the receptor cells are called rods and cones (rods containing a photopigment called rhodopsin, cones containing iodopsin). The sequence involves stimulation of receptor cells and transmission to bipolar cells, which synapse with ganglion cells. Neural signals travel along retinal ganglion cells axons to the lateral geniculate nucleus of the thalamus. From the lateral geniculate nucleus, axonal transmission continues to the occipital lobe of the brain.

Of necessity, the example has been oversimplified, but it provides a neural information-processing orientation that you will want to use for each sense organ. As you embark on this orientation, concepts such as receptive field, receptor potential, and sensory coding will be among those of central importance to you. Receptive field refers to the area of the surface of a sense organ that is served by a particular neuron. The concept is not limited to receptor cells. Study of receptive fields several steps removed from the actual stimulus can provide critical insights regarding how receptor surfaces are represented neurologically in the brain. In the case of vision, ganglion cells have been found to have concentric receptive fields with either excitatory center/inhibitory surround or vice versa. Major research in the area of visual receptive fields has been conducted by Hubel and Wiesel. Additional insights on the function of retinal ganglion cells are provided by the work of Barlow, Hill, and Levick (*Journal of Physiology*, 173 [1964], 377–407). P. Lindsay and D. Norman's *Human Information Processing*, in addition to its strength as an introductory reference source, provides excellent suggested readings lists in each topical area. W. T. Keeton's *Biological Science* (New York: Norton, 1980) or C. F. Levinthal's *The Physiological Approach in Psychology* (Englewood Cliffs, N.J.: Prentice-Hall, 1979) can provide additional references as needed.

Beyond the essential understanding of physiology and neural information processing, basic familiarity with a number of fundamental psychophysical terms and concepts will also be important.

- Dimensions of sensation — quality (what kind of sensation), intensity (how much of a sensation), duration (how long a sensation)
- Threshold (or Limen) — absolute threshold — minimum physical energy that will result in a sensory experience, method of limits (using a stimulus such as light, alternating intensity direction with each presentation), method of constant stimuli; difference threshold — j.n.d. (just noticeable difference), Weber's Law (and formula)/Fechner's follow-up

In studying any sensation, an experimenter characteristically begins with a given quality (e.g., light), then varies either the intensity or the duration. Because our receptor cells are not infinitely sensitive, the term threshold becomes prominent. Absolute threshold deals with the minimum physical energy that will result in a sensory experience; difference threshold deals with the minimum *change* in physical energy that will result in a sensory-detected change. For instance, absolute threshold involves the questions "Do you see it?" and "Do you hear it?" in either/or terms. In the difference threshold study, there is no question about your seeing or hearing a stimulus, the question now revolves around how much additional light or sound will be required before you can detect a change from the initial stimulus (in this case, the initial light or sound). Weber's classic work and formula pioneered in this area, and you will need to understand his work and be prepared for questions relating to it. Lindsay and Norman's work and L. Kaufman's *Perception: The World Transformed* (New York: Oxford University Press, 1979) can provide assistance with this portion of your review.

Vision and Audition

In terms of psychological emphasis, vision has been the most heavily studied modality in the sensory area, and audition has been next in prominence. Other sense modalities also receive attention, but not to the extent of these two. In keeping with this emphasis, I will begin with a review of vision and audition, then move on to other sensory modes.

In addition to a basic knowledge of neural information processing, you will also need to gain at least some familiarity with the following list of terms as you concentrate on the area of vision.

- Visual components — sclera; two-chamber concept: small front chamber including the lens, iris, pupil, and cornea, and large inner chamber including the retina, fovea, and neural connections leading to the brain; occipital lobe and optic chiasm
- Visual phenomena — accommodation, convergence, retinal disparity, involuntary eye movements (and their functions)

In studies of visual sensation, the retina assumes primary importance — specifically the rods and cones mentioned previously in our discussion. You will need to know the many distinctions between rods and cones (being able to compare them on such grounds as approximate numbers and distribution on the retina, shape, sensitivity to color and light, visual acuity, and neural connections). With such information, you will then be prepared to understand phenomena such as dark adaptation and the Purkinje Effect.

Not surprisingly, studies of sensory modalities have reached beyond the modalities themselves to the nature of the stimuli impinging upon them. In the case of vision, the most prominent "reach beyond" has encompassed color mixing and vision theory. Again, there are some general terms and concepts that you will need to understand.

- Color mixing — general understanding of where, for instance, violet, blue, green, yellow, and red are located within the wavelength spectrum; distinction between subtractive and additive color mixing and knowledge of the primaries within each; ability to distinguish the terms hue, saturation, and brightness
- Vision theory — Young-Helmholtz Trichromatic Theory, Herin ("three substance") Theory, Ladd-Franklin (compromise), negative after-effect phenomenon and its theoretical implications

Audition has similar aspects, mastery of which will be essential. In addition to background familiarity with neural information processing, the following will also be important.

- Auditory components — three parts of the ear: out —pinna, the visible structure plus the ear canal, middle — three-part bone structure (ossicles) including hammer, anvil, and stirrup, inner — oval window (actually a kind of "front door" letting in messages), cochlea (basilar membrane, hair cells of Organ of Corti, auditory nerve, round window); understanding of the general hearing process as it relates to the above parts; familiarity with the work of Georg von Bekesy
- Auditory phenomena — general hearing range sensitivity (in cycles per second); functions and threshold distinctions between "Boiler maker's ear" (nerve deafness) and deafness attributable to burst eardrum or bone ossification; stimulus-related terminology: pitch, loudness, and timber; understanding of tones, beats, and masking

Turning to auditory theory, you should delve into the following analyses, some of whose names will sound familiar to you while others will be entirely new.

- Auditory theory — Helmholtz Resonance (Place or "Piano") Theory, Rutherford Frequency (or "Telephone") Theory, Wever-Bray Volley Theory (a modification of the preceding)

The Chemical Senses

The chemical senses of taste and smell become our prominent concerns within this heading. The receptor cells for taste are located in clusters of cells known as the taste buds. Taste sensitivity is dependent upon a two-stage process that involves (1) the chemical stimulus penetrating the taste bud and (2) the chemical reaction that prompts the nerve impulse. Taste buds are served by branches of three cranial nerves (VII, IX, X) all of which terminate in the medulla or pons. The taste pathway subsequently reaches the posteroventral nucleus of the thalamus and terminates in the face somatic area of the cortex. Some of the most detailed work in this area has been done by Pfaffmann; his work entitled "Taste, Its Sensory and Motivating Properties," in *American Scientist*, 52, 1964; pp. 187–206 is among the most basic in this area. Knowledge about taste important to you includes data on:

- The four taste "primaries"
- General anatomy of a taste bud
- Neuroanatomy of the taste system

In smell sensitivity, the olfactory receptors are located in the roof of the nasal cavity. The olfactory epithelium contains columnar, basal, and olfactory cells; and the epithelium itself is bathed in mucous fluid — meaning that gases and mucous must be soluble in order to excite olfactory receptors. From the olfactory epithelium, axons extend to the olfactory bulb (a complex entity with its brain-destined networks of fibers and its reverberatory circuits). The final portion of the "journey" is via the olfactory tract to the cortex. What has been termed the primary olfactory cortex is actually a number of points in the ventral surface region. The region varies in size among species, depending on the relative importance of olfaction for the given species. Compared with other species, the area is notably small in humans. As you review the smell sensation, the following should be important to you:

- Olfactory bulb
- Olfactory epithelium and types of cells
- Olfactory neuroanatomy
- Nasal cavity
- Turbinate bones
- Relationship of olfactory system to other structures in the brain

Attempts to formulate theories of smell have not met with notable success. However, the work of Crozier, Moncrieff, and Adey demonstrates the theoretical progression that has occurred in the field.

The Skin Senses

In the late nineteenth century, experimenters observed that the human skin is not uniformly sensitive to different types of stimuli. In further investigations, areas of skin were circumscribed and, for instance, a cold stimulus was systematically applied to determine at what points a person would report feeling coldness. Similar mapping of the identical skin area was conducted for stimuli warmer than skin temperature. It became apparent that coldness and warmth were not being felt at the same points on the skin surface. Similar mapping was conducted with touch and pain stimuli, and again the sensations were not felt at identical points on the skin surface. Woodworth and Schlosberg (*Experimental Psychology* [New York: Holt, Rinehart & Winston, 1954]) give details of experiments that were conducted in this area. These experiments led to conclusions that there were at least four primary qualities of cutaneous sensation — touch, pain, cold, and warmth. Muller's doctrine of specific nerve energies, advanced fifty years earlier, was being supported. For review purposes, I will discuss the skin senses in the general categories of pressure, temperature, and pain. Receptor categories that will be important throughout this section will be (1) free nerve endings, (2) hair follicles, and (3) encapsulated end organs; and, as was true for the previous review sections, a general knowledge of neuroanatomy will also be important.

Pressure

Geldard formally defines pressure sensation as "tissue distortion, or the mechanical deformation of skin tissue." Pressure intensity is measured in grams per millimeter. As with other senses, the level of pressure sensitivity is different in different parts of the body. In general, the closer to the extremity, the more sensitivity there will be (making the center of the back, for instance, one of the least pressure-sensitive parts of the body). To fully understand pressure sensitivity, you should also look into such terms and concepts as the types of pressure receptors (encapsulated end organs, etc.) and touch blends (cold pressure, "wetness," etc.). Your goal should be a general understanding of the area and an acquaintance with its problems.

Temperature

As mentioned previously, evidence supports the suggestion of two receptor systems — one for warmth, one for coldness. Your knowledge in this area should include an awareness that cold receptors apparently are the smaller and more numerous. In addition, you should know something about cold and heat sensitivity in different parts of the body and the "three bowl" adaptation experiment of Weber.

Pain

There are many questions relating to the nature of pain and how to stop it effectively. Initial thought that pain was a direct function of tissue damage was quickly proven to be incorrect (when, for instance, it was found that major tissue damage could go hand in hand with minor pain sensation). The following are among the concepts you will need to understand:

- "Protopathic and epicritic" sensitivity (Henry Head)
- Two kinds of pain (and the possibility of two types of receptors)
- The classic theory of cutaneous modalities

In addition, you should be familiar with aspects such as the differential effects, and apparently very different pain-relieving functions, of aspirin versus a colleague anesthetic such as morphine.

Every sensory receptor discussed to this point has had the quality of being stimulated from outside the body and providing knowledge of events external to the body. In his well-known scheme, Sherrington classified such senses as exteroceptors, in contrast to interoceptors and proprioceptors. Neither of the latter two categories receives direct stimulation from outside the body. The sensory field of the interoceptors is the gastrointestinal tract (making them the organic or visceral sensors), and the "in-betweens" (receptors in subcutaneous tissue, deep-lying blood vessels, muscles, tendons, and bone coverings) are the proprioceptors — having the common characteristic of being stimulated mainly by actions of the body itself. Among the proprioceptors Sherrington includes the labyrinthine balance function of the inner ear. This labyrinthine sense is unique in that no other sense can make good on a claim to yield no sensations of its own. If you feel dizzy, the sensations that you experience are kinesthetic, pressural, viceral — but not labyrinthine. The kinesthetic sense (that tells you where your appendages are and what they are doing) is also among the proprioceptors. Within these general areas, there are some novel and classic studies with which you should be familiar, including Boring's "balloon" study of the gastrointestinal tract and the Cannon-Washburn technique for studying hunger sensation.

You now have gone through the spectrum of sense receptors. To the extent that you understand their neuroanatomy, physiological bases, and functioning, you are now prepared for a knowledgeable review of perception.

Perception

Earlier I said that sensation was physiologically based and that perception would build a bridge to learning. Let us look now at perception, the learning factor that makes a critical difference between what comes to us through our senses and what we individually *perceive* as having been received by those senses.

In contrast to what is actually received and transmitted, perception is our *mental organization* of what is out there. It is what we *say* we saw, heard, felt, etc. — as distinct from what actually was received. Perception, therefore, contains both the sensory element and the past experience that we bring to every situation. Vision again comes to the fore, and a school of thought known as Gestalt is responsible for the body of information concerning visual perception.

Whereas a thorough understanding of the term *stimulus* was relatively incidental to our previous discussions, it is essential for both perception discussions and our subsequent look at the learning area. Most definitions state that a stimulus is a physical agent that (given sufficient strength) activates one or a group of sensory receptors. Witnesses to an explosion, for instance, will find the explosion both a visual and an auditory stimulus. With such things as a traffic light, however, the stimulus will be in only one sensory modality. Having digested this all-important term, we can now take a look at the material on perception that you will need to review for the GRE. Major terms and concepts follow:

- Gestalt school of thought — Wertheimer, Koffka, Kohler
- Perception factors — Stimulus-related factors — prepotency of stimuli (brightness, contrast, movement), common perceptual organizations of stimuli (similarity, proximity, closure, figure-ground and its reversibility, continuity, common movement)
- Experience-related factors — shape, brightness, color, and size constancy, role of experience in "seeing" illusions — Muller-Lyer illusion, trapezoidal window (Ames window), distorted room, autokinetic illusion, phi phenomenon
- Perception theories — Ames (transactional), Brunswick (probabilistic)

Lindsay and Norman's chapter on "The Dimensions of Vision" and Zimbardo's chapter on perception will give you much of the data needed. For more depth, Kaufman's *Perception: The World Transformed* (New York: Oxford University Press, 1979) would be appropriate, but be careful not to get bogged down in small details.

The study of perception invariably calls for a distinction between "illusion" and "hallucination." For clarity, you can think of illusion as misperception of a stimulus and hallucination as response in the absence of any external stimulus. Inevitably, the discussion will go one step further, into extrasensory perception (ESP), and again some distinctions will be important.

- Definitional aspects of extrasensory perception — mental telepathy, clairvoyance, precognition
- Psychokinesis (or telekinesis)

In addition, you should be familiar with the work of J. B. Rhine at Duke University, known for his ESP cards. Extrasensory perception is not yet a generally respected area within psychological research, but some familiarity with it is in order.

We are all familiar with the expression "You see what you want to see!" This phrase suggests that we are motivated to see certain things — and perhaps *not* to see others. The relationship between motivation and perception has not been overlooked in psychological research, and I shall discuss that relationship when we look at the motivation area of psychology later in the review. For now, however, you should concentrate on familiarizing yourself with such things as perceptual defense, McGinnies's "dirty word" experiment, and Bruner-Goodman's "poor-boy/rich-boy" experiment. Zimbardo's introductory textbook is one of many sources providing direct accessibility to this information.

Taking inventory, we see that you have now been through the very difficult basic review sections on physiology, comparative psychology, sensation, and perception. In the sections that follow, you will begin to get glimpses of the "whole person" and of total human development.

Learning

The human glimpse may seem brief in this discussion of basic learning principles, but you will soon find that I have headed for practical applications of these principles that will affect all of you. Subsequent sections will cover cognition and complex human learning as well as developmental psychology (child development) and other areas of the discipline. In order not to flounder in those sections, you must master the basic learning principles. There are numerous terms and concepts you will need to know, so take a deep breath and plunge in.

- Basic definition of learning (and ability to contrast it with maturation)
- Species-specific constraints on learning
- Kinds of conditioning
  Classical (synonyms = respondent or Type-S)
    Pavlov
      conditioned stimulus (CS)
      unconditioned stimulus (UCS)
      conditioned response (CR)
      unconditioned response (UCR)
    basic conditioning techniques
      delayed (by far, the most prominent)
      trace
      simultaneous
      backward
  Instrumental (synonyms = operant or Type-R)
    understanding the term "reinforcement"
    Skinner's shaping techniques
    distinction between positive and negative reinforcement
    understanding of the following reinforcement schedules and their comparative effectiveness:
      fixed ratio
      fixed interval
      variable ratio
      variable interval
    familiarity with methods of reporting learning (number of correct responses, number of errors, and Skinner's cumulative response method)
    terminology relating to the learning curve
      acquisition
      plateau
      asymptote
      extinction
    transfer (or generalization)
      distinction between stimulus and response generalization
      distinction between positive and negative transfer
      understanding of the following transfer situations:
        proactive facilitation
        proactive inhibition
        retroactive facilitation
        retroactive inhibition

Dollard and Miller's four fundamentals of learning
  drive
  cue
  response
  reinforcement
 Harlow's "learning to learn" or learning set
 distinction between discrimination and generalization
 understanding of discriminative stimulus in contrast to negative discriminative stimulus
 general distinction between S-R and R-R relationship
Avoidance learning and punishment
 Mowrer's two-factor theory and "spread of effect"
 Skinner's views on effectiveness of negative reinforcement

For brush-up and review of these items, you should go to the learning chapter of a basic textbook. Kimble's work will provide additional depth. Whatever sources you review, it will be a good idea to come back to this term-concept list afterward to see where you are in your basic understanding. When you have mastered the list, you will be set to move on.

Cognition and Complex Human Learning

The learning principles that I have discussed until now hold true for animals as well as humans. Rats, cats, and pigeons (among others) can acquire and extinguish or can be classically and instrumentally conditioned, and Harlow found his learning set phenomenon in monkeys. But as soon as you get into such areas as thinking, language, mnemonic strategies, and computer models, you quickly leave the animals behind (with the possible exception of monkeys). The focus swings to humans and their learning behavior.

Because language constitutes the pivotal concept that leads to cognition, thought, and other human learning phenomena, it seems logical to begin with a review of verbal learning principles. Pioneering in this area was done by a nineteenth-century German named Hermann Ebbinghaus, enabling researchers to study human memory and forgetting by way of the nonsense syllable. Earlier, I mentioned the learning curve; now I must introduce the forgetting curve. It is useful to note that in verbal learning people normally forget more than 60 percent of what they learn within twenty-four hours after they "master" it. The forgetting curve for motor learning is vastly different, and you will need a clear comparative understanding of the two curves. In addition, the following terms and concepts will be important:

- Reminiscence
- Methods of measuring retention — recall (the essay test), reconstruction (the matching test), recognition (the multiple-choice test), relearning (and the concept of savings)
- Laboratory techniques — serial-position, paired-associates, free recall
- Theories of forgetting — decay theory (memory trace fade), interference theory (other learning inhibiting retention), motivated forgetting (repression of threatening memory)
- Kinds of memory — sensory, short-term, long-term
- Methods for improved remembering (retention aids) — massed versus distributed practice, overlearning, active recitation, chunking, mnemonic strategies, visual imagery, meaningfulness
- Serial position, von Restorff, and Zeigarnik effects
- Theoretical comparison of Skinner, Tolman, and Thorndike
- Programmed learning — teaching machines, computer-assisted instruction

To prepare for greater depth in cognition, thought, language, and problem solving, familiarize yourself with the following:

- Whorf hypothesis (language patterns as determinants of thought patterns)
- Brown hypothesis (thought primacy over language)
- Concept types — conjunctive, disjunctive, relational
- Linguistic analysis levels — phonological (and the phoneme), grammatical (morphemes and syntax), semantic
- Language learning theories — reinforcement (Skinner, Mowrer, et al.) inborn competence (Lennenberg, Chomsky, et al.)

People try to picture thought processes in order to study them and communicate regarding them. Although the mind may at one time have been compared to a sponge or a sieve, the onset of computer technology provided an input-output model that has gained prominence in research thought and discussion. G. Miller, E. Galanter, and K. Pribram (*Plans and the Structure of Behavior,* New York: Holt, Rinehart & Winston, 1960) were among the first to conceptualize thought in these terms, and it is not surprising that their model contained loops, branching, and the "if-then" conditions that are associated with a computer program.

Thinking has generally been characterized as a process that molds images, symbols, words, rules, and concepts into mental associations. Think of Reno or Las Vegas, for example, and a truckload of images and associations comes immediately to mind.

Intelligence

In any study of the mind, language, or thinking, you will inevitably encounter the concept of intelligence quotient (IQ). No review of the discipline of psychology could be complete without a discussion of this term and an attempt to convey a basic understanding of intelligence and its relationship to problem-solving and creativity. A definition of intelligence generally includes three elements: the ability to profit from experience, the ability to learn new information, and the ability to adjust to new situations. Theoretical work in the area has concentrated on the general nature of intelligence and whether it is a general, unitary factor or a combination of several specific factors. Scholarly work on this question began just after 1900 with Spearman's Two Factor Theory (a general-type factor and a specific-type factor). The next major name was Thurstone, who postulated seven factors in intelligence, and intelligence theory reached its peak of complexity with Guilford's Structure of Intellect (120 factors in three general classifications). The trend represented by these theories is indicative of the complexity of the term. In some respects, it is easier to measure intelligence than to discuss it theoretically.

Measurement began with Binet and Simon (French contemporaries of Spearman). Commissioned by the French minister of public instruction, they developed a test to determine which children could not profit from elementary instruction in the public schools. Their end product, later translated into English by Terman and named the Stanford-Binet, launched an era of intelligence testing in this country. In addition to creating the pioneering intelligence test, Binet and Simon gave prominence to the IQ concept and established a method for IQ computation. Other names and concepts important to the intelligence area include:

- The Wechsler Series of Intelligence Tests (and what distinguishes them from the Stanford-Binet) WAIS, WISC, WPPSI
- Awareness of Group Intelligence Tests (verbal and nonverbal) — Otis, Lorge-Thorndike et al.
- Nature-nurture controversy as it relates to intelligence (recent prominence in ethnic discussions associated with Jensen's work)

- Extremes of intelligence — knowledge of what IQ ranges accompany words such as gifted, above average, average, mildly retarded, moderately retarded, severely retarded, and profoundly retarded; Terman's classic studies of gifted children
- Intelligence effects of drugs and malnutrition during pregnancy

Although interest in intelligence measurement initiated the testing movement, applications of the technique spread quickly to the areas of aptitude, achievement, vocation, and personality. Aptitude is a narrower, more specific term than intelligence, and aptitude tests seek to measure much more specialized abilities (e.g., mechanical aptitude, musical aptitude, etc.) than general intelligence tests. To extend the distinction one step further, aptitude differs from achievement in that aptitude means potential for successful performance while achievement means actual performance. One could say that, on the basis of their test scores, two particular individuals are more *apt* to do well in mechanical tasks than two others. None of them has performed the tasks or become mechanically proficient as yet, but the test does predict their future performance. Your knowledge in the area should include an acquaintance with:

> SAT (Scholastic Aptitude Test)
> Vineland Social Maturity Scale
> Kuder Preference Test
> Strong Vocational Interest Test
> California Achievement Tests
> Sequential Tests of Educational Progress
> Stanford Achievement Test

Later, as you get into personality and clinical and applied areas, you will look at some representative tests in these areas and make critical distinctions between objective and subjective approaches to testing. For now, it is sufficient to note that intelligence testing "started something" that proliferated into many other areas. In addition to the introductory textbooks and the work of Anastasi, Frank Freeman's *Theory and Practice of Psychological Testing,* as well as numerous other references, may also prove helpful in your review of this area.

Cognition

A prominent voice in opposition to the intelligence test movement has been Jean Piaget. His keen theoretical mind, penchant for observing children, and background in Binet's laboratory equipped him for the unique contribution he has made to the field of cognition. Piaget's basic disagreement with Binet centered on the notion of structuring the response possibilities for a child. Piaget preferred to let the child be "in charge" of the situation, and he merely observed and sought to systematize what he saw. In short, he attempted to get a glimpse of the child's mental world and how it functioned. His experiments and observations have yielded a wealth of insights into the cognitive capacities of the young mind and the nature of cognitive development.

One of the major concepts stemming from Piaget's work has been conservation — a child's capacity to recognize equivalences when a specific form or arrangement changes. For example, if you took two identical glasses of lemonade and poured the contents of one of them into a thinner, taller glass, a five-year-old might tell you that there was more lemonade in the taller glass than in the original one. On the other hand, a seven-year-old who had witnessed the pouring procedure might chime in that both glasses really contained equal amounts, that the taller glass just appeared to have more lemonade in it. The seven-year-old has cognitively attained conservation in relation to such a demonstration, but the five-year-old has not yet reached such a point in his cognitive development. In addition to this concept, you should further acquaint yourself with the following:

- Conservation in number, substance, length, area, weight, volume (and the general age sequence in which a child normally would attain them)
- Adaptation
- Assimilation
- Accommodation

Problem Solving Creativity

If you were to take the expression "thinking and _____" and ask your listeners to fill in the blank, many of them would immediately say "problem solving." Much of our thought time is directed toward problem solving; thus, the process is a logical target for psychological inquiry. Several species engage in some form of problem solving — rats, cats, pigeons, monkeys, and humans among them — and the complexity level varies markedly. If you put a cat or a rat in a puzzle box, you would find that his method of problem solving would be strictly trial and error. Literally by accident, he would bump into the response that gained the desired result and would learn to repeat it in a similar future situation. Much of our own learning falls into this category, but humans and monkeys also demonstrate a phenomenon that Harlow called *insight*. Like an "aha" phenomenon, we seem to develop a capacity for solving problems that we have never encountered in the past, and it is this capacity that Harlow termed *learning set*. While set is our best friend in some problem-solving instances, it can be a barrier in others. Persistence of set, "functional fixedness," and deeply ingrained rules can sometimes prevent us from attaining the fresh, imaginative approach that some problems may require.

The next step in the problem-solving sequence is *creativity* or creative problem solving. Creativity is a phenomenon that most people can detect far more easily than they can define. "That was a creative idea!" and "She's imaginative and creative!" are much more familiar to us than "Creativity is _____." D. Krech, R. Crutchfield, and N. Livson (Elements of Psychology, rev. ed., [New York: Knopf, 1976], pp. 134–35) express the belief that the determinants of creative problem solving lie within (1) the stimulus pattern, (2) knowledge, and (3) the personality. They feel that the stimulus pattern, however, can cause individuals to become too rule-oriented and stimulus-bound so that their minds may tell them, as they approach a solution, that "A hammer can only be used for hammering!" or "A yardstick can only be used for measuring." Creativity implies the capacity to go beyond the conventional and traditional. But if one becomes stimulus-bound, his or her problem-solving methods are automatically limited to the conventional and unimaginative.

It is not surprising that knowledge can serve as both a help and a hindrance to creative problem solving. Everyone needs a certain amount of knowledge to solve a problem, but too many facts may lock him into the conventional. In the third area — personality — it appears that the creative person needs the ability to tolerate both frustration and ambiguity. Generally speaking, creativity presents an important field of investigation, which currently contains more questions than answers. Haimowitz and Haimowitz (*Human Development* [New York: Crowell, 1960], pp. 44–54) exhibit an awareness of the fascination held by the field — along with its unanswered questions. Additional names and concepts in the field that should be familiar to you include:

- Maier ("Practice makes blindness.")
- Maslow (self-actualization and creativity)
- Mednick (Remote Associations Test)

As you can see, creativity and intelligence are not synonymous — a fact demonstrated vividly by M. Wallach and N. Kogan in *Modes of Thinking in Young Children: A Study of the Creativity-Intelligence Distinction* (New York: Holt, Rinehart & Winston, 1965). For additional depth in the area of creativity, look into one of these:

    S. Arieti, *Creativity: The Magic Synthesis*.(New York: Basic, 1980).

    A. Rothenberg and C. Hausman, *Creativity Question*. (Durham: Duke University Press, 1976).

I have covered the vast areas of learning and cognition briefly, but, I trust, carefully and adequately for the purposes of this review. Next, I shall discuss developmental psychology, an even broader and more varied segment of the discipline.

Developmental Psychology

Developmental psychology, one of the most sweeping topical areas in the discipline, encompasses the psychological study of the child; that is, the child's physiological, comparative, sensory, perceptual, and learning characteristics. Thus, the study of child development actually involves everything we have been or will be talking about. For the sake of time and space, however, we will confine our discussion only to those concerns generally included in a course on the topic.

As Papalia and Olds point out in their introductory comments, child development centers upon the quantitative and qualitative ways in which children change over time. Not surprisingly, the quantitative changes are more easily measured because they are readily observable. The child's "quantity" changes in both weight and height, and in each instance the change can be systematically recorded. Qualitative changes pose greater problems for the would-be observer. For instance, how can one monitor a child's intellectual, emotional, social, and moral growth? And how does one determine the presence of creativity? Such questions quickly lead away from the straightforward instruments and answers that investigators rely upon in quantitative measurement.

The instruments and techniques necessary for qualitative measurement take various complexions. In the naturalistic approach, the investigator uses the method of Tinbergen and Lorenz, observing the child in his natural habitat. Large numbers of children are watched systematically at different ages, and these observations yield such data as the average age for walking, talking, parallel play, the presence of conscience, heterosexual interest, and so forth. Gesell and his associates compiled enormous amounts of observational data that enabled them to develop and publish a widely revered work and numerous articles on the average age for the emergence of specific skills and abilities in children.

Another technique, the clinical method of child observation, came into prominence with Piaget. With this method, the agenda is no longer strictly the child's in the sense that specific, open-ended questions are asked and responses are carefully studied. Whereas no intervention or structure is imposed under naturalistic observation, some intervention is evident in the clinical method — although individual freedom of response continues to be preserved. Piaget was able to use the clinical method to provide insightful glimpses into child thought processes, which previously had been totally unexplored.

A third, and most structured, measurement setting is known as the experimental approach. With this method, children may be grouped according to some established basis (e.g., age, socioeconomic status, etc.) and be "measured" by means of a standardized procedure, thus permitting response comparisons between groups. Statistical analysis of results enables the investigators to determine whether groups of children differ significantly on the skill or ability being measured. Everyone who has taken a school-administered IQ test has participated to some extent in a standardized, potentially experimental approach.

The development of a child begins at the point of conception, and prenatal development is divided into three stages — germinal (fertilization to two weeks), embryonic (two to eight weeks), and fetal (eight weeks to birth). Specific events are associated with each stage. During the germinal stage, there is rapid cell division and implantation on the uterine wall. In the embryonic stage, rapid differentiation of major body systems and organ development make the embryo particularly vulnerable to influences upon the prenatal environment. Because the mother is, in effect, the prenatal environment, the available research deals with such critical questions as the effects upon the embryo of maternal diet, drug and alcohol intake, and emotional state. Equally critical are considerations relating to illness, exposure to radiation, and mother-embryo blood compatibility. In the systematic, sequential development that is characteristic of man and animals, impaired development during the embryonic stage is major and permanent. Nature provides no opportunity for compensatory "make-up" work later in pregnancy. In the final stage, the body systems and organs of the fetus that were formed and differentiated during the preceding embryonic stage have the opportunity to grow.

At birth, new questions come into focus. Among them are concerns regarding the child's adjustment to the cold, bright, noisy environment beyond the womb. Physiologically, reflexes and sensory capacities are studied, and socially and emotionally, the mother-child relationship is carefully examined for possible links between the child's emotional adjustment and characteristics such as mode and schedule of feeding, maternal warmth, and the like.

During the first two years, the child's motor development is of primary import. Have his or her crawling, walking, etc. occurred on schedule? Invariably "the schedule" used as the reference point is the one created by Gesell.

If motor development proceeds without difficulties, language development begins to steal the spotlight. One of the most exciting days for parents is the day their child says his or her first word, and if that word proves to be in the "socially acceptable" category (ma-ma, da-da, etc.) the day is a joy indeed. Language development is equally exciting for child psychologists. It is obvious that a child receives and understands many words long before he or she can produce them, and, given the appropriate technology, the reception area may someday become an important exploration ground. For the moment, however, research emphasis centers on the accessible — language production.

Two broad categories in language production are prelinguistic (first year) and linguistic. E. and G. Kaplan ("Is There Such a Thing as a Prelinguistic Child?" in *Human Development and Cognitive Processes,* ed. J. Eliot [New York: Holt, Rinehart & Winston, 1970]) have further defined the prelinguistic category as encompassing the basic cry (first three weeks), sound variety beyond the basic cry (three weeks to four or five months), and babbling (last half of the first year). Babbling consists of vowel-like and consonant-like sounds articulated with imitations of adult intonation. One of the questions that fascinates theorists is whether the transition from babbling to recognizable words is a leap or a sequential step. A related question deals with exactly how the monkey differs from the human in the language area. At one time, language use was considered the standard by which humans were rated above monkeys and their relatives, but surprising and convincing studies with chimps have begun to erode that standard. Names with which you should be familiar in this area include: Kellogg and Kellogg (early study with "Donald" and "Gua"), Gardner and Gardner (recent work with "Washoe" and the American Sign Language for the Deaf), and Premack ("Sarah" and "plastic sentences").

Social and personality development become prominent research concerns as the child moves beyond the immediate family to his peer group, and obvious questions relate to the effects that early family influences have had upon the child's personality and social adjustment. Several personality theorists have spoken to these early years and their potential influence. Among the most prominent is Erikson, whose psychosocial theory suggests that foundations for basic trust, autonomy, and initiative are laid during the first five years of life. Freud's earlier theory took a sexual view, suggesting the possibilities of narcissism and fixations and the presence of Oedipal love characteristics. Dollard and Miller sought to combine the Freudian concept with learning principles, indicating that early experiences of hunger and crying in a child's dark bedroom could be the basis for later fear of the dark, overreaction to slight pain, apathy, and overeating. Many child psychologists who have a learning orientation concern themselves primarily with the present behavior of the child and the stimuli that prompt a given behavior. Nevertheless, few psychologists would be willing to defend a position that these early years are unimportant to the child's personality development and social adjustment.

For the preschool child — typically viewed as the three-to-five-year-old — mental development becomes an important concern. The effects of stimulus-enriched environments both in and beyond the home take on major importance, and most personal vocabularies now include the terms public kindergarten, private kindergarten, and day care center. Research has convinced several state school systems to develop kindergarten facilities for all five-year-olds, and the preschool years are being increasingly viewed as a time for learning as well as for social adjustment.

As the child begins school, he enters what child psychologists call middle childhood. Stretching from ages six to twelve, middle childhood is a critically important time for physical, mental, personality, and social development. Understandably, the development areas are complexly interwoven. A girl who grows quickly and is taller than her male peers, for instance, can expect a social experience that is quite different from that of a girl who is shorter. Erikson sees this period as a time when the child's energies are directed toward "industry" (i.e., school achievement). For many, this involvement leads to the frustration of failure and to feelings of inferiority. It also raises the question of a child's moral development strength in the wake of achievement pressure and competition. This developmental stage terminates with the onset of puberty.

Adolescence begins in the turmoil of puberty — a time of rapid physical and sexual development accompanied by conflicts and feelings that make the young person's life difficult and trying. Growth spurts, concern about physical appearance, nocturnal emissions, menstruation, and masturbation are among the factors combining to form the adolescent's complex adjustment picture. Erikson sees the young person at this stage as an individual making a search for identity; he also sees successful achievement of self-identity as essential for meaningful heterosexual love relationships. A search for identity is, in part, a search for values; and the young person's parental and peer group relationships become dominant factors in this search.

The preceding is a chronological approach to developmental psychology. An investigator in the field might take a more stratified approach (i.e., look at a child's emotional development from birth to age eighteen, take a similar look at mental development, etc.), but most developmental psychologists prefer to examine the child intact, looking at all aspects of a his or her development at each chronological point. As you review this area, the following are among the additional concepts and names that will be important to you:

- Distinction among reflex, instinct, and learned act
- Reflexes in the newborn — Babinski, Moro, Babkin, sucking, grasping
- Imprinting — Lorenz, Hess, Scott, Harlow
- Berkeley Growth Studies
- Early childhood cognitive/intellectual development (White's Harvard Early Education Project)
- Cross-cultural study of relationship between environmental stimulation and child intelligence (Kagan)
- The Gesell, Cattell, and Bayley scales (testing infant development)
- Social learning (Bandura)
- Conscience (Sears)
- Visual cliff (Gibson and Walk)
- Determiners of development — (Developmental level = heredity × environment × time)
- Relationship of heredity to maturation, environment to learning
- Hebb's six classes of factors in behavioral development
- General knowledge of comparative thresholds in the different sensory modalities at birth (e.g., Does a newborn have color vision? Is temperature sensitivity better developed than pain sensitivity?)
- Genetic terminology — Distinction between singly determined and multiply determined characteristics (Tryon's maze-bright and maze-dull rats); Mendel's law and the distinction between dominant and recessive traits; Distinction in twins — monozygotic versus fraternal

- Patterns of development and their meaning — cephalocaudal, proximodistal, general to specific
- Ability to compare the child's development patterns in the neural, reproductive, and somatic (general body growth) areas
- Familiarity with certain terms:— Dwarfism, Acromegaly, Down's syndrome, Klinefelter syndrome, Autism (Lovaas), Aphasia, PKU (phenylketonuria)

For reference purposes beyond introductory works, D. Papalia and S. Olds, *Human Development* (New York: McGraw-Hill, 1978) and L. Stone and J. Church, *Childhood and Adolescence*, 4th ed. (New York: Random House, 1979) are among the most readable. One of the most comprehensive works in the field is P. Mussen, H. Conger and J. Kagan, *Child Development and Personality*, 5th ed. (New York: Harper and Row, 1979). A strong case for early education in the home is made by B. White in *The First Three Years of Life* (Englewood Cliffs, N.J.: Prentice-Hall, 1975) and in his early education project summary work *The Origins of Human Competence*.

Motivation and Emotion

A quick browse through any graduate school catalog will indicate that motivation and emotion — while perhaps not inseparable terms — are often seen together.

Motivation

Motivation generally is defined as a social or psychological condition that directs an individual's behavior toward a certain goal. Drive, on the other hand, is a biological condition that performs a goal-direction function. The distinction is that a rat probably turns right in the T-maze because it has sensations of hunger or thirst, not to preserve its self-esteem. In the cases of both motivation and drive, we have to infer that they exist on the basis of what the animal or person does. We note the relationship between a stimulus and a response and then say, "Aha, the little four-legger was hungry!" or "Yep, I see a lot of love messages in the glances those two have been exchanging!" Each of these cases involves a stimulus (food pellet, lover) to which an organism responds (by turning right in the alley or sending affectionate glances). In short, on the basis of what we see, we infer.

To keep from switching terms in general discussion, the word *drive* is sometimes prefaced with "biological," "psychological," or "social." Our discussion of motivation will follow this pattern.

Biological Drives Biological or primary drives have certain common elements, including: (1) the maintenance and preservation of the organism, (2) homeostasis (the tendency toward achieving and maintaining a state of balance), and (3) the quality of preempting all other drives. Entries in this group include hunger, thirst, pain, breath, fatigue, warmth and cold, and bowel and bladder tension. The commonalities of biological drives can be easily illustrated. For example, if a person is hungry, his or her sonnet-writing and guitar-picking behavior stops temporarily (is preempted) until the hunger drive has been reduced. The tension of the drive itself creates a disturbing imbalance within the individual, requiring that the tension be relieved and balance be restored (homeostasis). The entire behavior sequence has survival at its root (maintenance and preservation of the organism).

Psychological Drives These drives have the common characteristic of seeking to establish mental-emotional well-being. Psychological drives include sex, curiosity, and gregariousness. Sex seems to have many biological drive characteristics. It does not qualify as a full-fledged biological drive entity, however, because its arousal is as actively sought as its reduction (not homeostatic), and, though it is essential for the survival of a species, it is not necessary for the survival of an individual organism (despite what your date may tell you!). Its power as a motivator is well known to advertisers, who utilize it as a selling aid for products ranging from magazines and entertainment to automobiles and cigarettes. Motivational research in this area has reached a point where even foods have been categorized as masculine or feminine.

The second major psychological drive — curiosity — is defined as a need to explore. Romanes, Thorndike, and Harlow have been among the researchers who have found that monkeys will perform a task or learn a response without any tangible reward except the opportunity to explore and discover. In one instance, the curiosity reward was the opportunity to see an electric train in operation. Translated to the human level, curiosity is exemplified by man's desire to know what is on the moon or on Mars or Venus. Curiosity is the penchant to explore, to discover, to know.

The third psychological drive — gregariousness — is the drive for affiliation among humans and other species. One yardstick for measuring emotional trouble in a friend might be the observation that he or she stays alone a good deal and does not mix. The capacity for interaction with others is seen as an aid in maintaining mental and emotional well-being.

Social Drives

Learning is the common element among drives in this category. We must learn to associate some kind of basic need gratification with these entries, or they never gain the capacity to motivate us. The normal means by which these entries gain their motivating qualities is an association with an element (food, maybe) that satisfies a primary drive. A person learns that with this element he or she can obtain whatever is necessary to satisfy biological or psychological drives. Entries in this category include money, achievement, and freedom from anxiety. You will inevitably encounter additional entries in some of the reference books you come upon. The above-mentioned entries — particularly money and achievement — will be found universally in your sources. Surprisingly, chimps have paralleled the human social drive for money. In an apparatus called a "Chimp-O-Mat," they have been known to work diligently for tokens that they could later exchange for food. The following are some additional names and concepts that will be important to you:

- Comprehensive study of motivation (Atkinson)
- nAch (McClelland)
- Social drives (Sarnoff)
- Curiosity (Butler)

Other related names and concepts will surface in the discussion of social psychology that appears later.

Emotion

Emotion is a logical companion of motivation. When we attain (or fail to attain) a goal, words like joy, anger, delight, and depression enter the picture. We express a feeling . . . an emotion. On the physiological side, emotional expression can prompt a number of changes, including:

- Striated muscle changes controlled by the central nervous system — facial expressions, vocal expressions, muscle tension, tremors, etc.
- Autonomic changes controlled by the autonomic nervous system and endocrine glands — heart rate, blood pressure, digestion, blood-sugar level and levels of acidity, adrenalin, and noradrenalin, metabolism, breathing rate, sweating

Measurement of emotions has been prominent in the areas of:

- "Lie detector" — breathing, heart rate, galvanic skin response (GSR)
- Pupil size — increase in pupil size signifying increased interest, pleasant stimulus, heightened mental activity

A theoretical question of long standing has focused on whether the cognitive, experiential aspects of an emotion precede physiological arousal or whether, on the other hand, the emotion is experienced as a result of the physiological arousal. Theoretical positions of importance to you include:

- James-Lange Theory (emotion a result of physiological arousal)
- Cannon-Bard Theory (neurological)
- Schachter adrenalin studies

Among the cues to use in detecting someone's emotions are:

- Verbal (least reliable, Mehrabian)
- Facial (reliable cross culturally for basic, simple emotions, Ekman)
- Situational context (essential to judgment of complex emotional expression, Frijda)

Studies of the general pattern and sequence of the development of emotion have provided important insights relating to the young child and, to "what comes first," emotionally-speaking. Two early sources of information in this area were Blatz and Millichamp's studies entitled "The Development of Emotion in the Infant" (University of Toronto Studies, Child Development Series, 1935, No. 4) and the Montreal Foundling Home Studies. At birth, a child exhibits emotion in the form of a general, undifferentiated excitement. Differentiation in the form of distress reaction appears at approximately one month of age, and the positive reaction of delight appears later (at approximately three months). Finer distinctions in each of the basic categories — distress and delight — then enter the picture and continue throughout life.

There is no doubt that prominent *learned* aspects are present in many emotional responses. For instance, a child may learn how much a cut finger hurts and how profusely to respond to such a trauma by the amount of parental fuss, alarm, and attention given similar preceding events. Where one child may cry a lot, another may hardly shed a tear — such is the parental "burden" in shaping human emotions.

Having completed this much of your review, you may feel both relieved and happy, that is, you may experience both a motivation and an emotion, companions throughout our existence. Motivation and emotion lead naturally into the next two areas of psychology that I shall discuss, social and personality. You will notice that I have put social psychology before personality. My reason is that I feel that personality builds a skillful bridge to the clinical and psychopathology areas that follow.

Social Psychology

Social psychology connects sociology and clinical psychology. Where the sociologist is concerned with the study of groups and the clinical psychologist works with the concerns and problems of the individual, the social psychologist studies the behavior of the individual within the group and the effects of the group upon the individual's behavior. If the area sounds sweeping to you, it is! This review spotlights some of the major areas of social psychology and discusses briefly certain aspects of each. In deference to the breadth of the field and the limitations of the review, however, a list of terms, concepts, and names concludes this section.

Attitudes and Attitude Measurement

If you were asked to select the most prominent area of research within social psychology, your best bet would be to select the study of attitudes. It is estimated that approximately half the research in the field deals with some aspect of attitude formation and change. Definitionally, many researchers in the field indicate that there are three components essential to the existence of an attitude: (1) cognitive, (2) emotional, (3) behavioral. If I know something about cars (cognitive), get a "fun charge" out of working on them (emotional), and frequently can be spotted under the hood of some four-wheeler (behavioral), I have an attitude about cars. Knowledge alone, without emotional feeling, does not qualify; and the only way an attitude can be detected is through some form of behavior (working on cars frequently, answering an opinion poll, etc.).

Because attitudes are a prominent concern, researchers in the field have spent quite a bit of time and effort designing and standardizing attitude measurement scales. The earliest efforts in this area were those of Thurstone. Following very rigorous procedures for item selection, he developed a scale technique known as "equal appearing intervals." This term encompasses both the underlying concepts and the procedures used in developing such a scale. For example, the experimenter might ask 200 people to act as judges, whose job would be to categorize a large group of statements that had been written on a specific subject (war, for instance). They would read each statement, decide to what extent it was favorable or unfavorable (i.e., for or against war), and place it in the category corresponding to their rating. There would be twelve categories into which the judges could sort these statements. Categories 1 or 2 would receive the statements that were felt to be strongly antiwar, while categories 10 or 11 would receive strongly prowar statements. As you can imagine, it would take a long time for 200 judges to sort a large group of statements into these categories.

When the judges had completed their sorting, the weeding out and selecting of statements for the final scale would begin. The best candidates for the final scale would meet two criteria: (1) low variability among the judges (meaning that a statement did not get placed into categories 1 or 2 by some judges and 10 or 11 by others), and (2) equal representation of all statement categories (meaning that the statements in the final scale would be equally distributed across the twelve-category range). The second criterion prompts the "equally appearing intervals" description associated with Thurstone scaling procedures. After the above series of steps, the resultant scale would be a collection of approximately twenty statements. Judges would then be asked to read those statements, checking the ones that were in agreement with their respective viewpoints on the subject. By adding the category weightings of these statements (1, 2, 4, 7, 10, 11, etc.) and obtaining a mean score, the scale administrator would be able to determine where in the twelve-category range the judges' attitudes on this subject happened to be. Scale results would indicate, for instance, whether they were prowar or antiwar.

Because the judging, categorizing, and statement-selecting procedures must be repeated for each subject on which one wishes to develop a Thurstone-type scale, it is easy to understand why attempts have been made to simplify scale-development procedures. One of the earliest and best-known attempts was that of Likert. Likert believed that it was important to have judges express their own attitudes on a subject rather than to ask them to make general "anti" or "pro" judgments in relation to others' attitude statements. In keeping with this belief, he developed a scaling procedure known as the "method of summated ratings." The response range on a Likert scale item encompassed five categories (strongly agree, agree, no opinion, disagree, strongly disagree). A strongly "pro" response on a given item was scored as a 5, and this meant that the person with the most prominent "pro" attitude on the subject received the highest overall score on a Likert scale. Correspondingly, the person with the strongest "anti" attitude on the subject received the lowest overall score on the scale. In this procedure, called "summated ratings," it is important that a person's score on each individual item in the scale correlates prositively with the person's overall score.

A number of scale measurement approaches concentrating on specific measurement purposes followed these early beginnings. One was Guttman's unidimensional approach in which he sought to measure a range of depth on a given attitude dimension. In a scale itself, he arranged this depth measurement sequentially. This means that, if a subject had a very slight agreement attitude on the attitude dimension, he or she would agree with the first item in the scale. If a subject had a stronger agreement attitude, he or she might agree with the first two scale items, etc. In theory, it was an approach whereby Guttman claimed the ability to discern what specific items in his scale the subject has agreed with, simply by knowing that person's overall scale score. In practice, prediction has not always been that neatly accomplished, but the method proved innovative and important.

Another specific-purpose scale was Bogardus's "social distance scale." This scale had a seven-phrase description range that could be used in relation to a number of different identifiable ethnic groups or nationalities. For whatever groups or nationalities that were being tested in a given situation, a person had a response range from (1) "would admit to close kinship by marriage" to (7) "would exclude from my country." Several modifications of this scale technique have been made — the best-known recent one being that of Triandis.

Osgood developed the "semantic differential scale." In this scale, the subject is given a concept — such as church, capital punishment, or whatever — followed by a series of bipolar adjectives (e.g., good-bad, honest-dishonest, clean-dirty, etc.). Between the two poles (good-bad, for instance) there are seven spaces, and the subject's job is to place a check in one of those spaces. A check in the spot next to "good" receives a score of 7 and, correspondingly, a check next to "bad" receives a score of 1. There are several sets of these bipolar adjectives, thus allowing for a large possible range in which scores can occur. Through factor analysis, Osgood has discovered three dimensions to be tested — evaluative, activity, potency. The first of these dimensions is tested with adjectives such as good-bad; the second with adjectives such as active-passive; and the third, with adjectives such as strong-weak. The key dimension, and the one measured most prominently within an Osgood scale, is the evaluative one.

Public opinion polling is familiar to us and constitutes another measurement approach in this area. Unlike the preceding approaches, public opinion polling seeks to obtain a response percentage figure that can serve as a base for comparison when subsequent polls are conducted on the same question or attitude dimension. The "white elephant" in this area, that served as a great lesson for subsequent pollsters, was a presidential poll conducted by the *Literary Digest* in 1936. The *Digest* used the telephone book as the source of names to be included in its sample. Conducting a poll using these names, the *Digest* predicted that Alf Landon would win the election by a landslide. When Roosevelt's strength at the ballot box smothered Landon's election hopes, it also smothered the *Literary Digest*. Because the *Digest*'s managers had failed to realize that the names in the phone directory did not constitute a representative sample of the voting public, they had polled an unrepresentative sample and correspondingly had made an erroneous prediction. The *Literary Digest* went out of business, but the lesson of representative sampling was remembered well by other would-be pollsters — especially George Gallup, whose American Institute of Public Opinion has become a byword in polling. Polling techniques have become very refined, and polls are depended upon heavily by certain groups, notably politicians. Pollsters warn, however, that they are not predictors of an outcome but, instead, monitors of an opinion as it exists within a sample at a specific time.

Scaling techniques continue to develop. Among current entries on the scene is Bem's Scale of Psychological Androgeny (a measure of sex-role stereotypes). If your androgeny scale score were low, you would be considered high in sex-role stereotyping and vice versa. Since current research emphases in the field provide needs for new or modified measuring instruments, the development of new scales and techniques will no doubt continue.

Two additional terms that should be mentioned under this heading are "behavioral" and "behavioroid." A behavioral technique is one in which the person being tested is asked to make a commitment to a certain behavior or course of action and to carry through with that behavior. In a behavioroid technique, the person is asked to make a commitment to a behavior or course of action but is not asked to carry through with the behavior itself. Say, for instance, I approached someone with the information that some school buses had broken down and I was forming a car pool to carry children across the city to their respective schools. I would be employing a behavioral approach if I actually asked that person to drive a group of children across the city. In the behavioroid approach, I would get the person's verbal or written commitment in favor of such a car pool, but I would not follow up with a later request that he or she perform the behavior.

Attitude Change

Among the best-known names in the area of attitude change is Festinger. His theory of cognitive dissonance has been the source of a broad range of experimentation in this field. In effect, Festinger's theory says that there is a tendency for people to seek a state of consonance between their attitudes and their behavior. Someone is in a state of consonance when his or her behavior in a given belief-area corresponds to his or her attitude in that area. After formulating his theory, Festinger's next step was to create a dissonance between the person's attitude and his or her behavior. He predicted that in order to regain the comfort that comes with consonance, the person's attitude would tend to change in the direction of the behavior that had been performed. For instance, a conscientious objector who had been forced to use a rifle in frontline army combat would begin to change his attitude in favor of this behavior.

Aronson and other researchers extended this theory to the area of initiation-type settings. If I go through some pretty unpleasant behavior in order to meet the requirements for joining a group, I justify having gone through this behavior by enhancing my valuation of the group. I say, in effect, "This is a tremendous group and well worth the initiation requirements I went through in order to join." If this seems farfetched, check with some friends who have joined a sorority or a fraternity recently and ask them whether they are glad they joined. Better yet, ask your dad or one of his friends whether he is glad he had the experience of basic training in the military. In each of these instances, one's tendency to say that the experience was worth the trouble is an example of cognitive dissonance — a means of self-justification.

Attraction and Affiliation

Determinants of Attraction

To answer the question of why persons are attracted to one another, several possible determinants have been mentioned and investigated. *Proximity* is one of the most prominent of these determinants. Whyte found that within a new housing development the single best predictor of social attraction and friendship development was the distance between houses. Friendship and social attraction were far more likely between persons living next door to each other than, for instance, between people living down the street from each other or in different blocks. Festinger and his associates did a similar study in an apartment complex containing several two-story buildings with five apartments on each floor. Social attraction and friendship patterns again were found to be most prominent in the next-door setting and weaker as one moved additional doors away from any given apartment. This finding introduced the concept of functional distance — functional because, although two or three doors away is not all that far in terms of actual physical distance, the principle of proximity still seems to hold.

A second determinant — *similarity* — has been investigated prominently by Newcomb, Byrne, and others. Newcomb put the variables of proximity and similarity in competition with each other by setting up a dormitory room assignment procedure and carefully assigning rooms on the basis of either similar or dissimilar interests and values. Of major concern was whether sheer proximity (being roommates) would determine attraction patterns or whether similarity in interests and values would be the major determinant in attraction. The outcome revealed that proximity operated short-range but that similarity determined the long-range attraction patterns. Byrne and his associates used a questionnaire technique to establish within their subjects either perceived similarity or dissimilarity to another person's attitudes. Typically, Byrne might present his subject with the results of a questionnaire that presumably had been filled out by another person — but actually had been based on the subject's responses to an earlier questionnaire. The subject's reactions yield strong evidence of attraction on the basis of perceived similarity (i.e., agreement between the subject's responses and those of the "other person"). This evidence of attraction holds even in situations where the perceived "other person" has been represented as being a member of a different ethnic group or nationality.

Aronson and Jones are among the leading researchers who have investigated a third determinant — *rewardingness* (and its ingratiation counterpart). In effect, they have found that individuals are attracted to persons who care about them and will be very wary about persons whose "care" seems to have within it the possibility of an ulterior motive. Concentrating on the rewardingness aspect of attraction, Aronson and his associates have also found that persons are more likely to be attracted to individuals who have evaluated them positively than to individuals who have negatively or neutrally evaluated them. A surprising finding was that attraction was most prominent in instances where the evaluation had moved from an initially negative one to an eventually positive one. The strength of the attraction in such instances is attributed to the combined effects of negative reinforcement (removal of an aversive stimulus) and positive reinforcement (positive evaluation); and this phenomenon provides the basis for Aronson's gain-loss model, cited later. Jones, working with ingratiation, found that persons are attracted to individuals whose positive evaluation does not carry the prospect of subsequent commitment or expectation. Counterpart to this outcome is the finding that flattery or ingratiation is most effective when directed toward an area in which the recipient has never been sure of having competence but has wished for such competence.

Anderson's work deals with *personal attributes* as a basis for social attraction. He is concerned with the general question of whether there are personal traits that people collectively find attractive. Using an adjective-rating approach, he found that the highest rating among 555 adjectives was invariably given to the traits of honesty, sincerity, and trustworthiness. Correspondingly, the lowest rating was given to words connoting liar or phony. Anderson is a pioneer in this area, and his work has been prominently utilized in the categories of attribution and person perception.

Zajonc has investigated the determinant of *familiarity* and has found it to be a prominent factor in social attraction. In one of his studies, he had persons look at Turkish words (totally meaningless to the viewing persons). He offered some words only one or two times, but showed others as often as twenty-five times. Following the viewing procedures, the persons were asked to define the words they had seen. The words seen most often were accorded the most positive definitions.

Attraction Models

Social psychologists have found it helpful in both their communication and their research to develop models of attraction. The following — briefly cited — are among the most prominent of these models:

Balance (A-B-X)

Developed through the work of Heider and the more recent theoretical concepts of Newcomb, this model is built upon persons A and B having attraction feelings toward each other and toward person or concept X. In the resulting A-B-X triad, the model indicates that consonance or state of balance exists when there is an even number of negative signs. Imbalance exists where there is an odd number of negative signs. For example, suppose that Jack likes rock music, his dad does not like rock music, and Jack likes his dad. The situation within this triad is imbalance (one negative sign). Balance can be restored if Jack changes his views about either rock music or his dad (bringing a second negative sign into the triad).

Obviously, all + signs in the triad also represent balance — both Jack and his dad liking rock music, and Jack liking his dad. The model is usually demonstrated as a triangular-positioned triad with signs placed between the entries. For example:

$$\begin{array}{c} \text{Student} \\ + \qquad\qquad + \\ \text{Parent} \quad - \quad \begin{array}{c}\text{Group}\\ \text{or Concept}\end{array} \end{array}$$

The balance model is frequently used in explaining and demonstrating a phenomenon such as cognitive dissonance.

Social Exchange Theory

Currently Gergen is one of the most prominent names associated with this theoretical view (see his booklet entitled *Psychology of Behavior Exchange* (Reading, Mass.: Addison-Wesley, 1969). Simply stated, the theory puts social attraction in the context of a person's rewards from interaction divided by the person's cost incurred in the interaction. When costs outrun rewards, social attraction can be expected to decline and disappear. Moreover, the most favorable fraction (rewards/costs) will be the front-runner when a choice must occur in social attraction. If, for instance, a college student is dating back home and on the campus, the back-home relationship must be proportionately more rewarding than the on-campus one to remain comparable in strength — maintaining the back-home relationship involves more cost. According to social exchange theory, people continually scan and evaluate reward/cost in their social relationships.

Complementarity Theory

Winch is associated with this view, the primary application of which is in the area of extensive, intimate relationships such as courtship and marriage. This theory says, in effect, that such relationships require that aspects of personality be complementary in order for the relationship to be successful. A guy and a gal who both have strong dominance needs would be seen as heading for disaster in such a relationship. Success in the relationship would be achieved only if a strong dominance need on the part of one person were met by a low dominance need on the part of the other (in effect, complementarity). Because it is relationship-specific and symbolically "messier," this theory runs no real interference with its tailor-made prospective opponent — the balance model.

Festinger's Social-Comparison

This model demonstrates how perceived similarity and social attraction tend to interact. Essentially, Festinger is saying that (1) people are attracted to persons they perceive as similar to themselves and (2) they perceive the persons to whom they are attracted as more similar to themselves than is really the case. Those "perceived similar others" take on special significance in ambiguous decision-making or opinion-forming situations. Given a situation in which we must deal with ambiguous or contradictory information in forming an opinion or making a decision, the decision, thought, or opinion of a "perceived similar other" becomes very influential. This may be part of the dynamic operating in the "two-step flow of communication," discussed later. The "snowball" effect within Festinger's concept is readily apparent — social attraction feeds perceived similarity, which feeds more social attraction, and so forth.

Aronson's Gain-Loss Model

In studies such as the one performed by Aronson and Linder, it was found that movement from a negative to a positive evaluation of a person led to stronger social attraction toward the evaluator by the person being evaluated than did movement from a neutral position toward positive evaluation. Aronson quotes Spinoza's observation that "hatred which is completely vanquished by love passes into love and love is thereupon greater than if hatred had not preceded it." Within this kind of situation, it has been suggested that a kind of double or compound reward operates, with (1) the removal of the aversive stimulus operating as negative reinforcement and (2) the presentation of a desired stimulus operating as positive reinforcement. Unofficially, this has been termed "Aronson's law of marital infidelity."

The woman who receives a compliment from a stranger finds that compliment more rewarding than an equivalent compliment received from her husband. The husband — beginning from a general position of positive reinforcement — lacks the capacity to be as rewarding as the stranger (who begins from a neutral position). Thus, the close friend or spouse constitutes a less potent source of reward but a strong and more potent source of punishment.

The distinction between attraction and affiliation, is that between positively evaluating other people (attraction) and simply being with other people (affiliation). Schachter conducted a classic series of studies on the affiliation dimension and found that, in a situation of experimentally induced stress, persons were discriminating in their choice to be with other people. Given an option of simply being with other people, being with other people experiencing the same situational stress, or being alone, those persons having only the choice of simply being with other people preferred to remain alone — while those persons having the choice of being with others in the same situational stress preferred affiliation over being alone. Schachter concluded that, in the presence of fear, misery loves miserable company. Conducting similar studies in which both unrealistic fear (anxiety) and realistic fear were introduced, Sarnoff and Zimbardo found that in high-anxiety settings persons preferred to remain alone. (This was interpreted as hesitancy to share their unrealistic fear with others because of the risk of embarrassment.) Thus, the research findings indicate that people have a tendency to affiliate with "similar situation others" in cases of high fear and a tendency to prefer being alone in cases of high anxiety.

Communication

Two tracks operate within this heading — verbal communication and nonverbal communication. The former deals with communication via words; the latter refers to ways in which social communication occurs without words.

Verbal Communication

Specific communication patterns and leadership styles are prominent research concerns within this area. Their relevance is also strongly felt in organizational areas of applied psychology though, and thus, to avoid duplicate review coverage, these topics will be considered in the Applied Psychology section. Janis introduced the concept of groupthink, which indicates the decision-making problems that can beset a group because of thought patterns that the sheer existence of the decision-making group can promote. He analyzed in detail the groupthink phenomena surrounding the Kennedy Administration's decisions that culminated in the Bay of Pigs invasion. Among the characteristics of groupthink are (1) illusions of invulnerability, (2) evolution of a rationale (justifying the group's decision), (3) belief in the morality of the group's decisions, (4) stereotyped views of the enemy, (5) conformity pressures, (6) self-censorship of critical thoughts (the individual censoring self and not expressing critical thoughts to the group), (7) mindguards (persons in the group who suppress information divergent from group opinion), (8) illusion of unanimity (an illusion of unanimity within the group despite unexpressed individual doubts).

Janis believes that groupthink is likely to occur when (1) the decision-making group is highly cohesive, (2) the group is insulated from other, more balanced information, and (3) the leader has preconceived notions of the correct policy to follow. To prevent groupthink, Janis underscores the importance of arranging group conditions in such a manner that individual thought and expression are encouraged.

Among media effects, the following terms are generally familiar:

- Two-Step communication flow — refers to the media communication pattern of first reaching the opinion makers in a given group or community (step 1) so that they will then influence their respective constituencies (step 2). The opinion makers need not be the "pillars" of the community, but they are those persons within any given group who have the basic opinion-reference function in that group.

- Media elite — refers to the pattern of influence associated with specific persons in a given communications medium. For instance, in television news there are certain commentators toward whom the rest of the television commentator community turn in developing their own approaches to news events. This term, therefore, refers to an influence within the medium itself.

Nonverbal Communication

Two avenues form the basic investigation areas here — kinesics and proxemics. *Kinesics* is the study of body language — the ways in which people unwittingly communicate through their gestures, facial expressions, body positions, etc. Pioneering work in this area was done by Birdwhistell. He concentrated upon the face and the development of a notation system for each aspect of facial expression. This approach was considered micro. A macro approach was undertaken by a Birdwhistell associate named Scheflen. Within Scheflen's approach, general patterns of interaction over a period of time were studied. Ekman has concentrated upon the posssibility of universal facial expressions and has spent much time studying the smile in various cultures. He concludes that the smile is a universal expression — a general communicator across all the cultures he has studied. Other research in this area includes the work of Kendon and that of Goffman. Possessing a theoretical mind, Goffman has been the stimulus for many research studies conducted in this area.

Proxemics deals with research relating to territoriality, that is, personal space, unseen dividing lines, and the dynamics of invading another's personal space. Key work in this field was spearheaded by Hall, who suggested four territorial zones — intimate, personal, social, and public. The first of these zones is believed to extend to approximately eighteen inches from the body; other zones become increasingly distant. Implications for urban crowding may be a future outgrowth of work in this area.

Persuasion

In this area, concerns relating both to noncoercive and coercive persuasion come into view. The latter includes brainwashing techniques and techniques formerly used in police interrogation; the former deals with general persuasion techniques as used in public speaking, advertising, and the like.

Techniques in General Persuasion

Several concepts have been advanced in this area. Among them is McGuire's inoculation theory, which states, in effect, that people can be "immunized" against a subsequent persuasive communication if they have been familiarized in advance with the persuasive arguments they are going to hear, and have heard counterarguments. Freedman introduced a foot-in-the-door technique that demonstrates that we are more likely to agree to a large, commitment-type request if we have agreed in advance to a smaller commitment request. This is the salesman's familiar approach of getting a small commitment now and returning to ask for a larger commitment later. Janis found an eating-while-reading effect that indicated that people were more likely to acquiesce to a request or agree with a viewpoint if it were presented during a pleasurable activity such as eating.

Additional concepts in this area include the sleeper effect (a communication that has no immediate effect but proves to have long-range influence), the primacy-recency effect (whether first-communicator or last-communicator position in a presentation sequence is most effective), and two-sided/one-sided communication (whether persuasive communication will be most effective if both points of view are presented or if only one view is presented). In primacy-recency, the major question is how long after the communication will the audience members be making their decision. If the decision is soon or immediate, recency would apply (i.e., the last communicator in the sequence would be the most influential). If the decision is distant, primacy would be most effective. Out of necessity, I have oversimplified this area. Communicator characteristics and credibility are among the additional concerns central to investigations undertaken here.

Techniques in Coercive Persuasion

Schein is associated with the study of brainwashing techniques and has subdivided the general approach into a physical phase and a psychological phase. The physical phase occurs first and includes such things as exhaustive, forced marches at night (accompanied by sparse food, little or no medical attention, the leaving behind of those who cannot keep the rigorous pace, and captor explanation that all this is made necessary by the ruthless aggression of the captured soldiers' armed forces). The psychological phase begins upon arrival at the captors' camp facility. Leaders are separated from the group, original insignia of rank are no longer recognized, prisoners are rewarded for informing on fellow prisoners, incoming mail is read and only the unpleasant news is relayed, prisoners are rewarded for making confessions of their "wrongs" against the captors and for "admitting" the burden of guilt they feel at having engaged in such unfortunate aggressive behavior. The ultimate goal is to gain converts to the cause of the captors, but Schein has observed that the goal is seldom realized. Although a number of prisoners have been found to make confessions and testimonials, few convert.

Groups

Conformity

Asch conducted early research in this area and introduced a line-judgment technique in which seven or eight persons acted as confederates in unanimously making an obvious error in judgment. Next, the unsuspecting subject was asked to respond. Findings indicate the subject's prominent tendency to go along with the obviously wrong judgment that has preceded. If confederate unanimity is broken, such conformity is far less likely.

Crutchfield developed an indirect means of imposing conformity pressure that relieves the need to have a large number of persons serve as confederates. His technique involves five individual booths, each equipped with a light panel. Via the panel, a subject presumably sees how persons occupying the other four booths have responded to questions. In actuality, each booth occupant is being given the same light-panel-response feedback from a control room. While this technique enables every participant to be a subject, it is one step removed from the conformity pressures imposed through direct interaction.

Hollander felt the necessity of moving beyond a conformity-nonconformity terminology. He believed that within the nonconformity category there could be both persons who were reacting against conformity and those who were behaving independently on the basis of their own preferences (regardless of the conforming trend). To characterize this distinction, he introduced the terms *anticonformity* and *independence* (replacing *nonconformity*).

Cooperation-Competition

Sherif and Sherif did a classic field study utilizing subjects from a boys' summer camp. Through prearrangements, they established two basic groups, which they soon found to be very hostile toward each other. The only technique that the investigators found effective in reducing this hostility was the introduction of a superordinate goal — a desirable corporate goal that neither group could accomplish alone (e.g., finding the problem with the camp's water supply, or getting the camp's disabled food truck moving again). Whereas merely bringing the groups together only served to aggravate the hostility, the superordinate goal proved effective in hostility reduction.

In a more formalized laboratory setting, Deutsch has studied the dynamics of cooperation-competition. His Acme-Bolt Trucking Game involves two players and a single main route to their respective destinations. The game has the capacity to give each player a roadblock potential, and Deutsch has found that when a player is given such threat potential he is very likely to use it.

Game decision theory (gaming) has also been prominently developed for investigating the dynamics of cooperation and competition in laboratory settings. A major distinction in this area is that between the zero sum game and the nonzero sum game. In the zero sum game, the gains of one player are made at the direct expense of the other; the nonzero sum game allows each player to make intermediate gains. The nonzero sum game has been prominently adopted in the characteristic research on cooperation-competition. A game involves a payoff matrix. Within a matrix, each player can make one of two choices. Each player knows in advance that the payoff will depend upon the choice made by the other player. In the "Prisoner's Dilemma," both players can make intermediate gains if they cooperatively refrain from trying to maximize individual gain. If they both try to maximize individual gains, they will both suffer great losses. The matrix concept allows several payoff possibilities to be established and investigated. Names prominent to this area include Thibaut, Kelley, and Tedeschi.

Violence

As a prominent social concern, violence and aggression have been natural subjects for social-psychological inquiry. Dollard and Miller gave an early conceptual framework to the field with the frustration-aggression hypothesis. Their hypothesis indicates that frustration (being blocked from a goal or having the goal removed) leads to aggression. Berkowitz has been concerned with the effects of aggression-eliciting stimuli upon a potential aggressor. He has found that the presence of weapons heightens both the likelihood and the level of aggression. Bandura has investigated modeling effects — for instance, the effect of viewing an aggressive model on television. He finds that a child's aggression is heightened immediately following observation of a model who has been rewarded for aggressive activity. In the case of television, Siegel has suggested that a more long-range result of violence viewing is the expectation that children come to associate with specific roles in society. One of the most blatant examples of this is the role-violence differential between male and female roles as socially communicated and defined. Wolfgang believes that our society has, in effect, legitimized violence. Among subtle sanctions he sees in support of this position are the society's support for physical aggression of parents toward their children and the institutionalization of sanctioned violence through wars. Zimbardo investigated vandalism, violence, and his concept of deindividuation. In effect, the latter indicates that when people lose their identity or become anonymous within the larger group, they are likely to engage in aggression and violence. Milgram conducted perhaps one of the most frightening investigations in this area. Through a shock-administering experiment, he found that people are surprisingly obedient to commands to administer high-level shocks to other people.

Helping Behavior

The investigation of helping behavior grew out of the scientific interest in thought-numbing incidents of violence. The catalyst was the Kitty Genovese murder in Manhattan in 1964, when thirty-eight persons were known to have watched the half-hour, gruesome ordeal. What was so shocking was the fact that no one tried to help or call the police. Darley and Latane spearheaded early investigations and, in their laboratory studies, found the number of other persons present to be a prominent variable — with the likelihood of anyone helping decreasing as the number of bystanders increased. Bryan, Test, and Piliavin have found the model variable to be important. If a model of helping has preceded the incident in which a person is called upon to help, the likelihood that that person will help is greater than the likelihood present in a no-model setting. Allen has found that directness of request is also important — that there is a greater likelihood of obtaining help when the help request has been specifically addressed to the would-be helper. Another variable, that has been found to be important by Darley et al., is the clarity of the helping situation — whether the person requesting help really is in an emergency situation.

Prejudice

Prejudice is defined as an attitude against an identifiable group, formed without knowledge of or familiarity with specific members of the group. The word *prejudice* gives definitional meaning and clarity to this attitude. Allport's *The Nature of Prejudice* summarized early work in the area, and Clark and Clark provided basic early work with young children. While the latter investigators found that young black children some years ago expressed a preference to be white, recent replications such as Hraba and Grant's have indicated that this preference pattern no longer exists. That turnabout may be interpreted as indicative of both personal and racial pride. Pettigrew — one of Allport's former students — is among the most prominent current research authorities in the area.

Personality

Adorno's *The Authoritarian Personality* took a post-World War II look at the question of whether attitudes (particularly anti-Semitism) were related to general personality traits and characteristics. The large, comprehensive study uncovered a relationship between the authoritarian personality and attitudes of anti-Semitism and prejudice. The authoritarianism scale developed within this study has been widely used in other contexts and is commonly referred to as the F-scale. Rokeach has extended this avenue of research and introduced the concept of dogmatism. Also related to this general area is the term *Machiavellianism* as introduced and investigated by Christie.

Status and Roles

In this area, I will briefly concentrate upon a handful of concepts and terms. Achieved-ascribed status distinction is between status attained on the basis of one's own achievement and status accorded on the basis of given characteristics such as family line, wealth, etc. Inter-role–intra-role conflict distinction is made between conflict experienced in meeting the expectations of two different roles (e.g., daughter and fiancée, son and fiancé) and conflict experienced in meeting expectations within a single role (e.g., professor and student differences in expectations for the role of college student). The former is "inter," the latter, "intra." Distributive justice refers to comparing your reward-minus-cost to that of another worker. If, for instance, one worker is not as well educated as another but earns more money, distributive justice does not prevail and worker discontent can be anticipated. Status congruence refers to a person's tendency to make all aspects of his status congruent.

Currently, the investigation of sex roles constitutes a major research emphasis within this area. Bem has introduced the term *androgeny* to refer to sex equality in status and role opportunities and expectations. Her Scale of Psychological Androgeny is one of the instruments used to measure the presence of sex-role stereotypes. Williams, Bennett, and Best have made a distinction between sex roles, sex-role stereotypes and sex-trait stereotypes — a distinction that they have built into their measurement instrument in this area. Their Adjective Checklist is used to determine the presence of sex-trait stereotypes.

Attribution Theory

A recent and growing area of investigation, attribution theory encompasses several of the topics already reviewed. The initial model in this area was Heider's analysis-of-behavior model:

$$\text{Behavioral effect } (E) = f (\text{Environment} + \text{Personal force})$$

Heider's formula states that behavioral effect is a function of environment and personal force. Research is concentrated upon determining the extent to which perceivers will attribute another person's behavior to external or internal causation. Jones and Davis have found that when external forces are strong and a person goes against those forces, the person's behavior is likely to be attributed to internal causation. Similarly, there is difficulty in attributing internal causation when the person's behavior is normative or in keeping with group behavior.

A quick look at findings in the broader spectrum indicates, for example, that when men and women perform equally well on a given task, women are seen as trying harder (Taylor, Kiesler et al.); people tend to perceive their own behavior as situationally controlled and that of other people as internally caused (Jones and Nisbett). Hastorf et al. have found that people with unusual histories (handicap, psychiatric hospitalization, etc.) will have any non-normative actions attributed to that background. In "Lennie B" experiments concerning the severity of accidents, Walster found that there is a tendency to attribute more responsibility to the person at fault (i.e., internal causation) when the accident outcome is severe than when it is mild. Perhaps one of the most telling findings was that of Jones — discovering our tendency to attribute very high or very low performance to internal causation. Hence, the familiar comment that "the poor are poor because they're lazy and don't want to work."

To explain why people attribute internal causality to others, Shaver formulated a defensive-attribution hypothesis suggesting that the prospect of bad or unfortunate consequences occurring by chance threatens self-esteem. It therefore becomes a kind of self-defense to attribute internal causation to others. Lerner's just-world hypothesis indicates that people like to believe that the world is just and that individuals get what they deserve.

Although it is somewhat superficial and oversimplified, I hope that this review section has given you some familiarity with the field of social psychology and its areas of research. In your further review, the concept-name-terminology sheet may provide a helpful checkpoint. As you seek mastery of concepts, names, and terminology, the following textbooks might prove valuable:

> J. Freedman, D. Sears, and J. Carlsmith, *Social Psychology* (Englewood Cliffs, N.J.: Prentice-Hall, 1981), three well-known psychologists touch upon major areas with more breadth than depth

> K. Gergen and M. Gergen, *Social Psychology,* (New York: Harcourt, Brace, Jovanovich, 1981), a highly-respected husband-wife team brings both authoritative depth and skillful readability.

> P. Middlebrook, *Social Psychology and Modern Life* (New York: Knopf, 1980), combines thoroughness and interesting presentation.

Social Psychology Review

CONCEPTS	NAMES	TERMS
Attitude Formation and Change		
Cognitive dissonance	Festinger	Definitional requirements for an attitude
	Aronson	
Measurement	Thurstone	Equal-appearing intervals
	Likert	Summated ratings
	Guttman	Unidimensionality
	Osgood	Semantic differential
	Bogardus	Social distance
	Remmers	
	Gallup	Quintamensional filtration
		Objective vs. projective
		Behavioral/behavioroid
Single stimulus factor	Kelley	"Warm-cold" variable

CONCEPTS	NAMES	TERMS

Attraction and Affiliation

CONCEPTS	NAMES	TERMS
Models		
Balance (A-B-X)	Newcomb/Heider	
Social comparison	Festinger	
Complementary	Winch	
Behavior exchange	Gergen	
Gain-loss	Aronson	
Attraction determinants	Whyte/Festinger et al.	Proximity
	Newcomb/Byrne	Similarity
	Aronson/Jones	Rewardingness/ingratiation
	Anderson	Personality attributes
	Zajonc	Familiarity
Affiliation	Schachter	Stress

Communication (Verbal)

CONCEPTS	NAMES	TERMS
Patterns	Bauer	Y/chain/wheel/circle/star
	Lewin/Lippitt/White	Autocratic/democratic
Group effects	Janis	Groupthink
Media effects	Klapper	Direct and indirect effects
		Two-step communication flow
		Media elite
		Third party

Communication (Nonverbal)

CONCEPTS	NAMES	TERMS
Proxemics (territoriality)	Hall	Personal space
	Ardrey	
Kinesics (body language)	Birdwhistell/Scheflen	Micro/macro
	Ekman	Universal expressions
	Kendon	
	Goffman	

Persuasion

CONCEPTS	NAMES	TERMS
Advertising	Markin	Freudian vs. existential
Coercive techniques		
Brainwashing	Schein	Phases: physical/psychological
Interrogation		Structured environment & intentional distortions
	McGuire	Inoculation theory
	Freedman	Foot-in-the-door technique
		Two-sided vs. one-sided communications
		Sleeper effect
		Primacy/recency

Groups

CONCEPTS	NAMES	TERMS
Conformity	Asch	Line judgment technique
	Crutchfield	Booth technique
	Hollander	Conformity/anticonformity/independence
		Idiosyncrasy credit
Cooperation-competition	Sherif and Sherif	Superordinate goal
	Deutsch	Trucking game
		Use of threat
Game decision theory (gaming)		"Prisoner's dilemma"
		Payoff matrix
		Zero and nonzero sum
	Thibaut/Kelly	Fate control
Risk taking	Wallach/Kogan/Bem	
Theories of collective behavior	Smelser	
	Freud	
	LeBon	

CONCEPTS	NAMES	TERMS

Violence

Frustration-aggression hypothesis	Dollard/Miller	Displacement
Aggression-eliciting stimuli	Berkowitz	Catharsis
Modeling	Bandura	
Socialization	Wolfgang	
Vandalism	Zimbardo	Deindividuation
Obedience	Milgram	

Helping Behavior

Analysis of determinants	Latane/Darley	
Model	Bryan/Test	
	Piliavin	
Directness of request	Allen	

Prejudice

Theoretical analysis	Allport	
Attitude/race dimensions	Rokeach	
Attitudes among children	Clark and Clark	Racial awareness
	Hraba and Grant	Racial self-identification
		Racial preference

Personality

Authoritarian personality	Adorno	
Dogmatism	Rokeach	
Machiavellianism	Christie	
Dimensions	Rotter	Internal/external control
	McClelland	nAch
	Kuhn	Self-concept
Person perception	Schlosberg/Woodworth	Recognition of emotions
	Anderson	Additive/averaging model
Perceptual defense	McGinnies	
	Bruner/Postman	

Status and Roles

Class and class measurement	Brown	Achieved/ascribed
		Interrole/intrarole conflict
	Homans	Distributive justice
		Status congruence
	Bem and Bem	Androgeny

General

Attribution theory	Shaver et al.	

Personality

You have all heard at one time or another the expression that he or she "has personality," and you have no doubt given thought to your own personalities at times. It is easier to spot personality than to define it, but the many definitions of the term carry the common elements of (1) relatively enduring qualities in our behavior, (2) uniqueness, and (3) comprehensiveness. "Jan swats a fly" says nothing about Jan's personality, because it is a statement about a behavior of the moment that has an automatic quality about it. In addition, everyone swats flies (even cows), so it really says nothing to distinguish Jan from anyone else. On the other hand, someone might say that "Jan reacts quickly and defensively to criticism." That person has said something about her personality — something that defines a relatively enduring characteristic distinguishing her from other people and having the comprehensive quality of being part of a total view of "Jan the person."

Review of this area logically centers on two categories: theory and measurement. The following lists will give you an idea of the familiarity that you will need in each of these categories:

- Personality theories
  Psychoanalytic (Freud)
    ego-analytic (Hartmann, Erikson)
  Psychodynamic
    individual (Adler)
    analytic (Jung)
    interpersonal relationship (Sullivan)
    cultural (Horney)
    sociopsychoanalytic (Fromm)
    learning interpretation of psychoanalytic (Dollard-Miller)
  Behaviorist
    radical behaviorist (Watson, Skinner)
    social behaviorist (Bandura, Rotter)
    reciprocal inhibition (Wolpe)
    two-factor theory (Mowrer)
  Phenomenological
    client-centered (Rogers)
    self-actualization (Maslow)
    transactional (Berne, Harris)
    logotherapy (Frankl)
    personal construct (Kelly)
  Trait
    physiognomy (Sheldon)
    functional autonomy (Allport)
    factor analysis (Cattell, Eysenck)
    personology (Murray)

Theory

A reasonable question at this point would be: Why don't personality theorists get together on a single, unified theory? The reason is that research in the field is not far enough along for the investigators to be in that enviable position. Dealing with and theorizing about the whole person is a complex task. The theorists themselves are well trained, thoroughly experienced clinical psychologists or psychiatrists who have dealt firsthand with people's adjustment problems. Their theories reflect their observations and the commonly recurring themes that they have encountered. Each theorist, in his own way, gets at important aspects of personality. All current theoretical views will at some point in the future seem as weird and archaic as early maps of the world seem now. But people's problems are occurring now, and efforts to systematize and understand in order to help must be made now, too.

Personality theory foundations began with Sigmund Freud in the 1890s. His psychoanalytic theory is by far the most thoroughly systematized of any personality theory in existence and has served as a basis for investigation by most subsequent theorists. Within the theoretical framework outlined, many terms and concepts are expressed. The major ones are listed here to assist you in your review.

- Psychoanalysis
  Divisions of the psyche — id, ego, superego
  Cathexis and anticathexis
  Defense mechanisms (repression et al.)

Psychosexual stages of development
    oral (passive-sadistic)
    anal (retentive-expulsive)
    phallic (Oedipus complex and castration fear – Electra complex and penis envy)
    latency
    genital
Conscious, preconscious, and unconscious
Thanatos and Eros (death and life instincts)
Parapraxes (slips of the tongue) and wit
Dreams and dream interpretation
Free association — the method of therapy

- Ego analysis
Ego as conflict-free sphere
Erikson's eight stages of man (covering personality adjustment throughout the life cycle)

- Psychodynamic
Adlerian terms:
    inferiority feeling and superiority striving
    social interest as a determinant of mental health
    family constellation (birth order and personality)
    predisposing situations for mental illness — organ inferiority, pampering, neglect
Jungian terms:
    archetype
    collective unconscious
    extraversion-introversion
    persona, anima, animus, shadow
    four psychological functions — sensing, thinking, feeling, intuiting
Sullivan terms:
    modes of cognition — prototaxic, parataxic, syntaxic
    emphasis on schizophrenic patients
    dynamisms
    personifications
Horney terms:
    role of culture in defining normality
    modes of relating — moving toward, moving against, moving away from
    womb envy (counterpart to Freud's penis envy)
Fromm terms:
    five types of love — brotherly, motherly, erotic, self, supreme being
    five human needs — relatedness versus narcissism (love), creativeness versus destructiveness (transcendence), brotherliness versus incest (rootedness), individuality versus conformity (identity), reason versus irrationality (frame of orientation and devotion)
Dollard-Miller terms:
    four fundamentals of learning — drive, cue, response, reinforcement
    four critical training situations (each with potential for adjustive or maladjustive learning) — feeding, cleanliness, sex, anger-anxiety
    four types of conflict situations — approach-approach, avoidance-avoidance, approach-avoidance, double approach-avoidance

- Behaviorist and Learning Theory
Watson-Skinner terms:
    larnyx movements and muscle twitches (Watson)
    operant conditioning
    shaping techniques
    positive reinforcement
    current social prevalence and inadequacy of punishment as a behavior controller

Bandura-Rotter terms:
  expectancies and values
  perceived value of reinforcers
  observational learning
  situational emphasis (in contrast to early childhood emphasis within psychoanalysis)

Wolpe terms:
  reactive inhibition
  reciprocal inhibition
  systematic desensitization

Mowrer terms:
  spread-of-effect phenomenon
  classically conditioned escape – instrumentally conditioned avoidance (his two well known factors)
  sign learning-solution learning (directly related to his two factors)

- Phenomenological

Rogerian terms:
  client-centered
  organized and goal-directed behavior
  basic striving to actualize, maintain, and enhance
  "This is Me" (well-known paper)

Maslow terms:
  need hierarchy theory of motivation
  five levels of need — physiological, safety, belongingness and love, esteem, self-actualization

Berne-Harris terms:
  script
  parent, adult, child
  contract

Frankl terms:
  existential vacuum and existential frustration
  collective neurosis
  life will and meaning

Kelly terms:
  personal constructs
  construct alternativism
  C-P-C cycle (circumspection, preemption, control)

- Trait

Sheldon terms:
  endomorph
  mesomorph
  ectomorph

Allport terms:
  cardinal dispositions
  central dispositions
  secondary dispositions
  integration of personality — the proprium
  transformation of motives — functional autonomy

Cattell terms:
  L, Q, and T-data — life record, questions regarding self, objective tests
  Trait elements

Eysenck terms:
  personality dimensions — introversion-extraversion, neuroticism, psychoticism

Murray terms:
- person-environment forces (needs and press)
- viscerogenic (primary) needs-psychogenic (secondary) needs
- specific psychogenic needs
- achievement (later pursued by McClelland)
- social approval

The preceding list will provide quick reference and rapid feedback regarding the personality theory aspects of your review.

Measurement

The second portion of this personality discussion centers on measurement — the use of formal instruments to tell psychological investigators about their subjects. Instruments in this collection vary from the highly objective to the highly subjective, and it might be helpful at this point to take a look at the various devices within that broad range and some major names within the different categories.

"Dean" of the objective measuring instruments is the Minnesota Multiphasic Personality Inventory (MMPI). Developed by McKinley and Hathaway in 1942, it stands as a milestone in objective personality measurement. The standardization process for the inventory was conducted with a wide range of persons judged to have specific psychological abnormalities, and as a person answers the 550 statements, his or her response patterns can be compared with those of the large standardization sample. Obviously, such comparison means that the inventory is oriented toward detecting abnormality. Similar scales patterned after the MMPI (e.g., Gough's California Personality Inventory) have been standardized on normal individuals and thus emphasize normality. In each of these tests, the scales are organized around the true-false statement — the test taker reads each statement and marks it either true or false. The subject's responses to the large number of statements then enable the psychologist, utilizing established procedures (or perhaps computer analysis), to develop a response profile. Objective tests of this nature have the advantage of ease of administration to large numbers of people simultaneously and ease of objective scoring. Nevertheless, the structured format of such tests does not allow unique individual expression.

Subjective measuring instruments are often described as projective techniques. In the projective technique a person is shown an ambiguous stimulus or life situation, and is asked to give his or her observations concerning it. The test format makes it relatively easy for a person to relate his own thoughts, concerns, and problems to the stimulus (generally without realizing that he or she is doing so). The term *projection* suggests casting upon something (or someone) "out there" that which is within. Were I depressed and lonely, for instance, I might see depression and loneliness in every life-situation picture presented to me, although the pictures did not specifically suggest such feelings. I would be, in effect, projecting onto the pictures the feelings that I have. Such techniques enable therapists to observe recurring themes and trends among subjects' responses, allowing them to get at major facets of their patients' concerns and thoughts.

The "dean" of projective techniques is the Rorschach Inkblot Test, a series of ten ambiguous-stimulus plates presented to a respondent. A life-situation instrument employing the projective-technique format is the Thematic Apperception Test (TAT) developed by Murray. Variations on each technique have been incorporated into subsequent measuring instruments (e.g., the Blacky Pictures Technique). Additional test names mentioned for purposes of familiarity include:

- Edwards Social Desirability Scale
- Taylor Manifest Anxiety Scale
- 16 Personality Factor (16 PF) Scale
- Allport-Vernon-Lindzey Study of Values

The list is not complete, of course, but it should be sufficient for review purposes.

In addition to the objective and projective techniques, there is a set of techniques that could best be described as behavioral or situational. The OSS — World War II predecessor to the CIA — mastered this set of techniques and utilized them prominently in their screening procedures. As an OSS applicant, one might have become involved in situational testing the moment he or she walked through the front door. Such tests were designed to judge individual performance and response in actual, structured settings — providing information essential to the OSS in its selection procedures. Understandably, there are practical limitations on broad, general usage of such a procedure.

To understand individuals, professionals observe carefully and theorize — developing measuring instruments to help pinpoint specific aspects of personalities. At some point in the distant future, the theories and measuring instruments now in use may seem ridiculously humorous and weird; but for now they constitute one of the major avenues for gaining increased understanding of emotional disturbances. Such understanding is the only source of hope for millions of people whose daily lives are an emotional, living nightmare, and it is these people toward whom you should now turn as you consider psychopathology.

Psychopathology

It is estimated that one out of every ten persons born in the United States will at some time in his life be hospitalized for mental illness. Equally striking is the fact that, at any given moment, half of all hospital beds in the United States are occupied by persons suffering from emotional disturbances. Moreover, it is estimated that 30 percent of all Americans have emotional disturbances not severe enough to require hospital care, yet severe enough to interfere significantly with their life adjustment. There is much emotional pain in our midst and, consequently, much attention centered in the area of psychopathology.

Frustration is considered a prime cause of many emotional problems. In specific terms, frustration is defined as the thwarting of a goal-directed behavior (by either blocking the path to the goal or removing the goal object). Although blocked paths often can be the source of learning and creativity, they also house the seeds of emotional disturbance. The frustrated person or animal may engage in direct attack upon the object of frustration. In human society, however, such attack is more likely to be displaced in subtle ways such as scapegoating (verbal or behavioral aggression toward innocent objects or people), free-floating chronic anger (a general cynicism brought to all situations), or suicide (anger directed toward oneself). Beyond the possibility of anger response, frustration may also produce regression (a person's return to a form of behavior characteristic of an earlier point in life) or fixation (a maladaptive response repeated again and again without any thought or logic). Thus, you can begin to see that frustration is often central to emotional disturbances.

Emotional disturbances themselves take several forms. A traditional psychological approach to these forms has been to adopt a medical model and classify each form on the basis of behavioral characteristics and symptoms. This classification approach has produced a general division into psychoneurotic and psychotic disorders. The psychoneurotic disorders (sometimes called simply "neurotic") have the common characteristic of anxiety (a painful state of tension). The psychoneurotic person remains behaviorally and cognitively in contact with his environment. Psychotic disorders, on the other hand, are more severe cognitive, emotional, and behavioral disturbances characterized by hallucinations, delusions, and perhaps cognitive disorientation or loss of contact with the environment. Within these two basic classifications, there are the following subcategories:

- Psychoneurotic disorders
  Anxiety reactions (persistent feelings of intense anxiety)

Phobic reactions (excessive fear of a specific external object or condition without logical justification)
    claustrophobia (closed-in places)
    acrophobia (high places)
    ochlophobia (crowds), etc.
Obsessive-compulsive reactions (e.g., the compulsive "hand-washer" who is obsessed with unrealistic fear of germs)
Dissociative reactions (memory becoming dissociated from other parts of one's personality through repression)
    amnesia (loss of memory, sometimes including failure to know one's own identity)
    fugue (loss of memory accompanied by physical flight from the conflict situation)
    multiple personality (very rare occurrence — existence of several self-contained, different personalities within the same person, as in the classic cases of Eve and, more recently, Sybil)
Conversion reactions or hysteria (an incapacitating bodily ailment such as arm paralysis without any underlying physiological basis)
Neurasthenic reactions (chronic physical and mental fatigue, again, without underlying physiological basis)
Hypochondria (imagined physiological disorders and "a medicine for everything")
Neurotic depressive reactions (strong feelings of dejection, inferiority, worthlessness, and hopelessness)

- Psychotic disorders
Organic (a function of brain-nervous system deterioration due to accident or disease)
Functional (without identifiable physiological basis)
    paranoid (strongly organized system of delusions relating to personal grandeur, persecution, or both)
    affective (extreme fluctuations in mood)
        manic-depressive
            manic type (overactivity characterized by delusion)
            mixed type (alternation of manic attacks and psychotic depressions)
        psychotic-depressive (self-condemnation having reached delusional proportions, person unable to function in daily life)
    schizophrenic reactions
        simple type (reduction in external attachments, impoverishment of human relationships, strong sense of apathy and indifference)
        hebephrenic (emergence of shallow, inappropriate emotion, such as giggling, in response to a human tragedy or a fatal accident)
        catatonic (motionless rigidity; an arm may remain indefinitely in the position to which it was moved)
        paranoid (elaborate delusions and hallucinations of persecution and/or grandeur; paranoid reaction mentioned earlier contains only delusions)

Beyond the psychoneurotic and psychotic disorders, the traditional classification system contains additional categories that will probably sound familiar to you.

- Sociopathic personality disturbance (lack of conformity to social norms)
Antisocial (emotionally shallow, in constant rebellion against society, unable to profit from experience or punishment, and incapable of loyalties to any person, group, or code)
Dyssocial (disregard for the usual social codes because of early upbringing in an abnormal environment, capability for strong loyalties fertile for exploitation; however, no sign of the rebellion element characteristic of the antisocial — e.g., the farmboy driver for Bonnie and Clyde)
Sexual deviation (sexual gratification in one of the following behaviors)
    exhibitionism ("streaking")
    voyeurism (the "peeping Tom")

fetishism (worship of a given object)
transvestism (wearing undergarments of the opposite sex)
sadomasochism (torturing a loved one = sadism; sexual self-punishment = masochism — e.g., needing to be severely whipped as a prelude for intercourse)

In addition, the term *psychosomatic disorder* is frequently used to refer to a physiological problem that results from stress, tension, and anxiety. The most familiar entry in this category would be stomach ulcers.

Looking at the entire list in survey fashion, one notes that the psychoneurotic disorders constitute the largest percentage of emotional disturbances. Within the psychotic disorders, schizophrenia is seen as the "wastebasket classification:" "When in doubt, label it schizophrenic!" Within sexual deviations, overt homosexuality was an entry until very recently. Between consenting adults, however, homosexuality is no longer considered pathological.

In my introductory comments on psychopathology, I used the terms "medical model" and "traditional" to lead into a discussion of this classification system. If you inferred from this wording that there were other professional views in the area of psychopathology, you were right. A strong body of opinion suggests that classifications do individuals an injustice — that they fit each individual into a square containing symptoms that are not uniquely his. Critics argue that treatment is then geared to the square (the label) rather than to the individual and his special problems. More will be said about each of these views in the next section on clinical (treatment) aspects. Meanwhile, you might find it interesting to read T. Szasz, "Mental Illness is a Myth," *New York Times Magazine*, June 12, 1966. The article has been reprinted in several sources, including: Robert Guthrie, ed., *Encounter* (Menlo Park, Calif.: Cummings, 1970), pp. 278–89.

One of the major concerns of psychopathology has been the question of underlying causes of abnormal behavior. Research scientists have found answers difficult and elusive — primarily because the research itself is difficult. For example, one of the classic studies on the possibility of an hereditary basis for schizophrenia was conducted by F.J. Kallman ("The Genetics of Mental Illness," in S. Arieti, ed., *American Handbook of Psychology* [New York: Basic Books, 1959]). Among identical twins, Kallman found that in cases where one of the twins had schizophrenia, the second twin also had it in 86 percent of the cases. A corresponding figure among fraternal twins was only 14 percent, suggesting a strong hereditary contribution to the disorder.

Physiology also plays a convincing role in many instances — notably with regard to blood protein content found to accompany functional psychoses. It is a case of being able to say, "We've found something physiologically different among these people, but why is the difference there and what is its significance?" Such findings raise further questions, as yet unanswered. To complicate the picture even more, life-history comparisons of normal and mentally disturbed persons have revealed marked differences in the areas of parental relationships, home and social environments, and traumatic emotional events. As you sort through what I have just said, you will grasp the complex interrelationship between heredity and environment. There can be little wonder why research in this area is so difficult — and equally little wonder why it must continue. As it does continue, we can expect increasingly closer cooperation between psychologists and physiologists; indeed, the finding of essential answers will depend heavily upon such cooperation. In the meantime, emotional disturbances exist and must be treated — which brings us to the clinical aspect of psychology, next in our review.

Clinical Psychology

Clinical psychology is, in effect, treatment psychology. Not surprisingly, treatment approaches reflect the viewpoints held by professionals in the areas of theory, measuring instruments, and psychopathology. To get acquainted with this whole area, a logical starting point is to examine the ways in which each theoretical viewpoint approaches the clinical aspect. For purposes of clarity, you should take your initial glimpse via the outline used in the personality discussions.

Psychoanalysis

The assumption is made in psychoanalysis that the personality's core elements are established in the first few years of life. Treatment, therefore, is oriented toward reaching back into those early years and "laying bare" the guilt and conflict in the situations where they occurred initially. In the classical approach to treatment, the method used for this uncovering process is free association (subject lies on his back on a couch with instructions to say everything that comes to mind). It is assumed that the relaxed setting and these instructions will enable the person to both become aware of and reveal thoughts that have been kept from awareness by the usual psychological defense system prominent within daily life. Dream interpretation is central to this process — dreams being considered, in Freud's words, "the royal road to the unconscious." In addition to dream interpretation, the Rorschach Test is frequently used as another means of probing the unconscious. Complete psychoanalysis can require several years (and, obviously, a sizable sum of money). It also requires a patient with a reasonable degree of intelligence and some capacity for thought and insight. The assumptions underlying such treatment are that a change in personality can occur only through return to "the scene of the crime" (that is, the source of guilt and conflict) and that the "laying bare" process will enable the person to initiate a desirable change.

Ego Analysis

Followers of this method believe that they have modified the classical psychoanalytic approach in the way Freud himself might have done if he were alive today. As the title suggests, this approach frees the individual from a "slavery" to id urges and promotes the importance of ego. Although free association and dream interpretation are still important parts of this view, the play-by-play "laying bare" process within early childhood is relieved somewhat by the ego emphasis. A primary goal of this treatment is an understanding of child-based conflicts, coupled with a wholesome strengthening of the person's ego.

Psychodynamic Analysis

In this and the above two approaches, the therapist talks with the subject in a one-to-one setting. However, psychodynamic treatment is less formal than psychoanalysis, and treatment does not include free association and the necessity for several years of treatment. Again, the goal is insight and self-understanding as the means of initiating behavior change. Specific methods used to reach this goal reflect the unique aspects of a given theoretical position. For instance, Adler's approach to insight might include replacing inferiority feelings with self-respect and social interest, while Jung's approach might feature a balance among the psychological functions of sensing, thinking, feeling, and intuiting. We could expect Sullivan to use spadework directed toward removal of lingering parataxic cognitions still present and problematic in our adult thinking. Horney would emphasize adjustment to one's culture and the development of effective modes of relating within it. Fromm's method stresses relationships that carry within them a love between equals and emphasizes a personality strong in relatedness, creativeness, brotherliness, individuality, and reason. As they begin to build the learning-theory bridge, Dollard and Miller seek to grant a person learning-based understanding of early childhood conflicts. Because of its learning base, the heart of this treatment approach rightfully belongs in the next section.

Behaviorist and Learning Theory

The general emphasis of this approach is to remove faulty learning and replace it with learning that enables the subject to function and cope effectively. Virtually all the terms that you encountered in classical and operant conditioning come into play here because of the learning principles that are utilized. Dollard and Miller speak of the process as counterconditioning, i.e., running an effective response in direct and strong competition with the person's current ineffective one. Because this theory is a bridge between psychotherapy and learning theory, emphasis is given to insight — the ability to realize how faulty learning occurred in the early years and the learning capacity to change current problem behavior on the basis of this knowledge.

Behavior theorists place little importance on insight. They view psychopathology as one or a combination of several noncoping behaviors, and their goal is to change those behaviors. The method for doing so is to establish a learning situation or, in some instances, a complete environment, within which predetermined behaviors can be systematically encouraged through reinforcement while other behaviors (considered problem behaviors) can be either ignored or punished (depending on the approach). This spectrum of approaches follows, generally, one of the subsequent classifications.

The behaviorist-learning theory techniques provide the most readily demonstrable results in behavior change. Such techniques operate on the premise that the primary goal must be to change the current, maladaptive behavior and that a time-consuming, expensive return to one's childhood for purposes of unraveling and new insight is not important. Behaviorists believe that a person does not need insight into childhood conflicts in order to effectively change current behaviors. It is a "now" orientation based on systematic structuring of stimuli and responses. The technique initially identifies the problem behaviors and develops a conditioning program to change the responses customarily given to problem stimuli. It lives up to its name — placing emphasis on observable *behavior* without concerning itself with intrapsychic constructs such as id.

Desensitization

Watson pioneered in this method when he created within a child intense fear of white rats and then proceeded to remove the fear by a systematic procedure containing gradual steps (white objects at a distance, then moved closer to the child and approximating the feared object more and more in each successive treatment session). What Watson instituted was a desensitization process. This approach is widely used in cases of intense fear and phobia. Suppose, for instance, that you had an intense fear of butterflies and you were a summer lifeguard at an outdoor pool. Butterflies would no doubt appear and might well cause you both problems and embarrassment. To desensitize you, a professional might first have you read about butterflies in general, then later about the species that bother you the most. Next, you might be asked to collect pictures of them. And, to pass your "final exam," you might be given a butterfly net with instructions to catch a butterfly and return it to the therapist. The entire procedure would constitute desensitization. A prominent, controversial name currently in the field is that of Wolpe. Wolpe's treatment approach begins with development of an anxiety stimulus hierarchy (careful listing of most-to-least anxiety-producing situations). He then teaches the subject to relax all the muscles in his body. Desensitization begins as Wolpe introduces one or two of the least anxiety-producing situations and asks the person to relax (a response in direct conflict with the individual's normal behavior in these situations). Subsequent sessions move systematically toward the more severe anxiety-producing situations, again with instructions to the subject to relax.

Observational Learning

This approach relies on observation as a means of relieving intense fear and anxiety. Suppose you were intensely afraid of dogs. If this approach were used in treating you, you would be asked to observe someone with whom you could identify closely as this person moved gradually closer and closer to the feared object (a dog). Because you would be observing from a safe place, the initial threat of direct contact would be greatly reduced. Eventually (in the final stage of observation), however, you would be called upon to join your model in petting a dog. Bandura developed this approach and continues to be the most prominent name in the area.

Conditioned Aversion

Anyone who has seen the movie *Clockwork Orange* is familiar with facets of this approach, which is used in cases where the subject finds great pleasure and positive reinforcement in some problem behavior. Sexual problems such as fetishism, transvestism, and some instances of homosexuality are among the behaviors treated by this method. Generally speaking, it is a method utilized when other methods have failed; and the subject must have advance knowledge of and give consent for any treatment. For example, suppose a man achieved great sexual satisfaction and orgasm while wearing women's undergarments. The treatment would involve his wearing the undergarments at the same time that a drug-induced nausea was making him feel quite ill. The pairing of his former source of great pleasure with the drug-induced nausea would continue. Over a period of time, the amount of drugs could be reduced, but the thoughts and feelings of nausea would continue to accompany the former pleasure objects. In other cases, the stimulus object might be same-sex nude photos (homosexuality), a drink of Johnny Walker Scotch (alcoholism), etc. The major objective is to develop the nauseous response as dominant over the former pleasure response, thus discouraging the problem behavior.

Changing Behavior Consequences

This technique emphasizes the manipulation of positive reinforcement. In general, it involves the withdrawal of positive reinforcement from maladaptive behaviors and the association of reinforcement with appropriate, adaptive behaviors. Suppose that problem child George frequently screams and kicks, uses derogatory language, and takes off his clothes. Normally, each of these situations gets his mother's attention (in effect, a positive reinforcement). Under this technique, however, the consequence of George's problem behavior would change because George's mother would be instructed to signal George when his behavior was disruptive. If the behavior continued he would be put in a dull, drab isolation room and brought out only when the behavior ceased. He would, of course, be praised whenever a behavior occurred that was appropriate and desirable. The technique involves all the specifics of the shaping process familiar to you from the learning section review. It is this type of procedure that is generally being referred to when you hear the term *behavior modification*.

Therapeutic Communities

In certain instances, a person's entire environment can be set up with systematic reinforcement contingencies. The mental hospital and the prison setting are two environments having such contingencies, and behavior modification techniques in these instances would seek to change reinforcements and consequences in such a manner that desired behaviors would be encouraged and motivation toward such behaviors would be prompted. In effect, a therapeutic community involves a total-environment usage of behavior modification techniques and the changing of behavior consequences. Ethics controversies enshroud some of these usages. Currently, the question of whether prisoners can be forced to rehabilitate within such a modification program is being emphasized. Such controversies can be expected to continue, as there are no simple solutions to them.

Phenomenological

Perhaps the least systematic collection of views are those found under this heading. The main idea holding this collection together is an emphasis on individual perception. In the perception discussions earlier in this book, it was indicated that perception combined the sensory experience (what is received physiologically) with past learning (what one expects to receive). Two people can wake up at the same hour on the same morning with very different outlooks on the day. These two people may encounter virtually the same events during the day, and yet one may have a positive outlook and exhibit optimism toward these events, while the other may demonstrate a negative outlook and pessimism. Phenomenologists believe that the essential goal of a clinical technique is to change the subject's perception of himself and his environment. Where such perception is hampering him, the technique seeks to free the individual to be what he can be. As Maslow once stated, "What a person can be, he must be." Translated into actual settings, the approach uses therapist-person discussions on a one-to-one basis. For persons such as Rogers, Berne, and Harris, various approaches to group therapy are also important techniques. Group techniques are less expensive for the individual, and they provide the person with an opportunity to see how other people will respond to him and to what he is saying in a safe, controlled setting. The basic premise throughout this approach is that if you can change perception, behavior will change as a consequence.

Trait

It seems fair to say that trait theorists are more concerned with theoretical approach than with clinical technique in behavior change. They believe that it is possible to predict behaviors and personality characteristics on the basis of specific, measurable traits. Professionals steeped in this approach make much use of objective measuring instruments such as the MMPI. Beyond their use of such instruments, their techniques for behavior change tend to be eclectic — combining the elements of several of the preceding approaches.

Chemotherapy

Before leaving this clinical discussion, a word should be said about chemotherapy — the use of drugs. Currently, the use of drugs is a common way of controlling hospital patients and assisting behavior change. In extreme cases, which formerly required the use of the infamous straight jacket, a patient may now be controlled by regular drug dosage instead. Where extreme behavior is being controlled, the drug administered may make its recipient seem almost totally out of touch with his immediate surroundings. On the other hand, medically administered drugs also enable many patients to function and hold jobs outside the institutional setting. It is difficult at this juncture to predict what chemotherapy's future will be — whether it will become the clinical mainstream or simply one of many techniques in prominent usage. For now, at least, it is very much with us — particularly in the institutional setting.

Electroconvulsive Shock Therapy

Another technique used within the institutional setting for specific types of disorders is electroconvulsive shock therapy, that is, electrical shock administered to the brain to produce a type of convulsion. Not surprisingly, this technique involves short-term memory loss. Cases in which this technique is used are usually those involving depression.

Understandably, this technique is controversial, especially since a similar convulsive reaction can be attained chemically rather than electrically. Both techniques are currently used in specific, controlled medical settings.

Having viewed the range of clinical techniques, from the couch and free association to chemotherapy and electroconvulsive shock, you now have an idea of the variety of methods that are directed toward the common objective of changing maladaptive behavior. We are a long distance from rebuilt-brain transplants, and, in the meantime, people need emotional help. Clinical techniques seek to provide such help and relieve the accompanying emotional pain.

Methodology

Because psychology is a social science, investigators in all aspects of the discipline adopt the scientific approach to new information. The scientific method is, in effect, an objective way of observing, describing, and classifying. It is quantitative, and quantitative classification must work with objectively measurable characteristics involving "more than" and "less than" relationships. Qualitative classification, on the other hand, involves simply categorizing on the basis of a specific characteristic, e.g., hair color. To gain some understanding of the distinctions, a brief look at the words *nominal, ordinal, interval* and *ratio* can prove helpful.

Numbers used in nominal ways are, in effect, labels. The number on your house or apartment falls into this category. The fact that your house number is 1054 and someone else's is 1020 does not mean that your house is bigger than the other person's. The numbers simply serve a labeling, categorizing function. Ordinal use of numbers involves rank ordering. Judges at the county fair use numbers in this manner. A given ordinal number can indicate more of a quality than another number, but it does not indicate that the distance between first and second, for instance, is equivalent to the distance between second and third. Ordinal is rank ordering of some characteristic and does not go beyond that ordering to any suggestion of equal intervals between. The latter suggestion is reserved for the interval aspect of quantitative number usage. Such intervals are judged to be equal. An applied example of this type of usage involves temperature. The difference between 90 and 100 degrees Fahrenheit is considered equivalent to the difference between 70 and 80 degrees Fahrenheit. Though these differences may not seem equivalent when you are trying to find relief from the hot sun, in thermometer and interval terms they are. A psychological example that approximates interval measurement is the intelligence test. Though currently embroiled in controversy, these tests were developed on the premise that intervals were equivalent — that 15 IQ points at one point on the scale were equivalent to 15 IQ points at another point on the scale. This kind of testing provides one of psychology's strongest bids for interval use of numbers. The final type of numerical quantity — ratio — presumes an absolute zero point. When you have been able to establish an absolute zero, you have reached a point where you can make statements such as "twice as much as" or "three times as much as." Psychologists are certainly not yet prepared to suggest that a person having a 150 IQ is twice as intelligent as a person having a 75 IQ. This type of number usage is possible in natural science, but social scientists have not yet discovered an absolute zero and must concentrate their number usage in the ordinal and interval areas.

To maintain objectivity, the scientific method adopts an established set of procedures to be followed in the testing of hypotheses. Suppose, for instance, that you had made general observations that seemed to link the eating of carrots with reading speed. To determine whether these observations had any scientific validity, you would need to develop an hypothesis to be tested. You would be hypothesizing that carrot eating affects reading speed.

As you translate this hypothesis into formally established testing procedures, this is what you would have:

Step 1: Set Up the Null Hypothesis

Null hypothesis means "no difference." Your null hypothesis would be that reading speed is not affected one way or the other by carrot eating. Actually, you believe that carrot eating has an effect on reading speed, so this hypothesis is one that you hope to disprove later in the procedure. You are hoping that the difference you find will be sufficiently great that you can disprove (reject) the null hypothesis expressed here.

Step 2: Collect the Data Sample

(A) Set up the experimental and control groups.

Through careful thought and planning, you will need to develop your experimental design. At this point, you must familiarize yourself with such terms as independent variable and dependent variable and learn their specific translation within your experimental situation. In this instance, the independent variable will be carrots — the stimulus element that is placed in the experimental situation to see whether it makes a difference in reading speed. The dependent variable will be reading speed — the response obtained in relation to the stimulus element introduced. To compare the responses of your experimental and control groups, you should administer carrots to the experimental group, no carrots to the control group. Because the control group will not be receiving the independent variable, this group will enable you to later determine to what extent an observed response change was a function of the carrot eating (independent variable) within the experimental group. Obviously, it is important to keep all other potential variables between the two groups the same. For example, you may want to use only girls (or boys) to remove the possibility of performance differences resulting from sex differences. The reading material that you select must be equivalent for the two groups, and you must be certain that there has been no previous familiarity with this material. It will be essential to measure the reading speeds of all subjects *before* you institute the independent variable in order to get an accurate measure of any changes in reading speed after the experimental group has gobbled its carrots. And it will be important to be sure that each person consumes the same amount of carrots. In addition, situational variables must be controlled — lighting must be equivalent for all subjects, etc. Having proceeded with care in subject selection and control of potential variables, you can move into the second aspect of data collection.

(B) Decide on a statistical procedure and collect data in a form compatible with that procedure.

One of the most deplorable and traumatic scenes that any statistician can relate involves the sight of someone on his doorstep who has collected a batch of data and now wants to know what he can do with it statistically. Such decisions must be made *before* the data is collected. The GRE will assume that you are very familiar with the range of statistical procedures and the experimental situations in which each should be utilized. But before you can get acquainted with the specific statistical procedures, you need a thorough understanding of the foundations upon which they are built. Therefore, take a brief look at some of the basic terms and concepts as presented below; I will also suggest books to which you can refer for additional review.

Distinction Between Descriptive and Sampling Statistics

The descriptive-statistics approach requires a person to specify a given population of interest and then collect measurements from *all* the members of that population. You can begin to imagine the difficulty of accomplishing this kind of measurement collection when you think of a population such as Democrats, Republicans, or Independents! The more typical situation would involve having measurement access to a smaller group selected from the larger population of interest. This smaller group is known as a sample, and the statistics used in analyzing data collected from the smaller group are known as sampling statistics. Analyzing the data from the sample — assuming that a sample that is representative of the population has been obtained — you can then make generalizations from the sample to the population.

Statistical Inference and the Concept of Random Sample

Statistical inference refers to sampling statistics and the process through which inference is made to whole populations through sampling procedures. Such inference requires careful attention to the concept of randomness in sampling. Randomness means that in selecting a sample each member of the specific population has an equal chance of being selected — that no weight or preference will enhance selection chances for some members and weaken those chances for others. As mentioned in the section on social psychology, public opinion polling relies heavily on the concept of random sampling.

Parameter-Statistic Distinction

Values obtained from populations are called *parameters*, and values obtained from samples are called *statistics*. Parametric tests (statistical procedures) are based on the assumption that the population from which a sample has been drawn is a normal distribution. Correspondingly, nonparametric tests are not dependent upon this normal distribution assumption. Most of the statistical procedures with which you will become familiar are parametric. Among the few nonparametric procedures you will need to know is the chi-square test.

Central Tendency

In any distribution, it becomes necessary to measure central tendency. Three methods of measuring are available — mean, median, and mode. Most statistical procedures rely upon the mean (an average of the scores in the sample). The median constitutes a midpoint of the sample scores, and the mode is the most frequently occurring score. Use of mean can lead to problems in distributions where there are a few extremely divergent scores. Because it is an average, it tends to be prominently influenced by these extreme scores. In such instances, the median as the midpoint score (half the scores greater than, half smaller than) makes a more appropriate measure of central tendency.

You might ask what happens to the mean of a distribution when a fixed number is added to each score in that distribution. The answer is that the mean value is increased by this fixed number. In similar fashion, if each score in a distribution were to be multiplied by a fixed number, the resulting mean would be the original mean multiplied by this fixed number. Division would have a similar effect. In summary, the same effect that has occurred with the individual scores in the distribution also occurs with the mean.

Variability

Variability refers to the relationship among all the scores in a distribution. Are they clustered closely around the mean, or are they widely scattered? The terms *variance* and *standard deviation* are measures of this variability. The standard deviation is, in effect, the positive square root of the variance. Interpretively, if you were comparing two standard deviations (one being 3.7 and the second being 1.2), you would know that the scores in the second distribution are generally closer to the mean and less scattered than the scores in the first distribution.

If you increase or decrease each term in a distribution by a fixed amount, the variance and standard deviation remain unchanged. In effect, you have not changed the "scatter" of the distribution around the mean. If each term in a distribution is multiplied by a constant, the original standard deviation would be affected in the same manner as every other score in the distribution (the resulting standard deviation being the original standard deviation times the constant).

Because a standard deviation squared would be its corresponding variance, the effect upon variance of multiplying each score in a distribution by a constant would be that of multiplying the original variance by the square of that constant. For example, if each score in a distribution were multiplied by 2 and the original variance had been 6, the resulting variance would be 24. Squaring the constant makes it 4, and 4 times 6 equals 24. In cases of division by a constant, division by the square of the constant would yield the resulting variance.

Z-scores

Imagine that Distribution 1 has a mean of 40 and a standard deviation of 2.5, while Distribution 2 has a mean of 40 and a standard deviation of 2.0. Now, if someone were to ask how a score of 45 in Distribution 1 would compare with a score of 46 in Distribution 2, a quick score comparison would be difficult to make, to say the least. The computation of z-scores is a way of translating these different standard deviations and different means into a common language that facilitates comparison. Computed as score minus the mean divided by the standard deviation, the z-score makes score comparisons quite simple. In the above example, for Distribution 1 a score of 45 minus 40 = 5. This 5 divided by the standard deviation of 2.5 produces a z-score of +2. In Distribution 2, 46 minus 40 = 6. This 6 divided by 2 produces a z-score of +3.0. Therefore, through the use of the z-score translation, it becomes easy to see that the score of 46 in Distribution 2 is significantly better than a score of 45 in Distribution 1. Note that the z-score in these instances was preceded by a plus sign. If the score had been below the mean, it would have been preceded by a minus sign.

Central tendency, variability, and z-scores are intricately related to the concept of a normal distribution. Because the z-score is based on the assumption of a normal distribution, it is possible to speak in terms of probabilities. In a normal distribution (which you can find outlined in table form in any basic statistics text), approximately 34 percent of the scores occur between the mean and a z-score of +1 (one standard deviation above the mean). Approximately 14 percent more occur between z-scores of +1 and +2 (between one and two standard deviations above the mean), and approximately 2 percent of the scores in the distribution occur beyond a z-score of +2. So, if we refer to Distribution 1 momentarily and ask what is the probability of a score of between 42.5 and 45, we can immediately state that probability as 14 percent. Because a normal distribution is symmetrical, exact percentages hold for scores occurring below the mean. For example, the probability of a score of between 35 and 37.5 in Distribution 1 would be 14 percent. Part of the data you will receive regarding your GRE performance will involve your percentile rank. That rank will indicate the percentage of test takers scoring either the same as or below you — a computation strikingly similar to the ones made above.

At this point, you can see the intricate relationships among the concepts of central tendency, variability, z-score, normal distribution, probability and percentiles. In fact, the decision-making concepts of significance level, Type I and Type II error, are based upon the rationale to which you have just received an oversimplified introduction. As you seek for more depth within one of the introductory statistics books, I would suggest that you attempt to gain a basic understanding of the following additional concepts and terms:

- Frequency distributions
  Frequency polygon and histogram (distinction important)
  Methods of data grouping
    terms *interval* and *frequency*
    method of computing mean, median, and mode in both nongrouped and grouped data
  Concept of normal distribution and the proportions of distribution scores occurring within 1, 2, and 3 standard deviations of the mean
  Concept of positive and negative skew and its effect upon the location of mean, median, and mode
  Percentile rank (its computation and meaning)
  Notion of probability as it relates to the normal distribution
  Concept of risk in decision making and the distinction between Type I and Type II error

Concept of significance level as it relates to probability and types of error
difference between one-tailed and two-tailed tests
understanding "degrees of freedom"
confidence interval and interval estimation
- Conceptual understanding of correlation and regression
scattergram
difference between positive and negative correlation
concept of best-fitting straight line in regression
- Dichotomous variables and binomial statistics

With this basic statistical background, you are now ready to consider different statistical procedures and the situations in which they are utilized. Among the most prominent testing procedures are the *t*-tests for (1) the difference between sample and population means, (2) two independent means, and (3) related measures.

A typical example of the *first* instance (difference between sample and population means) would be a situation in which the researcher knows a national average for the dimension he is measuring (e.g., average weight of twelve-year-olds) and now must determine whether the weight of 12 year olds in his sample is significantly different from the population mean (the national average).

To demonstrate the *second* instance (two independent means), suppose that a researcher wants to determine whether there is a significant difference between the IQ scores of twelve-year-old boys and those of twelve-year-old girls in a given school. The scores of the boys and those of the girls have been obtained independently and, in effect, the comparison is between two sample means. This kind of setting — a comparison of two independent means — is perhaps the most common and most often used *t*-test procedure.

In the *third* procedure (related measures) there is a relationship between the measures being obtained. For example, one might take the above group of twelve-year-old boys and give them an IQ test just before instituting an intensive educational program and then administer the IQ test again at the conclusion of the program. The *t*-test would be comparing two sets of measures obtained on the same people (before and after an experimental procedure was introduced) to determine whether significant change had occurred in their IQ scores. In addition to using this procedure to test the same people twice, it is possible to use it to compare the performances of matched groups. In such groups each member of Group 1 has been matched with a specific member of Group 2 in the critical dimensions (age, sex, background, etc.). On the rare occasions when developmental psychologists have been able to assemble a large group of identical twins, it has been the norm to assign identical twin A to Group 1, identical twin B to Group 2. By following a similar procedure for each set of identical twins, the researchers could be sure of matched groups since, for each person in Group 1, there was a person in Group 2 with identical hereditary background. The researchers could now institute an experimental procedure with one of the groups and test each group at the conclusion of the procedure to determine how much performance change was a function of the experimental procedure. Such comparisons could utilize the *t*-test for related measures.

Correlation

By its name, correlation suggests a co-relation. It is used to determine if there is any systematic relationship between two sets of measurements or observations. The correlation coefficient used to describe such a relationship is expressed in a range from +1 to −1. A zero would indicate no relationship, a +1.0 would indicate a perfect positive relationship, a −1.0 would indicate a perfect negative relationship, and a + or −1.1 or above would indicate that a computational error had been made. Correlation coefficients never exceed 1.0. It is important to realize that the degree of correlation is expressed by the number itself and not by its sign. For example, between the numbers +0.5 and −0.7 the greatest degree of correlation is expressed by −0.7. The sign merely indicates in what direction the relationship exists, and direction will become better understood as we consider the following situation.

Spearman Rank-Order Correlation

Suppose that two judges were ranking the entries in a dog show. To simplify the outcome, imagine that the rankings looked like this:

Dog	Rankings Judge 1	Judge 2
A	1	5
B	2	4
C	3	3
D	4	2
E	5	1

By comparatively scanning the above rankings, one can see that the dog ranked highest by Judge 1 was ranked lowest by Judge 2, that the dog ranked next highest by Judge 1 was ranked next lowest by Judge 2, and so forth. There is definitely a systematic relationship in a negative direction. Spearman's rho formula yields a correlation coefficient of -1.0. If the rankings in Judge 2's column had been reversed (1 for dog A, 2 for dog B, etc.), there would have been a perfect positive relationship between the judges' rankings, and the resulting Spearman rho coefficient would have been $+1.0$. Obviously, most judges are not likely to either agree or disagree this perfectly, so correction coefficients generally are less than 1.0.

Pearson Product-Moment Correlation

This correction procedure applies in situations where the researcher wants to determine whether there is a relationship between two groups of paired numbers. Pairing generally means that two scores exist for the same person; thus, in a typical situation utilizing this procedure, you would expect to have two sets of scores for each of several individuals and would now want to determine whether the scores were in any way related. To illustrate, imagine that you have just obtained IQ scores and foreign-language proficiency scores for a group of college sophomores. The question now arises of whether there is any relationship between intelligence and foreign-language proficiency. To answer the question, you conduct a Pearson Product-Moment Correlation on the two sets of scores. If the resulting correlation is in the $+.6$ range or above, there would appear to be a high degree of relationship between these two factors. You can begin to see how many factors and aspects of personal and social life can be examined with this method. For instance, correlations have been made between high school and college performance levels, and obviously correlations have been made between performance on the GRE and success in the graduate program.

Correlation does *not* mean causation. It means that a systematic relationship has been found between two factors. When government and foundation sources discovered a correlation between cigarette smoking and incidence of lung cancer, cigarette industry spokesmen were quick to remind the researchers that they had only found a relationship and could not suggest causation.

If you think for a moment, you probably will realize that this correlation involves the same basic setting described for the use of the *t*-test for related measures. The difference is that in the case of the *t*-test you are comparing the same measure (taken at two different times or in matched groups) and are looking for a significant difference instead of for a systematic relationship.

Point-Biserial Correlation

If, in the above-described correlation setting, one of the scores you obtained was dichotomous, you would need a Point-Biserial Correlation to conduct the correlation. Dichotomous suggests "either-or" in contrast to a score continuum. If you compare IQ scores with whether a person obtains an above-B or below-B grade-point average in college, the latter situation is dichotomous. In tabling that dichotomous situation for purposes of the correlation, you might want to represent the above-B performances by the number 1 and the below-B by 0. The IQ scores can occur in a large, continuous range, and therefore your comparison would contain one continuous and one dichotomous measure for each person.

Otherwise, the basic format would resemble the one that you would establish for the Pearson Product-Moment Correlation.

Chi-square

In discussing the nonparametric area of statistics, I mentioned that chi-square was one of the most prominent methods. Chi-square seeks to determine whether two variables are independent in a population from which a sample has been obtained. Chi-square deals with variables that are discrete categories rather than continuous measurements. For example, this statistic might be used to determine whether the variables of political party registration and sex are related. In the simplest chi-square settings, you would be working with two categories for each of the dimensions (in this instance, female-male and Democrat-Republican). The question is whether sex and political party affiliation are related in the population from which the sample was drawn. Because there are two discrete categories on each of the two variables, the resulting table resembles a square, four-paned window. In the procedure itself, you will obtain a value known as a phi coefficient (similar to a correlation coefficient) which can then be used to obtain a final chi-square value. Terms you can expect to find within chi-square procedures include *expected frequency, obtained frequency,* and *degrees of freedom*. Understanding of this statistic should come after you have worked your way through several examples. One of the basic introductory books in statistics can be a valuable reference source for this purpose. From a clear, simplified, conceptual presentation standpoint, I would recommend Weinberg and Schumaker's book (referenced at the end of this section, Page 56. The following is a list of other statistics:

- *F*-test and *F*-maximum test
- Analysis of variance
  Completely randomized design
  Factorial design — two factors, three factors
  Treatments-by-levels design
  Treatments-by-subjects design (repeated measures design)
  Treatments-by-treatments-by-subjects design
  Two-factor mixed design (repeated measures on one factor)
  Three-factor mixed design (repeated measures on one factor
  Three-factor mixed design (repeated measures on two factors)
- Latin square design

With the statistics listed above, work for *general* familiarity with situations in which they would be used rather than for mastery of their fundamentals. To calm any fears that you may be having, let me say that, where the *t*-test can only handle two groups of measures simultaneously, these measures have been devised to work with more than two sets of measures simultaneously. Bruning and Kintz's section introducing the different analysis-of-variance procedures can provide further clarity (and fear reduction). With regard to statistical procedures, your main objective is knowing the settings in which they would be used. For instance, suppose that a question on the GRE outlined five experimental formats and asked which one measured learning transfer, could you identify it? Basic familiarity both here and within the area of learning transfer will prepare you to answer such questions.

Books that can assist you in this review include the following:

James Bruning and B. L. Kintz, *Computational Handbook of Statistics* (Glenview, Ill.: Scott, Foresman, 1977), brief, narrative sections helpful in understanding design usages.

Leonard M. Horowitz, *Elements of Statistics for Psychology and Education*, (New York: McGraw-Hill, 1974), brief, introductory coverage of basics.

Kathleen Speeth, ed., *Introductory Psychology* (San Rafael, Calif.: Individual Learning Systems, 1971), mentioned here because Unit 1 is a kind of workbook section on statistics.

George Weinberg and John Schumaker, *Statistics: An Intuitive Approach* (Belmont, Calif.: Brooks/Cole, 1974), very easy to read and clearly presented.

That may have seemed like a mammoth second step, and it was — encompassing all basic understanding in statistics. Because you have now mastered these essential concepts, however, the subsequent steps in hypothesis testing can go quickly; and as you review them you will understand their underlying rationale.

Step 3: Set a Significance Level

In psychological research, the significance level is generally either .05 or .01. The .05 level indicates that you are willing to consider significant a difference that could occur by chance only five times in each hundred cases. The .01 level is more stringent, accepting as significant a difference that could occur by chance only one time in each hundred cases. Notice that the significance level is set before statistics are computed. This sequence is essential. Otherwise, an experimenter might decide after the fact which significance level he wanted — the decision then being based on the size of the difference actually found. Throughout your perusal of psychological literature, you will find expressions like "significant at the .01 level" or "significant at the .05 level." Be sure you understand both their meaning and how they relate to proportions under the normal curve and probability.

Step 4: Compute Statistics

Having selected the experimental design in Step 2 and the significance level in Step 3, you should find this fourth step self-explanatory. Depending on the design that you have selected, you may have a t-value, z-value, F-value, etc. In each instance, for the n or df in your experiment (based on the number of subjects you have in each group), you will refer to the appropriate table (z, t, F, etc.) to determine whether the value you have obtained is larger than the value required for significance at the level selected.

Step 5: Make Decision

If the number obtained in your computation is larger than the number found in the table for your significance level (at your appropriate n or df), you can reject the null (no difference) hypothesis. As mentioned earlier, every experimenter hopes that the difference he finds will be large enough for such rejection of the null. On the other hand, if the number you find in computation is smaller than the table value for your established significance level, you have failed to reject the null (meaning in this case that carrot eating did not have a significant effect on reading speed). Obviously, significant results are the prime candidates for publication in experimental-professional journals; and the findings most impressive to journal editors are those involving experiments in which a large number of subjects have been used. Relating all this to your specific situation, suppose that you selected the .05 significance level and obtained a z-score of 2.05 in your statistical computation. As you move to the appropriate column in the z-table (normal distribution table), you find that the score required for significance at the .05 level is 1.96. Since your score is larger, you can reject the null hypothesis and conclude that carrot eating has had a significant effect upon reading speed. The table reference will change as a function of the statistical procedure that you have selected, but the basic reference and decision-making procedure will remain the same.

You have now been duly initiated into the scientific method. This method is utilized by researchers in all areas of psychology in their quest for information and further understanding of behavior. Because of this prominence and virtual omnipresence throughout psychology, your understanding of its various aspects should be thorough.

Applied Psychology

Psychological concepts from all aspects of the field have their counterparts in practical settings, and throughout your daily experience you constantly encounter these applications. Signboards and cereal boxes utilize colors that will attract and hold attention in given intensities of light, speakers convey warmth and seek to influence opinions, newspaper ads strive to achieve the von Restorff (novel stimulus) effect, and movies appeal to motivations and emotions. Each of these methods is applied, and each is psychological. The specific intent of this applied psychology section, however, is to study industrial, human engineering, and organizational applications.

To gain a general perspective of this area, it may be helpful to concentrate briefly on each of these headings — industrial psychology, human engineering, and organizational psychology. They enable us to think of distinct concerns within the general framework of applied psychology, concerns that relate to one another like the threads of an intricate design in a woven fabric.

The term *industrial* implies production, and several aspects of this heading are product-related. Major considerations in this area include questions such as how to achieve both worker satisfaction and efficient production, how to match persons to the jobs for which they are best suited, and how to achieve high worker morale and motivation.

Human engineering relates more specifically to the workspace of the individual worker. Here, some of the primary aspects can be expressed in such questions as whether the lighting, temperature, and noise levels are such that the worker can be effective. Additional concerns relate to promoting smooth work flow and eliminating bottlenecks in the production process. Within the workspace of the individual employee, attention should be given to the location of equipment controls and to whether they are designed to promote both worker efficiency and safety. For obvious reasons, one workspace that has been of prominent human engineering concern is the airplane cockpit. Here again, the problem is how to promote both maximal efficiency and safety.

Organizational psychology introduces concerns relating to the nature and effects of an organization's hierarchical structure, communication patterns, processes in organizational decision making, and styles of leadership and leadership development. Where human engineering has a very specific focus upon workspace, organizational psychology takes a broad-range perspective. As you proceed with this review, you will find elements from each of these headings interwoven within the context of applied psychology.

As we think of the organization and the worker, a natural emphasis at the outset is on analyzing jobs and their performance requirements and correspondingly selecting personnel whose aptitudes best match individual job descriptions. It is more than just a question of whether a person has, for instance, the finger dexterity needed to quickly install screws in automobile door handles; it is equally a question of whether the individual's personality and interests are compatible with the job and the work environment. The gardening or camping enthusiast may be discontent in a tiny office cubicle, and a basically shy radio performer may be personally unsuited for work in the television medium. In each instance, the emphasis is upon making the proper person-to-job match.

Such matching requires the use of personnel selection techniques that can produce the aptitude, personality, interest, and achievement information necessary for appropriate assessment and decision making. The required test "arsenals" are large and, in many cases, specific to the requirements of a given work setting, but among them are familiar names from your review of cognition and complex human learning. Several of the aptitude tests are prefaced with the words Purdue or Minnesota, prominent test contributors in this area. Personality tests include the Bernreuter and MMPI, and interest tests include the Strong and the Kuder. Achievement tests range from a written test for factual knowledge to a performance test on a job-related task. Each instrument carries its unique function within the personnel selection process.

Once hired, the worker will continue to be evaluated, and the hiring organization must devise equitable, effective methods for appraising job performance. Such appraisals take on critical importance in areas such as wages and salaries, promotions, on-the-job training, and so forth. Likert-type checklist rating techniques and interview methods are among the procedures frequently employed in such appraisals. It is critical that appraisal procedures be sufficiently controlled to prevent a final evaluation based largely on the opinions of a single individual. It is equally critical to control for such elements as "halo" effect (the rater's tendency to give a totally positive evaluation to a person whom he or she likes) and constant error (the rater's general tendency toward leniency or harshness in evaluation procedures). It becomes obvious that, in order to be both effective and equitable, the components of an overall appraisal procedure must be skillfully designed and carefully implemented.

Beyond the person-centered aspects of selecting the appropriate individual and evaluating him equitably, there are major concerns relating to worker environment. In the specific work setting, these can be the human engineering questions of how to arrange equipment, knobs, lights, and traffic patterns to promote the least amount of lost motion and the most efficient worker performance. At the broader, organizational level, the question expands to that of the industry's general view of its workers.

The industrial view toward workers has never been a singular one that could be isolated in time and labeled unanimously scientific or consistently humanistic. Nevertheless, general climates have been evident during specific time periods in our nation's industrial history. The earliest climate, characteristic of the first quarter of the twentieth century, was one of scientific management. Within it, the emphasis was placed on production. Its principal advocates believed that work in general, and specific jobs in particular, should be defined clearly to the worker and that, given a knowledge of expectations and a product-designed work setting, reinforcements and punishments should be arranged in a manner designed to obtain highest output per worker input. This method sounds impersonal, and it is. Production emphasis, giving its attention to time-and-motion studies and piecework incentives, makes no provision for viewing the worker as a unique individual. In the purest sense, scientific management involves viewing the worker as part of the production machine.

The human relations approach emerged from the now classic "Hawthorne effect." While studying ways to improve lighting and production-oriented features of a specific work setting, management at the Hawthorne Plant of the Western Electric Company discovered that productivity was increasing in the absence of any changes in work setting. The only viable explanation for this phenomenon was the attention being given to the workers themselves, and the results provided convincing support for the view that one can increase productivity by increasing worker satisfaction. Workers were being viewed on an individual basis, and the philosophy that a satisfied worker is a productive worker gained a foothold. In some industries, counseling psychologists were hired with responsibilities for helping workers solve personal problems. Techniques were devised for making workers feel that they were participants in decision-making processes. Plant newspapers, suggestion boxes, and corporate sharing were among the changes that emerged. Industry was acknowledging the worker as a human being with feelings and needs.

Both the human relations and the scientific management approaches are currently found on the industrial scene. Also frequently used in evaluating specific organizations is the Blake-Mouton Grid, based on the premise that an efficient organization demonstrates strong and equal levels of concern for people and for production. This measure and several other current approaches within industry reflect an attitude to the worker environment that is both human and production-oriented.

The human relations approach has prompted numerous psychological studies of worker satisfaction. Katz and Kahn have applied the level-of-involvement model and suggest that certain jobs are inherently more satisfying than others because of the degree of worker involvement characterizing them. Utilizing Kelman's categories, they point to the job of guard as an example of minimal involvement in one's work. They see it as a compliance-type position that calls upon the person to simply "be there." Individuality, sense of personal worth, and involvement are lacking in the job itself. At the other end of the involvement spectrum, the manager and the creative worker have built-in opportunities to internalize their work. This means that their values and goals can be very much in keeping with the goals and objectives characterizing their work positions. Within their work responsibilities, they have a sense of personal input. One of the major challenges for management has been to take jobs such as that of guard and bring a sense of personal involvement to them. To define the situation from a slightly different perspective, Maslow suggested that the more a work position engages a person's potentialities, the deeper the satisfaction it provides. A kind of team approach has been used successfully in several industries to enhance the worker's sense of involvement. In coal mining, the perfection of conveyor systems destroyed team feeling and interaction among workers. It was a case where implementation of an obviously more efficient scientific method led to increased absenteeism and lower production. By contrast, miners working in teams felt a sense of responsibility to those teams, could identify with team goals, and received team support for their individual contributions.

A similar kind of distinction within industry has been made between the process and product models for workers. In the process model, the emphasis is "plugging in" the worker to an ongoing industrial process. The product model seeks to identify the worker with the final product. To accomplish such identification, an organization may take assembly-line workers and rotate them among different points in the assembly process. This rotation allows the individual worker to be involved with the product at different stages of completion, enhancing the possibility of his or her identification with the end product toward which his work is being directed.

Communication patterns and leadership styles profoundly affect the working climate and consequent satisfaction that a worker experiences. A communication pattern can promote either autocratic or democratic feeling throughout the work force and can do much to establish positions of power within the communication process. Consider briefly the following patterns of communication.

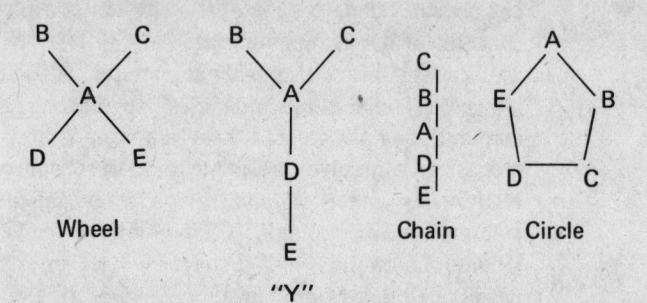

The wheel, "Y," and chain are centralized communication networks. They share the advantages of facilitating efficient performance of routine tasks, strengthening positions of leadership, and allowing for quick formation of stable patterns of interaction among group members. The most central position within each of these patterns is A, and the person occupying this position has built-in power, potential leadership, and the greatest likelihood of experiencing satisfaction. Peripheral positions such as C and E can be expected to experience the least satisfaction.

The circle is an example of a decentralized communication network. All positions have equal communication access. Although the decentralized network is less efficient than the centralized patterns, participants in such a circle-type pattern register much stronger feelings of satisfaction and seem better prepared to handle nonroutine, unpredictable situations than participants in the other patterns. One can readily see the variables in worker climate that can develop through communication network patterns.

In a specific communication setting — the interaction process of groups involved in decision making — Bales established analytical categories that have attained wide use and acceptance. His twelve categories are grouped in the following four areas:

(A) Positive reactions — Shows solidarity, shows tension release, shows agreement
(B) Problem-solving attempts — Gives suggestions, gives opinions, gives orientation
(C) Questions — Asks orientation, asks opinions, asks suggestions
(D) Negative reactions — Shows disagreement, shows tension increase, shows antagonism

Areas B and C are used to determine a group member's task orientation, and areas A and D are indicative of the member's sociability. Analysis centers upon the frequency of a person's interaction within each of the categories.

To point out another facet of the communication process operating within decision-making groups, Janis advanced the concept of *groupthink*. He believes that the highly cohesive group can foster a number of illusions among its membership. In discussing his illusion of invulnerability, Janis expresses the view that the group may decide to take risks that its members individually would not be willing to take. The illusion of morality involves the group's tendency to consider any actions that it may take as being moral. An illusion of unanimity indicates that while the group may appear to have made a unanimous decision, individual members may have censored themselves and silenced their dissent. Other factors in groupthink include shared stereotypes, rationalization, self-censorship, direct pressure, and mindguards. The cohesive group shares the benefits of high morale, but Janis points out the pitfalls that may affect such groups in their decision making.

Beyond personnel selection and the environmental factors of job satisfaction and involvement, human engineering also deals with the specific work setting and the analysis of environmental factors as they relate to worker efficiency. Such analysis deals with factors involving illumination, air flow, temperature, humidity, noise, music, number of hours in the work day, and rest periods. In addition, "human engineers" look at equipment design. In this regard, worker errors and their frequency are studied for insights that might lead to more efficient equipment design. Making dials easily readable and knobs easily accessible and distinguishable are part of the human engineering goal. As you board an airplane for some distant destination, you begin to take a strong personal interest in how well the human engineer has done his job. Efficiency in cockpit control-panel design is among the major concerns of human engineering.

Because industry cannot function without the consumers, marketing is of special corporate interest. Though some industries are meeting an already existing consumer need, other corporations must create a need among potential consumers. In either case, the marketing process must involve careful attention to consumers' attitudes, motivations, and perceptions. Instruments such as attitude surveys, questionnaires, and interviews assist the corporation in tapping consumer opinion. The relationship between sales and specific marketing techniques is carefully studied, and distinct changes in approach are made in response to generally negative attitudes from consumers and/or disappointing sales for a given product. Although marketing may seek to shape consumer behavior, it is also obvious that consumer response can shape an industry's product directions.

From the moment that you begin looking for a job, applied psychology is all around you. Personnel selection, general worker climate, specific work setting, and product sales combine to form a complex picture of which the following are among the central names and concepts:

- Adaptability test
- Bergen's scale
- Uhrbrock's scale
- Bernreuter Personality Inventory
- Communication network patterns
- Decision-making processes

- Dichter ("dean" of psychoanalytic marketing approaches)
- Edwards Personal Preference Schedule
- E. A. Fleishman
- W. J. Giese
- Interview techniques
- Job analysis techniques
- Performance appraisal techniques
- Minnesota and Purdue tests
- Wonderlic Personnel Test

The preceding list is a sampling. Beyond it, the *Journal of Applied Psychology* can help you gain familiarity with the topical breadth and range of experimental concerns within this area, and books such as the following can satisfy your reference and review needs:

> F. Kenneth Berrian, *Industrial Psychology* (Dubuque, Iowa: William C. Brown, 1967), brief coverage of the field in a short booklet.

> B. von Haller Gilmer, *Industrial and Organizational Psychology*, 3rd ed. (New York: McGraw-Hill, 1971), comprehensive textbook in the field.

> Ernest J. McCormick, *Human Factors Engineering*, 3rd ed. (New York: McGraw-Hill, 1970), a textbook in human factors, granting a survey-type approach to the field.

As in the other areas of your review, you cannot expect to gain Ph.D.-level mastery of applied psychology, but acquaintance and familiarity with its primary aspects will be important to you.

Sources for Further Reading

The following list contains books that can be used for further review in each of the subject areas on the Advanced Psychology Test.

Physiological and Comparative Psychology

Alcock, John. *Animal Behavior: An Evolutionary Approach.* 2nd ed., Sunderland, MA: Sinauer Associates, 1979.

Dewsbury, Donald and Dorothy Rethlingshafer. *Comparative Psychology: A Modern Survey.* New York: McGraw-Hill, 1973.

Eccles, John C. *The Understanding of the Brain.* 2nd ed., New York: McGraw-Hill, 1976.

Levinthal, Charles F. *The Physiological Approach in Psychology.* Englewood Cliffs, N.J.: Prentice-Hall, 1979.

Sensation and Perception

Geldard, Frank A. *The Human Senses.* 2nd ed., New York: John Wiley and Sons, 1972.

Kaufman, Lloyd. *Perception: The World Transformed.* New York: Oxford, 1979.

Lindsay, Peter H. and Donald A. Norman. *Human Information Processing: An Introduction to Psychology.* 2nd ed., New York: Academic Press, 1977.

McBurney, D. and V. Collings. *Introduction to Sensation and Perception.* Englewood Cliffs, N.J.: Prentice-Hall, 1977.

Learning and Motivation

Atkinson, John W. *Introduction to Motivation*. 2nd ed., Cincinnati: Van Nostrand Reinhold, 1978.

Hilgard, Ernest R. and Gordon H. Bower. *Theories of Learning*. 4th ed., New York: Appleton-Century-Crofts, 1975.

Schwartz, Barry. *Psychology of Learning and Behavior*. New York: Norton, 1978.

Cognition and Complex Human Learning

Ellis, Henry C. *Fundamentals of Human Learning and Cognition*. 2nd ed., Dubuque, IA: William C. Brown, 1978.

Foss, Donald J. and David T. Hakes. *Psycholinguistics: An Introduction to the Psychology of Language*. Englewood Cliffs, N.J.: Prentice-Hall, 1978.

Klatzky, Roberta L. *Human Memory: Structures and Processes*. 2nd ed., San Francisco: W. H. Freeman, 1980.

Lachman, Roy, Lachman, J. and E. Butterfield. *Cognitive Psychology and Information Processing: An Introduction*. Hillsdale, N.J.: Halsted, 1979.

Lindsay, Peter H. and Donald A. Norman. *Human Information Processing: An Introduction to Psychology*. 2nd ed., New York: Academic Press, 1977.

Neisser, Ulric. *Cognition and Reality: Principles and Implications of Cognitive Psychology*. San Francisco: W. H. Freeman, 1976.

Developmental Psychology

Hetherington, E. Mavis and Ross D. Parke. *Child Psychology: A Contemporary Viewpoint*. 2nd ed., New York: McGraw-Hill, 1979.

Mussen, Paul H. and John J. Conger. *Child Development and Personality*. 5th ed., New York: Harper and Row, 1979.

Papalia, Diane E. and Sally W. Olds. *Human Development*. New York: McGraw-Hill, 1977.

Social Psychology

Aronson, Elliot. *The Social Animal*. 3rd ed., San Francisco: W. H. Freeman, 1980.

Gergen, Kenneth J. and Mary M. Gergen. *Social Psychology*. New York: Harcourt, Brace, Jovanovich, 1981.

Middlebrook, Patricia N. *Social Psychology and Modern Life*. 2nd ed., New York: Alfred A. Knopf, 1980.

Wrightsman, Lawrence S. and Kay Deaux. *Social Psychology in the 80's*. 3rd ed., Monterey, CA: Brooks/Cole Publishing Co., 1981.

Personality

Hall, Calvin S. and Gardner Lindzey. *Theories of Personality*. 3rd ed., New York: John Wiley and Sons, 1978.

Maddi, Salvatore R., ed. *Personality Theories: A Comparative Analysis*. 4th ed., Homewood, IL: Dorsey Press, 1980.

Monte, Christopher F. *Beneath the Mask*. 2nd ed., New York: Holt, Rinehart, Winston, 1980.

Rychlak, Joseph R. *Introduction to Personality and Psychotherapy*. 2nd ed., Boston: Houghton Mifflin, 1981.

Psychopathology and Clinical Psychology

Coleman, James C. *Abnormal Psychology and Modern Life*. 6th ed., Glenview, IL: Scott, Foresman, 1979.

Lahey, Benjamin B. and Anthony R. Ciminero. *Maladaptive Behavior: An Introduction to Abnormal Psychology*. Glenview, IL: Scott, Foresman, 1980.

Martin, Barclay. *Abnormal Psychology: Clinical and Scientific Perspectives*. New York: Holt, Rinehart, Winston, 1977.

Methodology

Anastasi, Anne. *Psychological Testing*. 4th ed., New York: Macmillan, 1976.

Craig, James R. and Leroy P. Metze. *Methods of Psychological Research*. New York: Holt, Rinehart, Winston, 1979.

Graham, Kenneth R. *Psychological Research: Controlled Interpersonal Interaction*. Monterey, CA: Brooks/Cole, 1977.

Horowitz, Leonard M. *Elements of Statistics for Psychology and Education*. New York: McGraw-Hill, 1974.

Applied Psychology

Landy, Frank J. and Don A. Trumbo. *Psychology of Work Behavior*. Homewood, IL: Dorsey, 1980.

McCormick, Ernest J. and Daniel R. Ilgan. *Industrial Psychology*. 7th ed., New York: Prentice-Hall, 1980.

Wertheimer, Michael and Leon Rappoport. *Psychology and the Problems of Today*. Glenview, IL: Scott, Foresman, 1978.

CHAPTER THREE
Sample Tests

This section contains five sample Advanced Psychology Tests, each based on the actual exam. Their length, the type of question used (multiple choice), and their content approach the official test as closely as possible. By simulating actual testing conditions as you take these tests, you should be able to get a good idea of how well you are progressing in your review, which subject areas need more work, and what your prospects for success on the actual test should be.

How to Use the Sample Tests

Each test has an answer grid, answers with explanations, and a scale for evaluating your score in each subject area. Best results can be obtained by following a few simple procedures.

When taking a sample test, it is a good idea to simulate actual testing conditions. To do this, find a quiet area away from distractions. Have several sharpened pencils and a watch or suitable timer handy. Since the time allotted for the official test is 170 minutes, plan to limit yourself to this time span. Don't consult notes or the review section of this book while taking the sample test. Use the answer grid to record your answers.

After you have completed a test, check your responses with the correct answers for that test. (The answer explanations will help you understand any questions you might have missed.) Next, turn to the section at the end of the test entitled *Evaluating Your Score*. The different subject areas on the test are listed with abbreviations. To find out which areas you may need more work in, find the numbers in the Subject Area Chart that correspond with the numbers of the test questions you missed. The abbreviation next to that number will indicate which area that particular question deals with. In the space provided below the chart, record the total number of questions you missed in each of the subject areas. You can then check the Test Score Scale to see how your scores compare with the norm. To do this, subtract the number you had wrong from the total number of test questions in a certain area as shown on the Scale and compare the result with the 75th percentile number also given. Any score below this percentile indicates an area for more review. After you have determined which areas need more work, return to those sections in Chapter II.

By taking one test at a time and evaluating your score after each one, you can chart your progress and make the most of your review time.

Test One

Time 170 minutes

Directions Each of the following questions contains five possible responses. Read the question carefully and select the response that you feel is most appropriate. Then completely darken the space on your answer grid that corresponds with your choice.

1. Specific energy of nerves refers to
   (A) their electrical potential
   (B) a receptor's capability to give only one quality experience (e.g., auditory), regardless of how it was stimulated
   (C) a receptor's capability to give several different qualities of experience (e.g., temperature, pain, etc.), which vary with the quality of stimulus received
   (D) postsynaptic potential
   (E) presynaptic potential

2. Alpha wave would be most prevalent in which of the following instances?
   (A) deep sleep
   (B) REM sleep
   (C) eyes closed in relaxed, wakeful state
   (D) solving a multiplication problem "in your head"
   (E) eyes open in relaxed wakeful state

3. "In no case may we interpret an action as the outcome of the exercise of a higher psychical faculty if it can be interpreted as the outcome of the exercise of one which stands lower in the psychological scale." The quotation expresses
   (A) natural selection (Darwin)
   (B) law of imprinting (Lorenz)
   (C) law of phylogeny (Tinbergen)
   (D) theory of tropisms (Loeb)
   (E) law of parsimony (Morgan)

4. Alcohol, barbiturates, and bromides are classified as
   (A) amphetamines   (B) sedatives   (C) mood elevators
   (D) tranquilizers   (E) antihistamines

5. The animal laboratory would be the most likely work setting for which of the following comparative psychologists?
   (A) Lorenz   (B) Tinbergen   (C) Lashley   (D) Romanes
   (E) Morgan

6. An individual who receives normal sight following blindness in the early years of life
   (A) cannot achieve the skills of shape discrimination
   (B) will not develop the size-constancy aspect of perception
   (C) will adjust to the visual world almost instantly
   (D) will experience long-term muscle coordination problems because of changes in reference points
   (E) will have to relearn auditory and tactile associations necessary to accommodate the visual frame of reference

7. Inability to monitor the movements of one's feet and the absence of feedback regarding their position and relationship to the ground would suggest problems with the
    (A) labyrinthine sensory system
    (B) kinesthetic sensory system
    (C) thermal sensory system
    (D) visceral sensory system
    (E) peripheral sensory system

8. The perceptual theory known as "Sensory-Tonic" was developed by
    (A) Dember   (B) Wertheimer   (C) Werner-Wapner
    (D) Allport   (E) Ricco

9. To conduct a split-brain experiment, surgery must involve the
    (A) cerebellum   (B) reticular formation   (C) medulla
    (D) fissure of Sylvius   (E) optic chiasm

10. Kohler has found that with "squint glasses"
    (A) greater adaptation occurs than with inversion glasses
    (B) no adaptation occurs to the phi phenomenon experience
    (C) no adaptation occurs to the color-stereo effect
    (D) strong adaptation occurs to color-stereo but not to phi
    (E) surprising adaptation occurs to both color-stereo and phi

11. Which of the following would *not* be characteristic of a reflex?
    (A) involuntary
    (B) slow
    (C) consistent
    (D) fixed response to a specific stimulus
    (E) unaffected by learning

12. Which of the following is *not* closely related to attribution theory?
    (A) Nisbett's person perception
    (B) Kelley's covariation
    (C) Heider's dispositional properties
    (D) Festinger's cognitive dissonance
    (E) Gergen's role behavior

13. In Butler's work with monkeys, he found the greatest visual incentive in a door-opening task to be
    (A) a banana   (B) a Chimp-o-Mat   (C) another monkey
    (D) an electric train   (E) candy

14. The process of maintaining constancy in the normal internal environment of an organism is called
    (A) homeostasis   (B) adaptation   (C) consistency
    (D) physiological equivalence   (E) psychological motivation

15. As stimulus patterns become increasingly similar, reaction times based on stimulus discrimination
    (A) become shorter
    (B) become longer
    (C) remain unchanged
    (D) become shorter for auditory stimuli, longer for visual ones
    (E) become shorter for visual stimuli, longer for auditory ones

Questions 16–17 are based on the following passage.

One can think of collective behavior from a number of different, and unique, perspectives. On the one hand, the Marxian model suggests that workers will combine in revolt when their life situations become intolerable. A second perspective, expressed by LeBon, suggests that a crowd takes on characteristics such as impulsiveness and irrationality that are not necessarily characteristic of individual persons within the crowd. A third perspective, held by Freud, sees Oedipal implications in crowd behavior as individuals identify with the crowd leader, expressing a kind of familial love within this identification. Still a fourth perspective is seen in Turner's emphasis on the emergent-norm model — the theory that the ambiguity of a crowd situation prompts the crowd members to adopt as their norm the behavior of a handful of the group's most visible members. Hall adds an additional perspective with the suggestion that crowd behavior tends to violate personal space.

16. Which of the above perspectives would be *least* likely to associate crowd behavior with the immediate, environmental factors?
    (A) Marxian (B) LeBon (C) Freud (D) Turner (E) Hall

17. The view that speaks most directly to the concept of territoriality is that of
    (A) Marx (B) LeBon (C) Freud (D) Turner (E) Hall

18. Primaries in additive color mixing
    (A) are synonymous with subtractive color mixing
    (B) are blue, green, and red
    (C) are utilized in the mixing of paints
    (D) have become obsolete and no longer are used as theoretical reference
    (E) are blue, yellow, and red

19. In perceiving the distance of a sound, a person must depend heavily upon
    (A) complexity and resonance (B) brightness and saturation
    (C) dystonia (D) loudness and timbre (E) beats

20. Which of the following is the receptor organ central to pain sensitivity?
    (A) Meissner corpuscle (B) Krause end bulb (C) free nerve ending
    (D) lateral geniculate nucleus (E) muscle spindle

21. Which of the following was an unexpected finding among subjects in early sensory deprivation experiments?
    (A) delusions
    (B) hallucinations
    (C) "phantom limb" phenomenon
    (D) experience of motion parallax
    (E) convergence

22. A term unrelated to ESP is
    (A) clairvoyance (B) psychokinesis (C) psychosynesis
    (D) telepathy (E) telekinesis

23. In a Sarason-type experiment, Group 1 is told that it is not expected to finish its task, while Group 2 is told that it is expected to finish. Which of the following would be the anticipated result?
    (A) Group 1 finishes; Group 2 does not.
    (B) Both Group 1 and Group 2 finish with equal speed.
    (C) Group 2 completes more of the task than Group 1.

(D) Both groups experience a type of situational neurosis preventing performance on the task.
(E) The experimenter-monitored group — regardless of the instructions — finishes last.

24. Among the following, the conceptual term *least* important to Hull would be
    (A) habit strength   (B) reaction potential   (C) drive
    (D) stimulus   (E) interaction potential

25. Auditory receptor cells are located in the
    (A) anvil   (B) stirrup   (C) cochlea   (D) eustachian tube
    (E) pinna

26. In his own words, Tolman called his theoretical views
    (A) S-O-R psychology   (B) radical behaviorism   (C) purposive behaviorism   (D) dynamic behaviorism   (E) motivational behaviorism

27. In the early, classic experiments of Cannon and Washburn, their subjects were required to swallow balloons. This procedure enabled the experimenters to study
    (A) the amount of food intake
    (B) hormonal secretions
    (C) the physiological mechanism known as the "start" factor
    (D) dietary self-selection
    (E) gastric contractions of the stomach

28. Which of the following name combinations constitutes a from-then-till-now time sequence in motivation research?
    (A) James, McKinsey, Atkinson
    (B) Freud, Adler, Rank
    (C) James, McDougall, Atkinson
    (D) Freud, Skinner, Berne
    (E) James, McClelland, Freud

29. Which of the following would Dembo consider a primary determinant of level of aspiration?
    (A) force field   (B) negative valence   (C) past success or failure
    (D) ideal self   (E) real self

30. Sleepwalking and talking
    (A) occur primarily during the dreaming period
    (B) occur mostly in nondreaming stages, since the dreaming person is almost totally immobile
    (C) signify hypnagogic activity
    (D) correlate strongly with the incidence of alexia
    (E) occur far more frequently among women than among men

31. Which of the following is a neurotransmitter that inhibits or facilitates an action potential in the postsynaptic neuron?
    (A) thyroxin   (B) ESP   (C) IPSP   (D) acetylcholine
    (E) epinephrine

32. Which of the following is the control responsibility of the parasympathetic nervous system?
    (A) respiration increase   (B) pupil dilation   (C) heart-rate inhibition
    (D) salivation inhibition   (E) piloerection

33. Muscles are prominent and familiar examples of
    (A) receptors (B) affectors (C) end plates (D) effectors
    (E) ganglia

34. Lindsley's activation theory of emotion centers upon the role of
    (A) the limbic system
    (B) classical conditioning
    (C) the reticular formation
    (D) instrumental conditioning
    (E) the galvanic skin response

35. According to Atkinson, which of the following would be true?
    (A) Motivation deals with immediate influences on direction, vigor, and persistence of action.
    (B) Motivation is synonymous with perception.
    (C) Motivation is synonymous with emotion.
    (D) Motivation is synonymous with the study of behavior change.
    (E) Motivation deals primarily with intelligence.

36. When sleep is regularly and experimentally interrupted at the onset of dream activity, it is found that, on subsequent nights,
    (A) normal dream frequency is evident
    (B) normal dream length is evident
    (C) lower dream frequency is evident
    (D) much longer than normal dream length is evident
    (E) there is a surprising absence of any dream activity

37. *Incorrectly* paired are
    (A) spinal cord — a center for reflex behavior
    (B) medulla — centers for respiration and cardiac activity
    (C) ventricular system — glandular hormonal secretions into the blood
    (D) midbrain — conduction of impulses between higher and lower centers of the nervous system
    (E) cerebellum — coordination of sensory and motor impulses

38. Studies by Denenberg indicate that early handling tended to make animals
    (A) more fearful as adults
    (B) less active as adults
    (C) less emotional as adults
    (D) more active as adults
    (E) equivalent in all respects to nonhandled control animals

39. In the exhaustion stage of Selye's general adaptation syndrome, a person demonstrates
    (A) hyperventilation (B) apparent calm (C) GSR (D) more visceral activity (E) the alarm-type reaction

40. Hyperactivity through glandular secretion is most directly related to
    (A) the cerebellum (B) the gonads (C) the thyroid gland
    (D) the adrenal medulla (E) the Sylvian fissure

41. A person who is in the circus because he or she is nine feet tall and has very large hands and feet and a protruding jaw can attribute his or her physiological abnormality to an overactive
    (A) thyroid gland   (B) parathyroid gland   (C) adrenal gland
    (D) pancreas   (E) pituitary gland

42. The brain and spinal cord comprise the
    (A) sympathetic nervous system
    (B) parasympathetic nervous system
    (C) central nervous system
    (D) peripheral nervous system
    (E) somatic nervous system

43. A peculiar, intoxication-type behavior in which a person loses normal control of his emotions is characteristic of
    (A) fatigue   (B) oxygen starvation   (C) thirst   (D) hunger
    (E) sexual deprivation

Questions 44–46 are based on the following information.

Among theoretical approaches to personality the terms *nomothetic* and *ideographic* serve to identify two basically different avenues. The ideographic approach places emphasis upon the individual person as a unique entity; the nomothetic approach experimentally looks for personality factors and characteristics that are common to people in general.

44. Which of the following points might be made in defense of the ideographic approach?
    (A) The person's unique qualities constitute the essence of his or her personality.
    (B) Correlations designed to find common personality characteristics are essential for progress in the field.
    (C) The function of an organism in response to a specific stimulus is the key to personality study.
    (D) Personality is essentially a matter of physiochemistry and hormonal secretions.
    (E) Id, ego, and superego are the principal factors in personality.

45. Which of the following correctly pairs an advocate of the nomothetic approach with an advocate of the ideographic approach?
    (A) Rogers–Kelly   (B) Frankl–Perls   (C) Watson–Skinner
    (D) Maslow–Tolman   (E) Freud–Adler

46. Which of the following terms and concepts is *not* associated with the ideographic approach?
    (A) individual psychology   (B) client-centered therapy   (C) personal construct   (D) systematic desensitization   (E) Gestalt therapy

47. The Bunson-Roscoe Law
    (A) holds for photochemical processes
    (B) holds exclusively for audition
    (C) relates exclusively to pain sensitivity
    (D) holds for synesthesia
    (E) relates exclusively to kinesthesis

48. REM sleep signals
    (A) high GSR   (B) dreaming   (C) reciprocal innervation
    (D) stage IV sleep   (E) stage II sleep

49. The method of summated ratings refers to the _____ scale.
(A) Thurstone   (B) Likert   (C) Semantic Differential
(D) Guttman   (E) Bogardus

50. In the McClelland-type ring toss game, which of the following groups of men would be expected to take the most shots from an intermediate distance?
(A) those high in test anxiety
(B) those high in both test anxiety and achievement need
(C) those low in achievement need
(D) those low in both achievement need and test anxiety
(E) those high in achievement need and low in test anxiety

Questions 51–53 are based upon the following diagram.

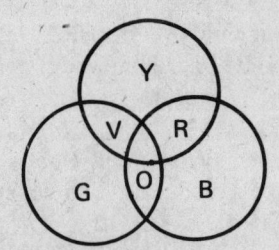

Key
V — Violet
G — Green
O — Orange
B — Blue
R — Red
Y — Yellow

51. Momentarily assuming the above diagram to be an accurate color wheel, what would be the after-image of exposure to red?
(A) yellow   (B) violet   (C) green   (D) orange   (E) blue

52. What combination of colors would produce green?
(A) violet and orange   (B) violet and red   (C) blue and yellow
(D) orange and red   (E) blue and red

53. What color would be the complementary of green?
(A) violet   (B) blue   (C) orange   (D) red   (E) violet-orange

Questions 54–56 are based upon the following diagram.

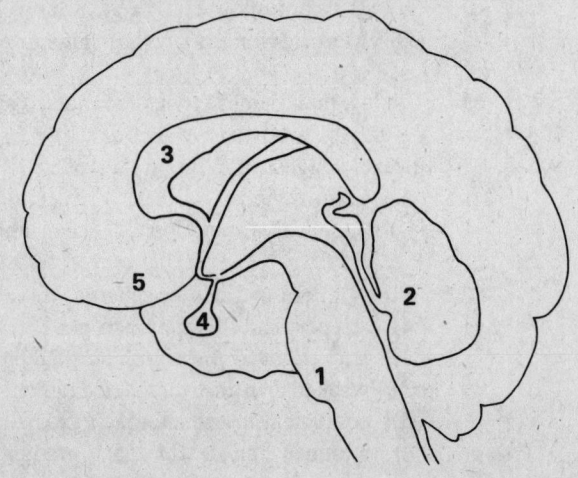

Assume that the human brain has been "halved" and that in the above drawing you are viewing from midbrain the central, interior portion of the right hemisphere.

54. Identify the rhinencephalon.
(A) 1   (B) 2   (C) 3   (D) 4   (E) 5

55. Locate the cerebellum.
    (A) 1   (B) 2   (C) 3   (D) 4   (E) 5

56. Find the corpus callosum.
    (A) 1   (B) 2   (C) 3   (D) 4   (E) 5

57. The pigeon reponds by pecking when the circular window is illuminated but does not respond when the window is dark. The illuminated window is a(n)
    (A) generalized stimulus
    (B) discriminative stimulus
    (C) unconditioned stimulus
    (D) reinforcement
    (E) discriminative response

58. The third stage of labor in childbirth is called
    (A) cervix dilation   (B) actual newborn emergence
    (C) the afterbirth   (D) breech   (E) vertex

59. Betsy is brown-eyed (heterozygous) and Bob is brown-eyed (heterozygous). The statistical likelihood of their producing a brown-eyed child is
    (A) 1 in 4   (B) 3 in 4   (C) 2 in 4   (D) 4 in 4   (E) 0 in 4

60. Research has related which of the following to maternal stress during pregnancy?
    (A) fetal activity   (B) reduced IQ   (C) personality instability
    (D) manic-depression   (E) psychosis

61. In the serial position effect
    (A) early items in a list are learned less quickly than middle items
    (B) uncompleted tasks are retained longer than completed tasks
    (C) prepotent stimuli are learned faster than other stimuli
    (D) middle items in a list are learned less quickly than early and late items
    (E) middle items in a list are learned more quickly than early and late items

62. Which of the following is produced by tactile stimulation of a newborn's cheek?
    (A) Babkin response   (B) Babinski response   (C) rooting response
    (D) Moro response   (E) grasping reflex

63. The fact that Siamese twins, connected at their backs, have been observed in alternate periods of sleep and wakefulness (e.g., one has been sleeping while the other is awake) suggests the importance of which of the following as a mechanism in sleep?
    (A) brain rhythms   (B) prolactin   (C) blood-sugar level
    (D) chemical stimulation   (E) epinephrine

64. In the Dollard and Miller schema, the avoidance gradient is
    (A) steeper than the approach gradient
    (B) equivalent to the approach gradient at all distances from the goal
    (C) weaker than the approach gradient near the goal
    (D) equivalent to the approach gradient when the goal is reached
    (E) stronger than the approach gradient when the goal is distant

65. The fact that a task interrupted prior to completion is remembered better than a completed task is called
    (A) proactive facilitation   (B) proactive inhibition   (C) Zeigarnik effect   (D) von Restorff effect   (E) serial position effect

66. Guthrie is most closely associated with which of the following in learning theory?
    (A) reinforcement   (B) habit strength   (C) contiguity of S and R
    (D) S-R connections   (E) cognitions

67. A person has just learned a new response to be substituted for an old one. Introduction of stress to the response situation will most likely
    (A) enhance responding
    (B) have no effect upon responding
    (C) interfere with responding
    (D) crystallize and "cement" the newly learned response
    (E) promote reminiscence

68. In toilet training, parents can expect
    (A) defecation control to precede urination control
    (B) urination control to precede defecation control
    (C) simultaneous defecation and urination control
    (D) defecation control by the end of the first year
    (E) the control pattern that was true in the parents' own childhoods.

69. Piaget calls the first two years of life the
    (A) concrete operations period   (B) preverbal period   (C) sensorimotor period   (D) formal operations period   (E) syntaxic period

70. "With the possible exception of old age, no other phase of individual development is so clearly marked by negative connotations and lack of positive sanctions." This is a reference by Goldblatt to
    (A) age 1
    (B) Erikson's age of automony versus shame and doubt
    (C) the general preschool period
    (D) early adolescence
    (E) early adulthood

71. In research with newborns, the cautious experimental hunch now being advanced is that
    (A) the point of diminishing returns
    (B) extinction
    (C) plateau
    (D) asymptote
    (E) learning terminal

72. In research with newborns, the cautious experimental hunch now being advanced is that
    (A) fast habituators may be brighter than slow habituators
    (B) slow habituators may be brighter than fast habituators
    (C) intelligence may be related to the presence and strength of initial reflexes
    (D) early onset of pleasant emotions in the newborn means healthy personality later
    (E) block design may be an accurate measure of intelligence as early as one month of age

73. The term *general-to-specific* in child development refers to
    (A) visual acuity   (B) auditory sensitivity   (C) motor movements
    (D) cortex development   (E) pain sensitivity

74. The neonate has well-developed
    (A) temperature-regulating mechanisms
    (B) pain sensitivity
    (C) immunity to various infections
    (D) lower torso
    (E) auditory acuteness

75. As one views the two-dimensional representation of a large, flat cobblestone area, the perception of distance is attained primarily through
    (A) linear perspective   (B) texture gradient   (C) motion parallax
    (D) closure   (E) continuity

76. The motor primacy principle in development means that
    (A) muscle development precedes neural development
    (B) striated muscle development precedes smooth muscle development
    (C) virtually any motor skill can be learned shortly after birth, if the infant is given sufficient training
    (D) maturation of neuromuscular structures to a given stage precedes ability to respond
    (E) motor development precedes glandular development

77. Scientific inquiry utilizing rules of logical inference from established premises and laws is known as
    (A) inductive   (B) reductive   (C) deductive   (D) teleological
    (E) probabilistic

78. Innate behavior patterns develop primarily as a function of
    (A) instrumental conditioning   (B) maturation   (C) learning
    (D) infant stimulation   (E) successive approximation

79. The newborn
    (A) vocalizes socially
    (B) smiles socially
    (C) tracks moving objects behind stationary objects
    (D) has the capability for basic learning
    (E) engages in babbling

80. In comparative physical growth curves, females
    (A) develop more slowly than males
    (B) develop more rapidly than males
    (C) develop at the same rate as males
    (D) develop more rapidly than males during the first six years and more slowly thereafter
    (E) develop more slowly than males during the first six years and more rapidly thereafter

81. If a female human fetus in the early stages of its development received large injections of androgen, which of the following could be expected in the newborn?
    (A) stillbirth
    (B) anoxia
    (C) brain damage
    (D) abnormal, exaggerated female sex characteristics
    (E) abnormal, exaggerated male sex characteristics

82. Which of the following constitutes a disadvantage of the rooming-in procedure with newborns?
    (A) Needs are met with minimal crying.
    (B) Trained nurses are easily accessible.
    (C) No adjustment required to handling by several people.
    (D) Constant demands are made upon the new mother.
    (E) Rigid feeding schedule is adhered to.

83. Continued improvement in the absence of further practice is known as
    (A) spontaneous recovery   (B) platikurtic   (C) savings
    (D) reminiscence   (E) recall

84. The PLATO system is
    (A) one of the early teaching-machine systems
    (B) a form of computer-assisted instruction
    (C) designed to test driver reaction times
    (D) designed to test pilot reaction times
    (E) designed to test nonreinforced (incidental) learning

85. In developmental terminology, PKU refers to
    (A) the effects of thalidomide
    (B) Down's syndrome
    (C) sickle cell
    (D) a hereditary enzyme deficiency
    (E) syphilis in the newborn

86. Which of the following contains the definitional elements necessary to obtain an intelligence quotient?
    (A) mental age divided by chronological age, quotient multiplied by 100
    (B) chronological age divided by mental age, quotient multiplied by 100
    (C) social age divided by mental age, quotient multiplied by 100
    (D) mental age divided by chronological age, quotient multiplied by 50
    (E) chronological age divided by mental age, quotient multiplied by 50

87. In a case where a person has intense fear of small rooms, the room serves as a
    (A) UCS   (B) CS   (C) CR   (D) UCR   (E) S(delta)

88. The process through which environmental information is received and labeled by the human is called
    (A) decoding   (B) generativity   (C) mediation   (D) encoding
    (E) programming

89. According to Piaget, the process through which a young child relates something he sees to something he already knows is called
    (A) accommodation   (B) assimilation   (C) convergence
    (D) concrete operation   (E) formal operation

90. Temporal conditioning
    (A) is synonymous with trace conditioning
    (B) is synonymous with delayed conditioning
    (C) is synonymous with simultaneous conditioning
    (D) presents UCS on a fixed time schedule
    (E) utilizes a CS that is in itself inherently rewarding

91. Existing research suggests that an active, outgoing, socially assertive child is most likely to have come from a family background that has been
    (A) warm and restrictive (B) distant and demanding (C) distant and democratic (D) warm and permissive (E) distant and permissive

92. Lorenz has suggested that
    (A) aggression is innate and biologically based
    (B) phonemes are the key factors in child language development
    (C) language determines thought processes
    (D) duck imprinting cannot be replicated in humans
    (E) the general notion of imprinting is not supported by experimental evidence

93. Punishment is most effective as an aid to learning when used
    (A) at the beginning of a series of trials
    (B) at the end of a series of trials
    (C) to extinguish previously rewarded responses
    (D) in combination with reward
    (E) in the middle of a series of trials

94. Theoretical separation between imagery and verbal processes has
    (A) not been supported by neurological investigations
    (B) been strongly supported by neurological investigations
    (C) been supported by investigations of the left temporal lobe only
    (D) been supported by investigations of the right temporal lobe only
    (E) been supported by the work of Kimura but not by that of Milner

95. Developmentally speaking, the earliest group in which a person participates is
    (A) dyadic (B) monadic (C) triadic (D) quadratic
    (E) parallel play group

96. Among the features by which we distinguish letters, a three-year-old child is proficient only in
    (A) curvature (U vs. V) (B) closedness (O vs. C) (C) direction (P vs. d)
    (D) size (a vs. A) (E) shape

97. Which of the following is stated by a null hypothesis?
    (A) significant difference
    (B) no significant difference
    (C) normal frequency distribution
    (D) minimized Type II error
    (E) .05 significance level

98. Which of the following has *not* been a finding within developmental psychology research?
    (A) The degree of mother responsiveness to a baby's needs affects the quality of the child's attachment to the mother.
    (B) Frequent mother-child separations during the first two or three years can produce anxious attachment.
    (C) The discipline technique of expressing disapproval through love withdrawal has been found to be one of the most effective.
    (D) Failure to form attachments to significant, caretaking persons during childhood relates to the inability to form close personal relationships in adulthood.
    (E) The young child is much more willing to explore strange surroundings when mother is present than when she is not.

99. The standard deviation obtained from a sample distribution of scores is
    (A) an inferential statistic
    (B) a descriptive statistic
    (C) a measure of correlation
    (D) a squared variance
    (E) a measure of central tendency

100. Which of the following would most greatly enhance the effectiveness of a film as a learning device?
    (A) passive review following the film
    (B) commentary during the film
    (C) brief introduction to the film
    (D) audience participation during the film
    (E) teacher participation after the film

101. Which of the following should be the source of greatest parental concern about a child's emotional health?
    (A) frequent laughing   (B) frequent noisiness   (C) long periods of sleep
    (D) frequent temper tantrums   (E) frequent crying

102. Current trends indicate that breast feeding is most prevalent among which of the following groups?
    (A) lower-class white mothers
    (B) lower-class black mothers
    (C) middle-class, well-educated mothers
    (D) middle-class, poorly educated mothers
    (E) all social strata

103. *Not* among the elements that Thurstone found comprising intelligence is
    (A) verbal comprehension   (B) memory   (C) reasoning
    (D) space visualization   (E) creative problem solving

104. In the present intelligence classification system, the former category of moron would now be included within
    (A) profoundly retarded   (B) educable   (C) severely retarded
    (D) trainable   (E) mildly retarded

105. In studying the relationship between test frequency and content mastery, a researcher finds a correlation of +1.20. On the basis of this finding, he can conclude that there is
    (A) strong positive correlation
    (B) strong negative correlation
    (C) low positive correlation
    (D) low negative correlation
    (E) a computational error

106. When asked what time it is, four-year-old Johnny correctly responds that it is 4:30. Johnny's time concept has developed
    (A) more rapidly than one normally would expect
    (B) more slowly than one normally could expect
    (C) through parental instruction and careful guidance
    (D) as a function of training received through a sibling
    (E) as a function of his work in spatial relations

107. Determining a rule of structure from incomplete evidence and then identifying items that fulfill the rule would be a demonstration of
    (A) interpolation (B) extrapolation (C) interposition
    (D) structuring (E) modeling

108. Among steps in problem solving, which of the following would occur earliest?
    (A) deriving and generating possible solutions
    (B) evaluating solutions
    (C) testing solutions
    (D) revising solutions
    (E) verifying solutions

109. Time and motion studies are the concern of
    (A) verbal learning psychologists
    (B) physiological psychologists
    (C) human engineering psychologists
    (D) social psychologists
    (E) clinical psychologists

110. Hebb found that "super span" tests involving long strings of digits repeated periodically after many intervening spans
    (A) left no memory trace
    (B) left a demonstrable memory trace
    (C) created unique number-span retention capacities
    (D) suggested strictly transient neural activity
    (E) suggested the "isometric digit" problem

111. In rote learning tasks, investigators have found that
    (A) most learning occurs during the last few learning trials
    (B) distributed practice is generally superior to massed practice
    (C) learning effectiveness is enhanced by delaying knowledge of results
    (D) all nonsense syllables have the same likelihood of being retained
    (E) most forgetting occurs in cases where the material was overlearned

112. Kohlberg indicates that at the most primitive level of moral development, morality is decided by
    (A) individual rights and social contracts
    (B) reward and punishment
    (C) individual conscience
    (D) social approval or disapproval
    (E) religious values

113. Telegraphic speech refers to
    (A) a child's first word
    (B) verbal expression that emphasizes only vowel sounds
    (C) the consistent use of three-syllable words
    (D) a child's early grammatical constructions
    (E) the basic consonant elements present in every language

114. In experiments such as Pavlov's surgical isolation of a portion of a dog's stomach, it has been found that the effect of food upon digestive processes depends upon
    (A) solely the tasting behavior
    (B) solely the swallowing behavior
    (C) solely the entry of food into the stomach
    (D) a combination of both the stomach and the mouth activities
    (E) neither the stomach nor the mouth activity

115. Which of the following is *least* characteristic of the kibbutzim?
    (A) professional caretakers for children in houses separate from those of the parents
    (B) marked retardation in the social and intellectual development of the children
    (C) parental visits primarily in the evenings and on weekends
    (D) a warm, permissive approach to toilet training
    (E) operation by the state

Questions 116–117 are based on the following diagram.

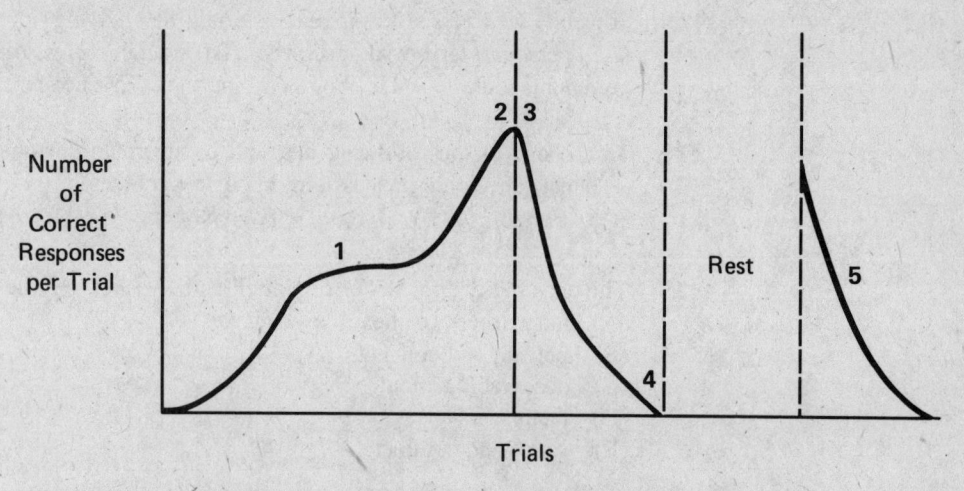

116. In the above diagram, the process of extinction began at which point?
    (A) 1   (B) 2   (C) 3   (D) 4   (E) 5

117. The phenomenon occurring at point A would be indicative of
    (A) asymptote   (B) extinction   (C) plateau   (D) reminiscence
    (E) spontaneous recovery

118. According to psychoanalytic theory, defense mechanisms develop as a function of
    (A) repression   (B) depression   (C) superego   (D) anxiety
    (E) reaction formation

119. Kelley's "warm-cold" experimentation demonstrated the effect of which of the following on a person's attitude toward a group speaker?
    (A) room temperature
    (B) the warmth or coldness of the speaker himself
    (C) the variation in a single descriptive adjective
    (D) the warmth or coldness of the experimenter
    (E) the warmth or coldness of the audience

120. Interpersonal attraction based on rewards and costs is a prominent aspect of the
    (A) theory of similarity
    (B) theory of complementarity
    (C) social exchange theory
    (D) theory of cognitive dissonance
    (E) distributive justice theory

121. Which of the following experimenters developed a test in which black and white dolls are presented to black and white children with the question, "Which one looks like you?"
    (A) Ammons   (B) Pettigrew   (C) Clark   (D) McCandless
    (E) Kelly

122. In Darley and Latane's "epileptic attack" study, the investigators found that a major determinant in eliciting a helping response was
(A) seeing someone else ask for help
(B) the number of other students that the individual thought had heard the victim
(C) the sex of the victim
(D) the age of the potential helper
(E) the degree of perceived seriousness of the situation

123. Someone well versed in proxemics would be studying
(A) personal, territorial space   (B) facial expressions   (C) mass communication   (D) brainwashing   (E) nonzero sum games

124. Which one of the following has said in regard to personality that every child is a scientist, developing and testing his own hypotheses?
(A) Freud   (B) Jung   (C) Rogers   (D) Allport   (E) Kelly

125. The personality approaches of Cattell and Eysenck rely heavily upon
(A) inner forces (cathexes-anticathexes)
(B) percept and concept
(C) observable action
(D) factor analysis
(E) script and contract

126. The therapy technique known as free association had its early beginnings in the work of
(A) James   (B) Freud   (C) Watson   (D) Jung   (E) Brucke

127. The terms *script* and *contract* are prominent within which of the following approaches?
(A) psychoanalysis   (B) systematic desensitization   (C) reciprocal inhibition   (D) implosive therapy   (E) transactional analysis

128. Definitionally central to personality as viewed within behaviorism is
(A) inner motivation   (B) percept and concept   (C) observable action
(D) reenactment of birth trauma   (E) factor analysis

129. Within Newcomb's A-B-X model, if person A likes X, person B likes X, and person A dislikes person B, the triad is said to be
(A) cooriented   (B) asymmetric   (C) congruent   (D) bipolar
(E) inoculated

130. In Adler's approach to personality, the presence of an inferiority complex within a person will be followed by
(A) heightened sexual activity   (B) need for maternal love   (C) desire for peace
(D) superiority striving   (E) thanatos

131. The Likert-type scale does *not* use
(A) a large number of judges
(B) an internal consistency analysis of items
(C) a high total-score indicator of "anti" attitude
(D) semantic differential techniques
(E) written statements to which the subject responds

132. When Berkowitz refers to the F-A hypothesis, he means
    (A) frustration-affection
    (B) frustration-aggression
    (C) feeling-affect
    (D) feeling-aggression
    (E) fixation-accommodation

133. In the Allport-Vernon-Lindzey scale, which type of person will most highly value the search for truth and order?
    (A) economic   (B) philosophical   (C) theoretical
    (D) aesthetic   (E) religious

134. Brown believes that the basic category governing our lives and actions is
    (A) roles   (B) class   (C) caste   (D) stereotypes
    (E) occupation

135. Which of the following characterizes a nomothetic approach to personality?
    (A) assuming commonalities among people
    (B) assuming the uniqueness of each individual
    (C) seeking functional explanations for behavior
    (D) seeking hereditary explanations for behavior
    (E) subscribing to "the whole being greater than the sum of its parts"

136. Kagan's work reopens debate and challenges the basic assumptions regarding
    (A) a critical early-childhood period in social development
    (B) a critical early-childhood period in cognitive-intellectual development
    (C) a critical early-childhood period in emotional development
    (D) the Erikson psychosocial stages
    (E) the Freudian views regarding thanatos

137. A decision to establish status on the basis of individual income, education, and occupation utilizes the
    (A) objective method   (B) reputational method   (C) subjective method
    (D) situational method   (E) projective method

138. Given the words *sunshine, weather, bastard,* and *beauty,* McGinnies would expect:
    (A) equal tachistoscopic exposure time for perception and reporting of each of these words
    (B) longer tachistoscopic exposure time for perception and reporting of the word *bastard*
    (C) shorter tachistoscopic exposure time for perception and reporting of the word *beauty*
    (D) shorter tachistoscopic exposure time for perception and reporting of the word *sunshine*
    (E) longer perception time and shorter reporting time on the word *bastard*

139. Which of the following makes the most prominent use of statistics in its scoring procedures?
    (A) Rorschach Test   (B) TAT   (C) Blacky Test   (D) MMPI
    (E) Sentence Completion Test

140. The general message about early childhood that can be gleaned from personality theorists is that that period is
    (A) not very critical to long-term development

(B) critically important to later personality development
(C) critical in the physiological sense but not in the social
(D) critical in the social sense but not in the physiological
(E) important only in terms of language development

141. Aronson and Mills's study involving "frank discussion of sexual matters" revealed that strength of initiation
    (A) does not correlate with group attraction
    (B) has strong positive correlation with group attraction
    (C) has weak positive correlation with group attraction
    (D) has strong negative correlation with group attraction
    (E) has weak negative correlation with group attraction

142. The Oedipal conflict is successfully resolved when the child
    (A) identifies with the opposite-sex parent
    (B) identifies with the same-sex parent
    (C) achieves satisfactory toilet training
    (D) has been satisfactorily weaned
    (E) adjusts to the anger-anxiety conflict

143. Existing research would suggest which of the following as an approach to problems of prejudice?
    (A) simply bringing the groups together
    (B) engaging the groups in competitive activities
    (C) developing a superordinate goal
    (D) initiating a letter-writing program between groups
    (E) individual psychotherapy

144. Selecting colors for a sign that must show up prominently at dusk, one might be best advised to choose
    (A) red   (B) yellow   (C) orange   (D) violet   (E) pink

145. One of the major reasons that circadian rhythm has become a focus of attention in studying pilots is its relationship to
    (A) sleeplessness   (B) anemia   (C) apraxia   (D) fatigue
    (E) strokes

146. A desire to guide and contribute to the development of a generation younger than oneself would *not* be characteristic of
    (A) generativity   (B) genital stage   (C) self-actualization
    (D) narcissism   (E) social interest

147. The socially "good" or "proper" within Freudian theory is conceptually defined as the
    (A) id   (B) ego   (C) superego   (D) archetype
    (E) preconscious

148. A primary problem encountered in treating drug addicts, alcoholics, and sociopaths is
    (A) their contentedness with their present life style
    (B) their lack of effective verbal communication skills
    (C) their related sexual problems
    (D) their consistently low IQ levels
    (E) resistance from families and close relatives

149. Someone suffering from an involutional psychotic disorder typically manifests either
    (A) depression or obsession   (B) obsession or regression   (C) regression or depression   (D) depression or paranoia   (E) paranoia or regression

150. Multiple personality is a specific disorder classified as a form of
    (A) psychosis   (B) neurosis   (C) schizophrenia   (D) paranoia   (E) delusion

151. Freud first became familiar with the concept of "talking cure" through an association with
    (A) Charcot   (B) Breuer   (C) Bennett   (D) Selye   (E) Rank

152. The person smokes a cigarette and, because of earlier drug administration, becomes nauseous in a technique known as
    (A) chaining   (B) therapeutic community   (C) extinction   (D) aversive conditioning   (E) reciprocal inhibition

153. Which of the following would most accurately describe the delusional situation in which a person believes others are talking about him?
    (A) delusions of sin and guilt
    (B) hypochondriacal delusions
    (C) delusions of grandeur
    (D) nihilistic delusions
    (E) delusions of reference

154. Eysenck's personality framework contains which of the following among its main dimensions?
    (A) parapraxic-syntaxic
    (B) depressive-obsessional
    (C) introversion-extraversion
    (D) hysteric-psychopathic
    (E) adaptive-maladaptive

155. The soldier who in the heat of battle curls up in a fetal position and cries is demonstrating
    (A) phobia   (B) regression   (C) projection   (D) psychosomatic disorder   (E) hypochondriasis

156. Elevators seem to "close in" and small rooms create feelings of fear that seem unbearable in
    (A) anxiety reaction   (B) claustrophobia   (C) acrophobia   (D) ochlophobia   (E) obsessive-compulsion

157. Fundamental to all sensitivity and encounter groups is
    (A) open interaction
    (B) nudity
    (C) the breakdown of defenses through the use of fatigue
    (D) an attempt by each member to "shock" the group
    (E) the arrangement of chairs in a semicircle and the presence of two trained therapists

158. Which of the following statements is incorrect?
    (A) Wolpe's method has been used with homosexual patients.
    (B) Behavior and reinforcement therapists include Skinner and Lindsley.

(C) Behavior therapy has been attacked on grounds that it threatens man's freedom.
(D) ESB is in common usage as a therapeutic technique.
(E) Frankl's logotherapy seeks to remove the existential vacuum experienced by the patient.

159. A man went on a fishing trip and did not return home. Much later, he was discovered in another part of the country with a new marriage, family, and job and no recollection of his previous family or identity. His emotional disturbance would be classified as
(A) amnesia (B) fugue (C) multiple personality
(D) conversion reaction (E) affective reaction

160. A respectable president of a corporation greets people who come by his office by shaking hands with only his little finger; then he excuses himself long enough to wash the finger thoroughly in his adjacent lavatory. His behavioral symptoms indicate
(A) schizophrenia (B) paranoia (C) obsessive-compulsion
(D) pyromania (E) anxiety reaction

161. A person thinks that he sees a snake moving stealthily through the weeds on a distant hillside. As he gets closer, he discovers that it was only a dark piece of rope. This is a perceptual phenomenon known as
(A) telekinesis (B) illusion (C) delusion (D) hallucination
(E) motion parallax

162. Statistics on psychopathology indicate that since 1900
(A) childhood schizophrenia incidence has increased
(B) autism has increased
(C) mental disorders stemming from alcoholism have decreased
(D) psychosis incidence in people under forty has not increased
(E) mental disorders as a function of age have decreased

163. A person is completely unresponsive, stares blankly into space, and never moves. He or she shows symptoms related to
(A) paranoia (B) hebephrenic schizophrenia (C) catatonic schizophrenia (D) simple schizophrenia (E) dyssocial reaction

164. In Bandura's behavioral psychotherapy, a withdrawn child in a kindergarten room would be reinforced for
(A) remaining alone (B) joining the group (C) drawing a picture
(D) writing his name (E) playing with blocks

165. A team approach to therapy in which the entire life situation and the activities of the patient are brought into the therapeutic plan is known as
(A) milieu therapy (B) sociotherapy (C) nondirective therapy
(D) nonanalytical therapy (E) Gestalt therapy

166. "Sour grapes" is an example of the defense mechanism called
(A) reaction formation (B) compensation
(C) compartmentalization (D) rationalization (E) projection

167. The effectiveness of psychotherapy as a treatment for mental disorders has been
(A) disproved completely through research
(B) proved conclusively in several recent experiments
(C) difficult to demonstrate conclusively

(D) recently classified as a "closed book" question — no longer an issue in psychology
(E) most difficult to demonstrate within behavior therapy

168. In which of the following would spontaneous recovery be most likely?
(A) paranoid state   (B) involutional psychotic reaction
(C) sexual deviation   (D) stuttering   (E) psychopathic antisocial reaction

169. Abreaction would be most common as a result of
(A) psychosurgery   (B) metrazol shock therapy   (C) electroconvulsive shock therapy   (D) LSD therapy   (E) psychotherapy

170. Each of the scores in a distribution has been multiplied by 7. The standard deviation is
(A) increased by 7
(B) increased to 7 times its original value
(C) increased by its original value divided by 7
(D) increased by 14
(E) unchanged from its original value

171. An inanimate object would be central to which of the following sexual deviations?
(A) voyeurism   (B) masochism   (C) fetishism
(D) pedophilia   (E) sadism

172. *Not* part of a symptom nucleus for neurosis is
(A) inadequacy   (B) fearfulness   (C) tension
(D) egocentricity   (E) high stress tolerance

173. Which of the following would seem unrelated to the "anniversary reaction"?
(A) specific age attainment by the patient
(B) awareness of the age of a family member when tragedy befell him
(C) specific day of the week
(D) wholesome potential to act as "releaser"
(E) divorce and remarriage

174. For best research control of genetic factors, which of the following should be used in experimentation?
(A) newborns   (B) siblings   (C) identical twins
(D) factor analysis   (E) longitudinal approach

175. One type of test reliability is
(A) the degree to which the test measures what it is intended to measure
(B) the degree to which repeated measurements give the same score result
(C) the degree to which the test measures content
(D) the degree to which it is predictive
(E) the degree of thoroughness

176. For simple testing of differences between the means of an experimental and a control group, a researcher would be likely to use
(A) chi-square   (B) t-test   (C) correlation   (D) regression
(E) F-test

177. That its findings cannot be checked by other researchers is a criticism frequently leveled at proponents of
(A) behaviorism   (B) eclecticism   (C) functionalism
(D) introspectionism   (E) neobehaviorism

178. A political gathering precedes election night by two months. Given a choice of speaking positions on the program, a political candidate would be wise to choose to be
    (A) the first speaker
    (B) the middle speaker
    (C) the last speaker
    (D) either the first or the last speaker
    (E) in any of the three speaking positions

179. Given a grouping of data that is heterogeneous, you can expect a standard deviation to be
    (A) small
    (B) large
    (C) small if sample size is small
    (D) large only if sample size is large
    (E) below .9

180. A disreputable jeweler would have the best chance of selling an inferior diamond in which of the following display settings?
    (A) positioned on red velvet under red light
    (B) positioned on blue velvet under blue light
    (C) positioned on blue velvet under red light
    (D) positioned on red velvet under blue light
    (E) positioned on yellow velvet under blue light

181. Persons on stage will be noticed if _____ light is beamed upon their blue outfits.
    (A) red   (B) orange   (C) yellow   (D) violet   (E) pink

182. In a "stop smoking" campaign, which of the following persons would be most likely to quit successfully?
    (A) a lady who has read statistics on cancer research
    (B) a lady who knows the mg. tar content of her cigarette
    (C) a lady who hears an expert deliver a talk on the subject
    (D) a lady who hears one of her friends deliver a talk on the subject
    (E) a lady who personally delivers a talk on the subject

183. Psychodrama is a form of which of the following managerial training techniques?
    (A) incident   (B) case   (C) sensitivity   (D) role playing
    (E) free association

184. Which of the following is *not* a characteristic of teaching-machine instruction?
    (A) small, graduated steps   (B) knowledge of results   (C) multiple-choice format   (D) essay, reconstruction-type format   (E) immediate feedback

185. In screening applicants whose employment would involve winding small electronic coils, which of the following would be most useful?
    (A) intelligence tests   (B) pursuit rotor   (C) personality tests
    (D) finger dexterity tests   (E) electrical knowledge tests

186. In which of the following settings would a victim be most likely to receive help?
    (A) several men watching the mishap
    (B) several women watching the mishap
    (C) several members of a mixed group watching the mishap

(D) three people watching the mishap
(E) one person watching the mishap

Questions 187–189 are based on the following choices.

Given a normal distribution with a mean of 68 and a standard deviation of 10, use the following set of choices to answer questions 187–189.
(1) .68
(2) .84
(3) .16
(4) .32
(5) none of the above

187. What is the probability of a score above 78?
(A) 1   (B) 2   (C) 3   (D) 4   (E) 5

188. What is the probability of a score below 48?
(A) 1   (B) 2   (C) 3   (D) 4   (E) 5

189. What is the probability of a score either below 58 or above 78?
(A) 1   (B) 2   (C) 3   (D) 4   (E) 5

190. A personnel selection test that requires previous knowledge and mastery of a given body of material is, in effect,
(A) an aptitude test   (B) an achievement test   (C) an intelligence test
(D) a test for creativity   (E) a test for sociability

191. The fact that repeated administrations of a particular test result in consistent scores is evidence of
(A) validity   (B) reliability   (C) split-half correlation
(D) objectivity   (E) reliability and consistency

192. An experimenter investigates test anxiety in military academy cadets by utilizing galvanic skin response measurement. The GSR represents
(A) dependent variable and operational definition of anxiety
(B) independent variable and operational definition of anxiety
(C) intervening variable and operational definition of anxiety
(D) only operational definition of anxiety
(E) only dependent variable

193. Terman's study of gifted children would be considered
(A) latitudinal   (B) longitudinal   (C) laboratory method
(D) representational method   (E) nomothetic

194. Which of the following scales could be developed and implemented with the least amount of standardization?
(A) Thurstone type   (B) Remmers type   (C) Likert type
(D) Stanford-Binet type   (E) Osgood type

195. In a specific hearing test for children, *separate* tones are presented in a range of frequencies and intensities. The child is given general instructions to press a button whenever he hears a tone. This test is an application of the
(A) method of limits   (B) difference limen   (C) paired-comparisons method   (D) differential-threshold method   (E) Fechner method

196. Among human engineering principles relating to man-machine systems, a familiar control principle states that the best system provides
    (A) only one action pathway to achieve a given effect
    (B) at least six action pathways to achieve a given effect
    (C) at least two action pathways to achieve a given effect
    (D) a maximum of three action pathways to achieve a given effect
    (E) a maximum of four action pathways to achieve a given effect

197. The function of "white noise" is to
    (A) intensify the decibel level of existing noise
    (B) reduce the decibel level of existing noise
    (C) blot out or "overshadow" existing noise
    (D) accomplish synesthesia
    (E) rehabilitate in cases of temporary hearing loss

198. In comparison with centralized networks, which of the following constitutes a distinct advantage of the decentralized communication network?
    (A) increased worker productivity
    (B) quickly formed interaction stability
    (C) more rigid structure
    (D) increased worker satisfaction
    (E) fewer messages required for making a given decision

199. To convert a standard deviation into a variance, one must
    (A) take the square root of the standard deviation
    (B) divide the standard deviation by N
    (C) multiply the standard deviation by $1/z$
    (D) multiply the standard deviation by N
    (E) square the standard deviation

200. Researchers in kinesics believe that
    (A) the territorial space concept is a myth
    (B) findings will have relevance to parent-child communication and understanding
    (C) the future of the field will be primarily within proxemics
    (D) Hall's work is the field's pinnacle achievement
    (E) interpersonal communication is primarily verbal

Test 1: Answer Comments

1. (B) Specific energy of nerves refers to a receptor's capability to give only one quality of experience (e.g., visual, auditory, etc.), regardless of how it was stimulated.

2. (C) Alpha waves are most prevalent when a person is in a relaxed, wakeful state with his or her eyes closed.

3. (E) Referred to as Occam's razor or "Morgan's canon," the quotation states a basic interpretive principle in comparative psychology.

4. (B) Alcohol, barbiturates, and bromides are classified as sedatives.

5. (C) The question deals with a basic difference in study methods among comparative psychologists. Lorenz, Tinbergen, and Romanes are part of a European naturalistic observation tradition; Morgan used the problematic anecdotal method; Lashley has been a major contributor within the American experimental laboratory approach.

6. (E) The individual receiving normal sight after several years of blindness must relearn the auditory and tactile associations necessary to accommodate the visual frame of reference.

7. (B) The kinesthetic sensory system enables us to monitor the movements of our feet and know their position in relation to the ground.

8. (C) Werner-Wapner developed the perceptual theory known as "Sensory-Tonic." It states, in effect, that any percept is determined by the interaction between sensory (afferent) and proprioceptive (tonic) activity.

9. (E) Because each eye is neurally connected to each cerebral hemisphere, split-brain experiments make surgery on the optic chiasm essential.

10. (C) Kohler found no adaptation to the color stereo effect when wearing "squint glasses." Squint glasses are prism-type filters worn over the eyes.

11. (B) A reflex is quick and immediate.

12. (D) Currently an area of prominent attention in social psychology, attribution theory involves the processes through which a person interprets the motivations underlying another person's behavior and, in effect, attributes causality. The work of Nisbett, Kelley, Heider, and Gergen is central to this area; that of Festinger is not.

13. (D) In his work with monkeys, Butler found the greatest visual incentive to be an electric train in motion.

14. (A) The process of maintaining constancy of the normal internal environment of an organism is called homeostasis.

15. (B) As stimulus patterns become increasingly similar, reaction times become longer because stimulus discrimination is more difficult.

16. (C) Freud's perspective places primary emphasis upon the presence of unresolved personal conflicts brought by the individual to the crowd situation.

17. (E) Hall's concept of personal space is, in effect, a concept of territoriality (i.e., of protecting one's personal "turf").

18. (B) The primaries in additive (light) color mixing are blue, green, and red. Primaries in subtractive (pigment) color mixing are blue, yellow, and red.

19. (D) To perceive the distance of a sound, a person must rely heavily upon loudness and timbre (sound wave complexity).

20. (C) The free nerve ending is the receptor organ central to pain sensitivity.

21. (B) Sensory deprivation researchers found the unexpected occurrence of hallucinations, as though the subjects were compensating visually for their lack of stimulation.

22. (C) Although it sounds similar to ESP terms, psychosynesis is a "clunker" (meaningless distractor).

23. (C) In the Sarason-type study, experimenter-conveyed expectation of task completion prompts better subject performance.

24. (E) Although the terms *habit strength*, *reaction potential*, *drive*, and *stimulus* are integral to Hull, the term *interaction potential* is not.

25. (C) Auditory receptor cells are located in the cochlea, the point at which transformation to neural impulse occurs.

26. (C) Tolman called his learning theory views *purposive behaviorism*.

27. (E) Cannon and Washburn's procedure was designed to study gastric contractions as the potentially critical factor in the experience of hunger.

28. (C) James was one of the prime movers in motivation research, followed by McDougall and, more recently, Atkinson.

29. (C) Dembo and his associates have found past success or failure a critical determinant of level of aspiration.

30. (B) Sleepwalking and talking occur in stage IV sleep while dreaming occurs during REM stage I.

31. (D) A neurotransmitter inhibiting or facilitating an action potential in the postsynaptic neuron is acetylcholine.

32. (C) Heart-rate inhibition lies within the responsibilities of the parasympathetic nervous system.

33. (D) Some of the best, most common examples of effectors are skeletal muscles.

34. (C) Lindsley's activation theory of emotion is based upon the function of the reticular formation in organismic arousal.

35. (A) In Atkinson's view, motivation deals with immediate influences on direction, vigor, and persistence of action.

36. (D) Dreaming appears essential to the human organism, and dream overcompensation will occur in sleep that follows that in which dreaming has been interrupted and virtually prohibited.

37. (C) The ventricular system supplies the brain and spinal cord with cerebrospinal fluid.

38. (D) Denenberg found that early handling had the long-range effect of making animals less fearful and more active in adulthood.

39. (E) The alarm-type reaction is demonstrated in the exhaustion stage of Selye's general adaptation syndrome.

40. (C) High levels of thyroxin output from the thyroid gland would be associated with hyperactivity.

41. (E) The pituitary gland secretes hormones related to body growth and maintenance. The fact that a person is nine feet tall and in the circus can be attributable to pituitary gland malfunction.

42. (C) The central nervous system contains the brain and the spinal cord.

43. (B) An intoxication-type behavior in which a person loses control of his emotions is characteristic of oxygen starvation. This result has been produced in experimental settings in which a person inhaled carbon dioxide.

44. (A) That a person's unique qualities constitute the essence of his personality is a point frequently made in defense of the idiographic approach.

45. Freud's psychoanalytic approach is nomothetic and Adler's individual psychology approach is distinctly idiographic.

46. (D) Whereas individual psychology, client-centered therapy, personal construct, and Gestalt therapy focus upon individual uniqueness (idiographic), systematic desensitization is a general approach often used in cases of phobia.

47. (A) The Bunson-Roscoe Law holds for photochemical receptors. It is sometimes called the reciprocity or photographic law and expresses a reciprocal relationship within vision between intensity and time.

48. (B) REM (rapid eye movement) stage I sleep signals dreaming.

49. (B) The Likert scaling technique is known as the method of summated ratings, expressing a relationship between a person's high score on individual response items and an overall high score on the scale.

50. (E) In a ring-toss game, McClelland found persons high in achievement need and low in test anxiety were taking intermediate-level risks.

51. (C) Utilizing this diagram, the after-image of red would be the color directly across from it in the color wheel — green.

52. (A) According to this diagram, violet and orange combined would produce green — the color that occurs between them in the sketch.

53. (D) In this case, the complementary of green would be red — the color directly across from it.

54. (E) The rhinencephalon is an area in the brain stem that contains primitive cortex and subcortical structures relating to olfaction and emotion. It is the oldest portion of the cerebral hemispheres.

55. (B) Located adjacent to the occipital lobe and the brain stem, the cerebellum coordinates movements necessary for maintenance of balance and posture.

56. (C) This heavy bundle of fibers — the *corpus callosum* — connects the two hemispheres of the brain.

57. (B) The discriminative stimulus is, in effect, the stimulus distinctly associated with reinforcement; therefore, this stimulus must have characteristics that clearly distinguish it from other potential stimuli.

58. (C) The three stages, sequentially, are cervix dilation, actual newborn emergence, and afterbirth. The third stage involves delivery of the placenta with its accompanying amniotic and chorionic membranes.

59. (B) Heterozygous indicates the presence of genetic potential for either brown-eyed or blue-eyed children. Because brown eyes are a dominant characteristic, only one among the four possible combinations would result in blue eyes.

60. (A) Positive correlations have been found between the amount of maternal stress during pregnancy and the extent of fetal activity.

61. (D) In serial position effects, the first and last items of a list are learned most quickly.

62. (C) Rooting response, in effect a search for the nipple, is prompted by tactile stimulation of a newborn's cheek.

63. (A) The observations of Siamese twins yielded early indicators that brain rhythms had a central function in sleep. Subsequent research began moving away from the chemical theory of sleep toward a search for brain mechanisms.

64. (A) Avoidance is steeper, meaning that it will take on prominence and power as a person approaches the goal.

65. (C) The Zeigarnik effect suggests better retention of uncompleted tasks than of completed ones.

66. (C) One of the theory aspects most prominently identified with Guthrie has been the word *contiguity* (closeness) in reference to stimulus and response.

67. (C) Newly learned responses are much more vulnerable to stress than their well-established predecessors.

68. (A) Physiological readiness for defecation control occurs in the young child before similar readiness for urination control. The latter must await sphincter-muscle development.

69. (C) Piaget speaks of three basic periods in cognitive development — sensorimotor (birth to two years), concrete operations (two to eleven years), and formal operations (eleven to fifteen years).

70. (D) Goldblatt is describing the combination of capability and prohibition that besets the early adolescent period of development.

71. (D) Asymptote refers to the physiological limits of learning capability in contrast to plateau, a temporary level-off in performance beyond which additional learning will become evident.

72. (A) The potential relationship between speed of habituation in the infant and intelligence is currently prominent in child psychology research. Initial findings have been encouraging.

73. (C) Massive motor movements (e.g., movements of whole arms or large portions of the body) precede more specific motor movements (e.g., those of wrists or fingers).

74. (C) The newborn has a natural immunity that wears off during its first six months.

75. (B) With the cobblestone representation described, distance perception would be primarily a function of texture gradient.

76. (D) The motor primacy principle refers to maturation as preceding response capability.

77. (C) Deductive reasoning combines separate elements of existing knowledge to reach a conclusion. Such reasoning is in contrast to the inductive approach, which takes the "known" as starting point and makes an intuitive leap toward the unknown via hypotheses.

78. (B) The terms *innate* and *maturation* both refer to hereditary elements in behavior.

79. (D) Such basic learning capability is evident in both the newborn and the late fetal stages of development.

80. (B) This male-female growth differential is especially evident during early adolescence — when many girls are embarrassingly taller than their male counterparts.

81. (E) Large injections of androgen (a male sex hormone) have been known to produce abnormal, exaggerated male sex characteristics in the female newborn.

82. (D) While the rooming-in procedure gives the mother closeness to the newborn and prompt responsiveness to infant needs, the potential price is that of constant demands upon the new mother.

83. (D) Reminiscence constitutes performance improvement without intervening practice on the task.

84. (B) In computer-assisted instruction at the University of Illinois, the letters stand for Programmed Logic for Automatic Teaching Operations.

85. (D) The letters refer to phenylketonuria, a defect in the enzyme that metabolizes phenylalanine. Uncorrected by dietetic measures, the disorder can cause brain damage and mental deficiency.

86. (A) The Stanford-Binet formula is IQ = MA/CA × 100.

87. (B) Fear is a conditioned response (CR) to the conditioned stimulus (CS) of a small room.

88. (D) The encoding (labeling) process is essential to human language and thought.

89. (B) Assimilation is a Piagetian term describing the cognitive process of relating a perceived stimulus to the conceptual information that a child already has.

90. (D) A regular, fixed time schedule is the critical factor in temporal conditioning.

91. (D) Warmth and permissiveness are positively correlated with outgoing, socially assertive characteristics in children, whereas similar correlation is not found for distant, restrictive, demanding, authoritarian family settings.

92. (A) Lorenz's work centers on the biological bases for behavior and spans a range from imprinting to the innate aspects of aggression.

93. (D) Punishment, in combination with a presented behavioral alternative and an associated reward, enhances effectiveness.

94. (B) Brain mapping and localization of functioning has been one research area supporting this separation of processes.

95. (A) The earliest group is the mother-child dyad.

96. (B) The capacity for distinguishing letters on the basis of closedness is characteristic of the three-year-old. More sophisticated distinctions such as curvature will occur later.

97. (B) The null hypothesis is, in effect, the "no difference" hypothesis that a researcher hopes to be unable to accept on the basis of his research findings.

98. (C) The work of Hoffman and others indicates that love withdrawal as a discipline technique can produce overdependence upon adult approval. Explaining how the behavior is harmful and undesirable (a reasoning method) has been found to be more effective.

99. (B) The number of scores in a distribution, the measure of central tendency, and the measure of variability are three measures generally called descriptive statistics. On the basis of one's description of the sample, the investigator can make inferences about the probable characteristics of the specific population that could not be measured in its entirety (inferential statistics).

100. (D) Active involvement of an audience enhances learning effectiveness.

101. (D) Frequent temper tantrums among children constitute an emotional health signal to be heeded.

102. (C) Middle-class, well-educated mothers are the group most prominently utilizing the breast-feeding method in child rearing. This practice reflects their prominent concern for cognitive-emotional-social development in young children.

103. (E) Thurstone's elements included verbal comprehension, numerical ability, perceptual speed, space visualization, reasoning, word fluency, and memory.

104. (E) Moron referred to the IQ range between 50 and 70, now covered by the "mildly retarded" classification.

105. (E) A score indicating highest possible, i.e., perfect, correlation would be 1.00. Any figure higher than 1 is erroneous.

106. (A) Such time-concept mastery would be characteristic of the six-year-old.

107. (B) Extrapolation, by definition, involves making inferences on the basis of existing data or facts.

108. (A) Deriving and generating possible solutions is a problem-solving step preceding evaluation, testing, or revision.

109. (C) Time and motion studies in work settings are a prominent aspect of human engineering.

110. (B) Hebb found such a digit-span memory trace to be demonstrably evident.

111. (B) In rote-learning tasks, the advantage of distributed practice over massed practice has been observed. Although the specific reasons for this advantage are not completely understood, reduction in the fatigue element, opportunity for periodic repetition, and the possibilities for reminiscence have been among the suggested ones.

112. (B) Kohlberg is a prominent researcher in the area of moral development within children and has been very strongly impressed by the importance of reward and punishment in moral determinations.

113. (D) Telegraphic speech refers to the child's early grammatical constructions. These spontaneous speech patterns are observed when the child is about two years of age and frequently are attempts to imitate parental speech. Such attempts are characterized by the omission of prepositions, articles, suffixes, etc. Representative of telegraphic speech would be a sentence such as "Go mommy store."

114. (D) Both stomach and mouth activities appear to have important roles in the digestive processes relating to food.

115. (B) The kibbutzim — collective farm — concept in childrearing is an Israel-based, state-supported approach which involves professional caretakers providing twenty-four-hour-per-day child care in a communal setting outside the home of the natural parents. Parental visits occur primarily in the evenings and on weekends. The child development atmosphere is characterized as warm and permissive. Recent studies indicate that these children are equal in physical, social, and intellectual development to their Israeli counterparts who have been raised in private homes.

116. (C) At point C there began a steady decline in number of correct responses per trial, indicating that reinforcement had been withdrawn and that the extinction process was underway.

117. (A) A temporary leveling in the response acquisition curve is known as an asymptote. Such leveling is followed by an increase in the number of correct responses per trial.

118. (D) Initiated theoretically within psychoanalysis, defense mechanisms have the function of reducing the anxiety caused by fear that an id impulse may emerge.

119. (C) The Kelley experiment demonstrated the tremendous change in attitude that can be produced by the variation of a single word in a description. A subsequent speaker gave to various individuals descriptions that contained within them either the word *warm* or the word *cold*. Evaluations of the speaker varied accordingly.

120. (C) The social-exchange theory of interpersonal attraction speaks of continually changing balances between reward and cost in any given interaction.

121. (C) The well-known Clark procedure utilized comparative presentation of black dolls and white ones to study prejudice in children.

122. (B) Darley and Latane found that the major determinant in eliciting help was the number of other students that the individual thought had heard the victim.

123. (A) Proxemics is the study of personal, territorial space. In the American culture, it is believed that each person has a kind of "invisible shield" approximately eighteen inches from his or her body. Anyone who comes closer than this and who is not an intimate friend is violating the person's territorial, personal space.

124. (E) Kelly views every child as a scientist forming constructs and testing hypotheses.

125. (D) Cattell and Eysenck are prominently concerned with factor analysis — e.g., correlation and grouping of traits.

126. (B) The therapeutic technique known as free association was initiated by Freud and remained central to his work throughout his career.

127. (E) The transactional analysis of Berne makes prominent use of the terms *script* and *contract*.

128. (C) Behaviorism focuses upon observable behavior and the means through which a person's environment can be restructured to effect a change in problem behavior.

129. (B) The triad is in a state of asymmetry or imbalance. Symmetry would be achieved if the triad contained an even number of negative (dislike) components. Such would be the case if person A liked person B, person A disliked X, and person B disliked X. Obviously, symmetry would also be attained if the triad contained no negative components — person A liking person B, person A liking X, and person B liking X.

130. (D) Adler believed that the major personality energizer was not a sexual drive (psychoanalytic view) but a superiority striving.

131. (D) Osgood developed and utilized semantic differential techniques. Likert's scaling technique preceded Osgood and was totally unrelated to such techniques.

132. (B) The F-A hypothesis in Berkowitz's usage refers to the frustration-aggression hypothesis: that frustration will be followed by aggressive behavior.

133. (C) In Allport-Vernon-Lindzey scaling, a person rating high in theoretical value would espouse a search for truth and order.

134. (A) Brown discounts the social categorizing based on class and believes that the more basic and relevant set of categories would be roles.

135. (A) The nomothetic approach assumes commonalities among people (e.g., that we all have id, ego, and superego, for instance).

136. (B) Kagan's research challenges the long-held premise of a critical period in cognitive-intellectual development. His study is cross-cultural, dealing with children who would be deprived of their usual habitat at the critical age for cognitive-intellectual development.

137. (A) Status determination on the basis of individual income, education, and occupation would be characteristic of the objective method — determining fixed criteria and placing people within them.

138. (B) As a taboo word, McGinnies would expect "bastard" to take longer tachistoscopic exposure time for perception and reporting.

139. (D) The Minnesota Multiphasic Personality Inventory utilizes a very rigorous statistical procedure for analysis.

140. (B) While some of their explanatory views vary, most personality theorists see early childhood as critically important to later personality development.

141. (B) Aronson, Mills, and others in the field of cognitive dissonance have found the amount of initiation to be positively correlated with an individual's degree of attraction to a group. Because your fraternity or sorority initiation was rigorous, for example, the group may be more attractive to you than a fraternity or sorority would be to someone who did not have such a rigorous initiation.

142. (B) The Oedipus complex — sexual attraction to the opposite-sex parent — is resolved when the child identifies with the same-sex parent.

143. (C) Notably, the "Robber's Cave" research of Sherif would underscore the development of superordinate goals as a positive approach to prejudice-related problems.

144. (D) The color corresponding to shortest wave length would show up most prominently. In this color grouping, violet holds that comparative position.

145. (D) Circadian rhythm — a cyclic body rhythm — has been studied in commercial pilots because of its relationship to "jet lag" (crossing time zones) and fatigue.

146. (D) Narcissism is complete devotion to self-pleasure. One of the behaviors exemplifying narcissism would be masturbation.

147. (C) Within Freud's psychoanalytic theory, moral regulations and restrictions are the province of the superego, which functions in the context of (1) ego ideal or a perfection striving, and (2) conscience or psychological punishment and guilt.

148. (A) Contentedness with present life style and insufficient desire to change are major problems in the treatment of drug addicts, alcoholics, and sociopaths.

149. (D) An involutional psychotic disorder is typically characterized by either depression or paranoia.

150. (B) Multiple personality is a form of dissociative reaction, a rare neurotic disorder.

151. (B) Breuer introduced Freud to the concept of "talking cure" — a method that Breuer had tried successfully in hysteria cases. Freud later utilized the concept in his free-association method.

152. (D) This method is aversive conditioning, one of the last resorts therapeutically when other methods have proved ineffective and the problem behavior is a source of pleasure.

153. (E) One's delusional belief that other persons are talking about him is known as delusions of reference.

154. (C) Two of Eysenck's major classification categories for maladaptive behavior are introversion and extraversion. Among his other major dimensions are neuroticism-nonneuroticism and psychoticism-nonpsychoticism.

155. (B) The soldier curled up in a fetal position and crying is manifesting maladaptive regression behavior.

156. (B) The person who experiences fear and anxiety in small rooms or elevators would be expressing claustrophobia.

157. (A) Although nudity, fatigue, etc. have specific encounter-group prominence, open interaction characterizes all sensitivity and encounter groups.

Sample Tests **101**

158. (D) ESB means electrical stimulation of the brain and has no relationship to electroconvulsive shock techniques occasionally used within clinical psychology.

159. (B) The combined elements of amnesia and geographical flight are indicative of the dissociative reaction known as fugue.

160. (C) This man has an obsessive fear of germs that prompts him to engage in compulsive — often embarrassing — hand-washing behavior.

161. (B) Misperception of an actual stimulus is a basic characteristic of illusions.

162. (D) Statistics indicate that the incidence of psychosis in people under forty has not increased since 1900.

163. (C) Lack of movement is indicative of catatonic schizophrenia. Muscular rigidity and motionlessness are characteristic of this disorder.

164. (B) In his behavioral psychotherapy settings, Bandura would reinforce a withdrawn child for joining the group.

165. (A) In milieu therapy, the family, close associates, and natural setting become parts of the therapeutic process.

166. (D) One of the classic rationalizations is the "sour grapes" phenomenon. As the story goes, the fox could not reach the grapes he wanted and rationalized that it was just as well because they were sour anyway.

167. (C) Demonstrations of the effectiveness of psychotherapy treatment are very difficult because it is often infeasible to form either a control group or groups of matched subjects.

168. (A) Of the disorders listed, spontaneous recovery would be most likely within the paranoid state. In each of the other instances, some form of therapy is virtually essential.

169. (E) Abreaction refers to the expressing of pent-up emotions. It is most likely to occur within psychotherapy.

170. (B) The standard deviation increases by the same multiple as each of the scores in the distribution — in this case, 7.

171. (C) Sexual stimulation attained from the sight or closeness of a given object or type of object is characteristic of fetishism.

172. (E) One of the characteristics of neurosis is low stress tolerance.

173. (E) Although Pollock's "anniversary reaction" involves such elements as specific age attainment, specific day of the week, and awareness of the age at which tragedy befell a family member, it has no direct relationship to divorce or remarriage. The reaction holds that wholesome potential acts as a "releaser" and involves emotionally reliving a highly stressful event on its calendar anniversary date.

174. (C) Research control of genetic factors is most effectively achieved through the use of identical twins.

175. (B) Statistical reliability of a test refers to the extent to which repeated administrations will give the same score result. In addition, a test must also have validity — that is, it must measure that which it was constructed to measure (e.g., intelligence, mechanical aptitude, etc.).

176. (B) The t-test would be used for simple testing of differences between the means of experimental and control groups.

177. (D) One of the basic problems with the structuralist school of Wundt and Titchener was the fact that their method of introspection did not permit confirmation of results by other researchers — a basic criticism leveled by functionalists and, later, behaviorists.

178. (A) Two months before election night (a comparatively long time), a political candidate stands the best chance of being remembered if he is the first speaker on the program. If, on the other hand, it is the day before the election, being the last speaker is the wisest choice.

179. (B) With a heterogeneous data grouping, standard deviation would be large. Homogeneous data would suggest a small standard deviation.

180. (B) The blue light would bring out the blue pigment in the velvet, making the diamond look beautiful and irresistible. The other combinations of light-pigment mentioned would not have comparable effectiveness.

181. (D) Blue is "next door" to violet on the subtractive color wheel; thus, because hues rarely are pure, the violet light would accentuate the blue pigment.

182. (E) A lady who personally delivers a talk on stopping smoking would be most likely to quit successfully. She is — through her personal involvement — more likely to believe the arguments and experience a consequent behavior change than a lady who merely has heard the information passively.

183. (D) Psychodrama was popularized as a therapeutic technique by Moreno. It involves patients taking the roles of persons related to their conflict situation.

184. (D) Graduated steps, knowledge of results, immediate feedback, and multiple-choice format characterize teaching machine instruction, but sentence completion is not an aspect of such methodology.

185. (D) In this situation, a finger dexterity test would most closely approximate the actual task for which the individuals are being screened.

186. (E) Research indicates that the greater the number of persons watching a mishap, the lower the likelihood that any one of them will render help to a victim.

187. (C) Since it is one standard deviation above the mean, the probability of a score above 78 is approximately 16 percent.

188. (E) Below 48 would be a score lower than two standard deviations below the mean, an approximate 2-percent probability.

189. (D) This item refers to the area beyond one standard deviation to each side of the mean — approximately 32 percent.

190. (B) Previous knowledge and mastery of a body of material would characterize an achievement test.

191. (B) Consistent scores on repeated administrations would be evidence of test-retest reliability.

192. (A) GSR measure here is both the dependent variable (subject response) and the operational definition on which the presence and extent of anxiety will be determined.

193. (B) Terman's follow-up study of several gifted children at different points in their lives was one of the best-known longitudinal studies.

194. (E) The Osgood-type semantic differential scale could be implemented with the least amount of standardization. Its administration ease and flexibility are its primary assets.

195. (A) Many hearing tests involve a practical application of the psychophysical method of limits — presentation of fixed stimuli at frequencies both above and below threshold.

196. (A) In human engineering control principles, the best system provides for only one action pathway to achieve a given effect. With more than one pathway, the result could be inefficiency and confusion.

197. (C) "White noise" serves to blot out or "overshadow" existing noise.

198. (D) Increased worker satisfaction has been found within decentralized communication networks.

199. (E) Standard deviation can be expressed as the square root of the variance. Therefore, one can obtain a variance by squaring a standard deviation.

200. (B) Kinesics researchers believe that their study of nonverbal communication and body language will have critical importance in understanding and relating to children.

Test 1: Evaluating Your Score

Abbreviation Guide

PC	Physiological/Comparative
SnP	Sensation/Perception
LM	Learning/Motivation/Emotion
CHL	Cognition/Complex Human Learning
D	Developmental
PrS	Personality/Social
PyCl	Psychopathology/Clinical
M	Methodology
Ap	Applied

Subject Area Chart

Use this chart to determine the subject matter covered by each question in Test 1.

1.	PC	21.	SnP	41.	PC	61.	CHL	81.	D
2.	PC	22.	SnP	42.	PC	62.	D	82.	D
3.	PC	23.	LM	43.	LM	63.	D	83.	CHL
4.	PC	24.	LM	44.	PrS	64.	LM	84.	CHL
5.	PC	25.	SnP	45.	PrS	65.	CHL	85.	D
6.	SnP	26.	LM	46.	PrS	66.	LM	86.	CHL
7.	SnP	27.	PC	47.	SnP	67.	CHL	87.	LM
8.	SnP	28.	LM	48.	PC	68.	D	88.	CHL
9.	PC	29.	LM	49.	PrS	69.	CHL	89.	D
10.	SnP	30.	PC	50.	LM	70.	D	90.	LM
11.	PC	31.	PC	51.	SnP	71.	LM	91.	D
12.	PrS	32.	PC	52.	SnP	72.	D	92.	D
13.	LM	33.	PC	53.	SnP	73.	D	93.	LM
14.	PC	34.	PC	54.	PC	74.	D	94.	CHL
15.	SnP	35.	LM	55.	PC	75.	SnP	95.	D
16.	Ap	36.	PC	56.	PC	76.	D	96.	D
17.	Ap	37.	LM	57.	LM	77.	M	97.	M
18.	SnP	38.	LM	58.	D	78.	D	98.	D
19.	SnP	39.	LM	59.	D	79.	D	99.	M
20.	PC	40.	PC	60.	D	80.	D	100.	CHL

101.	D	121.	PrS	141.	PrS	161.	PyCl
102.	D	122.	PrS	142.	PrS	162.	PyCl
103.	CHL	123.	PrS	143.	Ap	163.	PyCl
104.	CHL	124.	PrS	144.	Ap	164.	PyCl
105.	M	125.	PrS	145.	Ap	165.	PyCl
106.	D	126.	PrS	146.	PrS	166.	PyCl
107.	CHL	127.	PrS	147.	PrS	167.	PyCl
108.	CHL	128.	PrS	148.	PyCl	168.	PyCl
109.	CHL	129.	PrS	149.	PyCl	169.	PyCl
110.	CHL	130.	PrS	150.	PyCl	170.	M
111.	CHL	131.	PrS	151.	PyCl	171.	PyCl
112.	D	132.	PrS	152.	PyCl	172.	PyCl
113.	CHL	133.	PrS	153.	PyCl	173.	PyCl
114.	LM	134.	PrS	154.	PyCl	174.	M
115.	D	135.	PrS	155.	PyCl	175.	M
116.	LM	136.	Ap	156.	PyCl	176.	M
117.	LM	137.	PrS	157.	PyCl	177.	M
118.	PrS	138.	PrS	158.	PyCl	178.	Ap
119.	PrS	139.	PrS	159.	PyCl	179.	M
120.	PrS	140.	Ap	160.	PyCl	180.	Ap

181.	Ap			
182.	Ap			
183.	Ap			
184.	Ap			
185.	Ap			
186.	Ap			
187.	M			
188.	M			
189.	M			
190.	Ap			
191.	M			
192.	M			
193.	M			
194.	Ap			
195.	Ap			
196.	Ap			
197.	Ap			
198.	Ap			
199.	M			
200.	Ap			

Record the number of questions you missed in each subject area.

PC —   CHL —   PyCl —
SnP—   D —   M   —
LM —   PrS —   Ap —

Test Score Scale

The first number given is the number of questions in the test in that subject area. The number in parentheses indicates the 75th percentile score. To determine how well you scored in each subject area, subtract the number of questions you missed in a certain area from the total number of questions in that area. Compare the result with the 75th percentile number. If it is lower than 75%, you probably need more review.

PC —23(18)   CHL —18(14)   PyCl —25(19)
SnP —15(11)   D   —28(21)   M   —17(13)
LM —22(17)   PrS —30(23)   Ap —22(17)

Test 2: Answer Grid

1. A B C D E	21. A B C D E	41. A B C D E	61. A B C D E	81. A B C D E
2. A B C D E	22. A B C D E	42. A B C D E	62. A B C D E	82. A B C D E
3. A B C D E	23. A B C D E	43. A B C D E	63. A B C D E	83. A B C D E
4. A B C D E	24. A B C D E	44. A B C D E	64. A B C D E	84. A B C D E
5. A B C D E	25. A B C D E	45. A B C D E	65. A B C D E	85. A B C D E
6. A B C D E	26. A B C D E	46. A B C D E	66. A B C D E	86. A B C D E
7. A B C D E	27. A B C D E	47. A B C D E	67. A B C D E	87. A B C D E
8. A B C D E	28. A B C D E	48. A B C D E	68. A B C D E	88. A B C D E
9. A B C D E	29. A B C D E	49. A B C D E	69. A B C D E	89. A B C D E
10. A B C D E	30. A B C D E	50. A B C D E	70. A B C D E	90. A B C D E
11. A B C D E	31. A B C D E	51. A B C D E	71. A B C D E	91. A B C D E
12. A B C D E	32. A B C D E	52. A B C D E	72. A B C D E	92. A B C D E
13. A B C D E	33. A B C D E	53. A B C D E	73. A B C D E	93. A B C D E
14. A B C D E	34. A B C D E	54. A B C D E	74. A B C D E	94. A B C D E
15. A B C D E	35. A B C D E	55. A B C D E	75. A B C D E	95. A B C D E
16. A B C D E	36. A B C D E	56. A B C D E	76. A B C D E	96. A B C D E
17. A B C D E	37. A B C D E	57. A B C D E	77. A B C D E	97. A B C D E
18. A B C D E	38. A B C D E	58. A B C D E	78. A B C D E	98. A B C D E
19. A B C D E	39. A B C D E	59. A B C D E	79. A B C D E	99. A B C D E
20. A B C D E	40. A B C D E	60. A B C D E	80. A B C D E	100. A B C D E

101. A B C D E	121. A B C D E	141. A B C D E	161. A B C D E	181. A B C D E
102. A B C D E	122. A B C D E	142. A B C D E	162. A B C D E	182. A B C D E
103. A B C D E	123. A B C D E	143. A B C D E	163. A B C D E	183. A B C D E
104. A B C D E	124. A B C D E	144. A B C D E	164. A B C D E	184. A B C D E
105. A B C D E	125. A B C D E	145. A B C D E	165. A B C D E	185. A B C D E
106. A B C D E	126. A B C D E	146. A B C D E	166. A B C D E	186. A B C D E
107. A B C D E	127. A B C D E	147. A B C D E	167. A B C D E	187. A B C D E
108. A B C D E	128. A B C D E	148. A B C D E	168. A B C D E	188. A B C D E
109. A B C D E	129. A B C D E	149. A B C D E	169. A B C D E	189. A B C D E
110. A B C D E	130. A B C D E	150. A B C D E	170. A B C D E	190. A B C D E
111. A B C D E	131. A B C D E	151. A B C D E	171. A B C D E	191. A B C D E
112. A B C D E	132. A B C D E	152. A B C D E	172. A B C D E	192. A B C D E
113. A B C D E	133. A B C D E	153. A B C D E	173. A B C D E	193. A B C D E
114. A B C D E	134. A B C D E	154. A B C D E	174. A B C D E	194. A B C D E
115. A B C D E	135. A B C D E	155. A B C D E	175. A B C D E	195. A B C D E
116. A B C D E	136. A B C D E	156. A B C D E	176. A B C D E	196. A B C D E
117. A B C D E	137. A B C D E	157. A B C D E	177. A B C D E	197. A B C D E
118. A B C D E	138. A B C D E	158. A B C D E	178. A B C D E	198. A B C D E
119. A B C D E	139. A B C D E	159. A B C D E	179. A B C D E	199. A B C D E
120. A B C D E	140. A B C D E	160. A B C D E	180. A B C D E	200. A B C D E

Test Two

Time 170 minutes

Directions Each of the following questions contains five possible responses. Read the question carefully and select the response that you feel is most appropriate. Then completely darken the space on your answer grid that corresponds with your choice.

1. In _____ experiments, mallard duckling imprinting on a moving dummy is studied at varying time periods after birth.
   (A) Hebb's   (B) Hess's   (C) Scott's   (D) Harlow's
   (E) Webb's

2. The perceptual phenomenon of apparent tilt is
   (A) heavily dependent upon brightness and hue
   (B) a function of saturation
   (C) lease prominent among persons relying on bodily clues
   (D) related to intelligence
   (E) strongly dependent upon retinal disparity

3. The cerebellum functions prominently in which of the following areas?
   (A) heart activity   (B) blood pressure   (C) muscle-movement coordination   (D) verbal association   (E) respiration

4. Historically, the European and American approaches to comparative psychology distinctly differed in the prominence given to
   (A) intelligence   (B) behavior   (C) learning   (D) memory
   (E) naturalistic observation

Questions 5–7 are based on the following information.

For 200 ninth-grade students whose IQ scores were available, Guilford and his associates were able to obtain divergent production scores. The findings are presented in the table.

DP Score	60–69	70–79	80–89	90–99	100–109	110–119	120–129	130–139	140–149
50–59						1	3		1
40–49						2	4	1	
30–39			2	3	4	11	17	6	2
20–29			1	3	10	23	13	7	
10–19	1	5	3	9	11	19	7	3	1
0–9	1	3	1	4	10	11	2		

Intelligence Quotient

5. On the basis of this table, it would be appropriate to make the interpretation that there is
   (A) a direct, one-to-one relationship between IQ and divergent production
   (B) an almost perfect negative relationship between IQ and divergent production (the lower the IQ, the higher the likelihood of divergent production)

(C) apparently a complete absence of relationship between IQ and divergent production
(D) greater likelihood of divergent production in the 120–129 IQ range than in the 110–119 range
(E) greater likelihood of divergent production in the 100–109 IQ range than in the 130–139 range

6. Interpretations of data such as those presented in this table would rely heavily upon the assumption that the children
   (A) were in the same school
   (B) participated in standardized testing and scoring procedures
   (C) were of the same sex
   (D) received their testing on the same day within the same test setting
   (E) represented all parts of the country

7. The table data suggest the greatest statistical likelihood of divergent production by persons in which of the following IQ groups?
   (A) 60–69 (B) 70–79 (C) 120–129 (D) 130–139
   (E) 140–149

8. In Brady's work with "executive monkeys," those that developed ulcers had
   (A) mother-deprived backgrounds
   (B) father-deprived backgrounds
   (C) sibling-deprived backgrounds
   (D) capacity to control shock onset
   (E) no capacity to control shock onset

9. Transfer of excitatory or inhibitory potential between neurons occurs at a point called the
   (A) synapse (B) receptor (C) nerve ending (D) effector
   (E) synopsis

10. Sound vibrations in the ear create neural impulses received in which of the following cortex locations?
    (A) temporal lobe (B) central fissure (C) occipital lobe
    (D) parietal lobe (E) auditory lobe

11. Pitch is determined by
    (A) amplitude (B) complexity (C) frequency (D) decibels
    (E) amplification

12. The autokinetic effect is most commonly demonstrated with which of the following stimuli?
    (A) a spot of light in a darkened room
    (B) lights flashing on and off in a patterned sequence
    (C) lights rotating around a single, central spot of light
    (D) a color wheel containing a black-white color disc
    (E) a steady blue light consistently viewed near dusk

13. Alcohol consumption
    (A) shortens reaction time
    (B) lengthens reaction time
    (C) shortens auditory reaction time while lengthening visual
    (D) shortens visual reaction time while lengthening auditory
    (E) shortens all except pain reaction time

14. Which of the following is an *incorrect* pairing?
    (A) spike potential — the nerve impulse, characterized by a very rapid change of neuronal potential
    (B) threshold — a transition from graded potential to spike potential
    (C) absolute refractory period — complete depression following a spike
    (D) all-or-none law — refers to and focuses upon graded potential
    (E) autonomic system chemical transmitters — acetylcholine, norepinephrine

15. An EEG pattern of approximately ten pulsations per second, occurring when a person is awake, is
    (A) beta   (B) alpha   (C) theta   (D) delta   (E) gamma

16. The concept of equipotentiality was formulated on the basis of a systematic experimental program conducted by
    (A) Lindsley   (B) Tolman   (C) Lashley   (D) Skinner
    (E) Terman

17. Which of the following is an *incorrect* statement?
    (A) Receptive disorders such as agnosias and sensory aphasias are primarily localized in the posterior cerebral cortex.
    (B) Expressive disorders such as apraxias and motor aphasias are primarily localized in the frontal lobes.
    (C) Alexia is a type of visual aphasia associated with word blindness.
    (D) Apraxia refers to disturbances in audition, commonly called word deafness.
    (E) Inability to write or say a word that has been perceived is a type of aphasia.

18. Perceptual phenomena have been most prominently explored within
    (A) structuralism   (B) Gestalt   (C) behaviorism
    (D) functionalism   (E) eclecticism

19. Experiments related to extensive sensory deprivation
    (A) have never been performed with human subjects
    (B) provide evidence of ulcers in humans
    (C) have revealed schizophrenic-type responses among human subjects
    (D) have revealed hallucinatory responding in human subjects
    (E) have revealed an overwhelming autokinetic effect

20. Which of the following is *not* a taste primary?
    (A) bitter   (B) sour   (C) sweet   (D) salty   (E) bland

21. The inability to recognize printed words because of brain damage is called
    (A) kinesthesia   (B) somatic aphasia   (C) labyrinthine aphasia
    (D) alexia   (E) acromegaly

22. The fact that a cold-blooded animal can remain alive and make coordinated muscle movements for some time after decapitation is possible because of
    (A) spinal cord sufficiency for complicated patterns of reflexive behavior
    (B) pons activity and increased compensatory functioning
    (C) the role of the cerebellum in reflexive behavior
    (D) inhibitory postsynaptic potential
    (E) facilitating (excitatory) postsynaptic potential

23. A physiological psychologist would be most likely to find the term *reciprocal innervation* in discussions related to
    (A) EEG
    (B) digestion
    (C) heartbeat
    (D) muscle movements in walking
    (E) subsequent learning interfering with previously learned responses

24. When a subject's sleep is interrupted during nondreaming periods rather than during dreaming periods
    (A) subsequent sleep patterns equivalent to dream-period interruption are noted
    (B) significantly higher subsequent dream attempts are noted
    (C) subsequent dreams are much longer than usual
    (D) significantly lower than normal subsequent dream attempts are noted
    (E) subsequent dream attempts normal in both frequency and length are noted

25. The capacity for detecting the direction of incoming sound is
    (A) prominent among persons with hearing in only one ear
    (B) possible only when hearing exists in both ears
    (C) frequently termed monaural hearing
    (D) explained within the Young-Helmholtz theory of audition
    (E) heavily dependent on the Meissner receptor

26. The SOC one passes through going from sleeping to waking is called the
    (A) twilight zone   (B) hypnagogic state   (C) hypnotic trance
    (D) hypnopompic state   (E) syntonic state

27. The lowest frequency in brain waves occurs within the
    (A) alpha rhythm   (B) beta rhythm   (C) gamma rhythm
    (D) delta rhythm   (E) theta rhythm

28. Broca's area of the brain is related to
    (A) speech   (B) balance   (C) coordination necessary in walking
    (D) sexual arousal   (E) hearing

29. The earliest emotion evident in the newborn is
    (A) delight   (B) shame   (C) shyness   (D) excitement
    (E) affection

30. *Not* among stimulus cues that can aid perception of depth is
    (A) texture   (B) light and shadow   (C) relative position
    (D) linear perspective   (E) convergence

31. Tinbergen's fixed action patterns
    (A) are elicited by a complex arrangement of external stimuli
    (B) are hormonally induced without reference to external stimuli
    (C) are elicited by simple, specific external stimuli
    (D) are synonymous with Watson's concept of nest habits
    (E) are instrumentally conditioned

32. Which of following mobilizes the body be secreting epinephrine in stressful situations?
    (A) adrenal cortex   (B) pituitary   (C) gonads   (D) pancreas
    (E) adrenal medulla

33. Receptors generally referred to as chemical are
    (A) temperature and pain
    (B) visual and auditory
    (C) auditory and temperature
    (D) temperature and pressure
    (E) gustation and olfaction

34. The Frequency Theory of Audition is best suited to explain hearing in
    (A) the low frequency range
    (B) the high frequency range
    (C) the intermediate frequency range
    (D) all frequency ranges
    (E) the specific range between 3,000 and 10,000 cycles per second

35. Which of the following is an endocrine gland controlling growth and stimulating other endocrine glands?
    (A) pituitary   (B) adrenal   (C) thyroid   (D) parathyroid
    (E) pineal

36. Rat experimentation investigating the role of the cerebral cortex in sexual behavior indicates that
    (A) sexual behavior survives fairly extensive cortical destruction in male animals
    (B) the cerebral cortex is essential for copulation to occur in females
    (C) the cerebral cortex has no effect upon the ordering of responses that make up the pattern of sexual behavior in females
    (D) complete cortical destruction has no effect on arousal in male animals
    (E) cortical destruction affects motor but not sensory and perceptual functions

37. The study of motivation had its primitive, early beginnings with
    (A) Wundt and Weber
    (B) Fechner and Hull
    (C) Freud and James
    (D) Breuer and Charcot
    (E) Jung and Adler

38. Which of the following was *not* a facet of Freud's work having importance within the field of motivation?
    (A) underlying motives expressed consciously in disguised form
    (B) the function of unconscious processes in motivation
    (C) unconscious determinants of thought and action
    (D) relation of everyday slips and errors to underlying motivations
    (E) the manner in which habit combines with drive to express the content of emotion

39. Putting animals in puzzle boxes to study their intelligence was initially undertaken by
    (A) Darwin   (B) James   (C) Thorndike   (D) Atkinson
    (E) Lewin

40. Hebb's consolidation theory of memory trace expresses the position that
    (A) a type of learning consolidation activity occurs simultaneously with the learning event, "locking in" the memory trace instantly
    (B) a type of learning consolidation activity occurs for minutes and even hours after the learning event
    (C) electroconvulsive shock impairment of long-term, but not recent, memory provides basic support for his theoretical position

(D) children fit his theoretical model but adults do not
(E) adults fit his theoretical model but children do not

41. "A group of individuals capable of interbreeding under natural conditions and reproductively isolated from other such groups," most directly constitutes a definition of
(A) phylum   (B) class   (C) order   (D) family   (E) species

42. At which of the following ages would you expect clock time concepts to be mastered initially by a child?
(A) two years
(B) three years
(C) four years
(D) between five and six years
(E) between seven and eight years

43. Reaction time
(A) decreases with age up to approximately forty years
(B) increases with age up to approximately forty years
(C) decreases with age up to approximately thirty years
(D) increases with age up to approximately thirty years
(E) decreases with age throughout the life span

44. Auditory sensations are transformed from "air waves" to nerve impulses by the
(A) vestibular system   (B) pinna   (C) ossicles   (D) cochlea
(E) round window

45. Studies of emotion involving transections at various levels of the brain stem in animals reveal that
(A) the integrated "attack reaction" found in normal animals remains intact
(B) organization of intense emotional responses apparently occurs at a level above the midbrain
(C) auditory stimuli retain their normal effectiveness in evoking emotional responses
(D) visual stimuli retain their normal effectiveness in evoking emotional responses
(E) there are no emotional response differences distinguishable from those found in normal animals

46. The terminal point for efferent fibers is
(A) the spinal cord
(B) the central nervous system
(C) the cerebral cortex
(D) muscles or glands
(E) the myelin sheath

47. When Tolman summarized Watson's definition of emotions, he did so in terms of
(A) field theory
(B) law of effect
(C) law of exercise
(D) stimuli and responses
(E) sensations and perceptions

48. A term collectively describing muscles and glands is
(A) receptors   (B) effectors   (C) innervators   (D) affectors
(E) constrictors

49. The Ames room was specifically designed to test
    (A) shape constancy (B) size constancy (C) motion parallax
    (D) interposition (E) continuity

50. Experiments that have been able to restrict a specific visual input to a specific location on the retina have found
    (A) increased stimulus clarity
    (B) slight, but not total, fading
    (C) gradual and complete fading
    (D) partial Ganzfeld
    (E) increased visual concentration capacities

51. Which of the following has been experimentally associated with LSD use?
    (A) permanent insanity
    (B) increased creativity
    (C) therapeutic growth and insight
    (D) cognitive experience similar to psychosis
    (E) telekinesis

52. Which of the following is most deficient in color vision?
    (A) turtles (B) fish (C) rats (D) monkeys (E) humans

Questions 53–56 are based on the following hearing diagram.

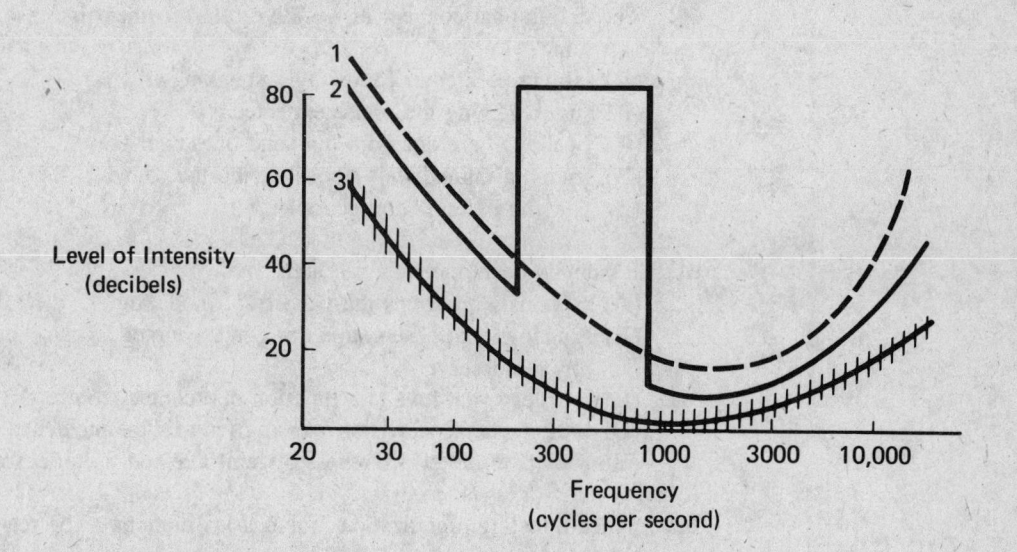

53. Which of the above lines would indicate nerve damage?
    (A) 1 (B) 2 (C) 3 (D) 1 and 3 (E) all of the above

54. Which of the above lines would suggest ossification?
    (A) 1 (B) 2 (C) 3 (D) 1 and 3 (E) all of the above

55. Which of the above lines would be unusually acute for human hearing?
    (A) 1 (B) 2 (C) 3 (D) 1 and 3 (E) all of the above

56. Which of the above lines would represent the effects of aging?
    (A) 1 (B) 2 (C) 3 (D) 1 and 3 (E) all of the above

Questions 57–59 are based on the following drawing.

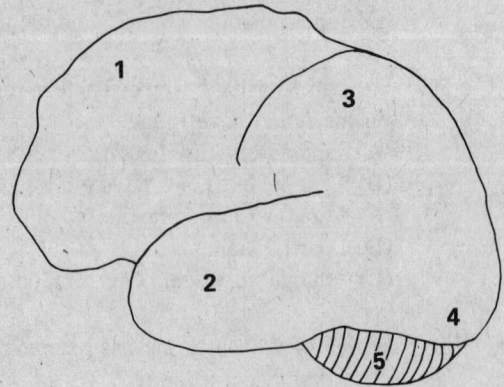

57. Audition functions would be located in which of the above cerebral areas?
(A) 1   (B) 2   (C) 3   (D) 4   (E) 5

58. Which of the above areas has cerebral responsibility for vision?
(A) 1   (B) 2   (C) 3   (D) 4   (E) 5

59. Which of the above brain areas is responsible for muscle coordination and posture?
(A) 1   (B) 2   (C) 3   (D) 4   (E) 5

60. The definitional concept of negative reinforcement is most central to which of the following?
(A) sitting on a chair following a spanking
(B) not receiving the praise expected
(C) walking barefoot from hot sand onto cool grass
(D) running immediately upon hearing the sound of the school bell
(E) staying indoors after school

61. Bandura's developmental research
(A) seriously questions the validity of modeling
(B) suggests that observation of aggressive models can prompt aggressive behavior by the observer
(C) suggests that love is a function of "contact comfort"
(D) suggests that television viewing reduces the incidence of aggressive behavior
(E) points to the effectiveness of reinforcement in toilet training

62. When a testing organization includes instructions to be read verbatim to each test-taking group, the organization is concentrating upon
(A) dependent variables   (B) intervening variables
(C) standardization   (D) reliability   (E) validity

63. During the third through the eighth week of pregnancy, the developing child can be accurately referred to as the
(A) prenate   (B) zygote   (C) embryo   (D) fetus
(E) blastocyst

64. Developmental research suggests a possible relationship between anxiety in the expectant mother and
(A) premature birth
(B) fetal brain damage

(C) defective hearing
(D) color blindness
(E) the incidence of crying behavior in the newborn

65. Of the following malfunctions, the one *not* pituitary-based is
    (A) acromegaly (B) dwarfism (C) giantism
    (D) disproportionately large hand (E) cretinism

66. Experiments with Hopi Indian children have suggested that the point at which a child begins to walk is primarily a function of
    (A) learning (B) intelligence (C) maturation
    (D) environment (E) modeling

67. Which of the following is *not* associated with the "visual cliff"?
    (A) the names Gibson and Walk
    (B) the question of depth perception
    (C) the suggestion of possible innate capacity
    (D) comparison of child and animal performance
    (E) the question of retinal disparity and convergence

68. Research evidence suggests highest aggression among boys who come from which of the following home settings?
    (A) broken (B) father-absent (C) father-present
    (D) mother-present (E) parents-deceased

69. Piaget's initial phase of cognitive development is subdivided into
    (A) two stages (B) five stages (C) three stages (D) four stages (E) six stages

70. Through test apparatus that, in effect, asks the newborn what he visually prefers, which of the following is found to be most preferred?
    (A) bright-colored triangles
    (B) bright-colored squares
    (C) pictures of toys
    (D) pictures of pets
    (E) pictures of the human face

71. Checking a newborn male child via EEG, EMG, EOG, and respiration monitoring, would reveal which of the following?
    (A) total absence of REM sleep
    (B) some irregularities in respiration
    (C) no body movement during sleep
    (D) no reflex smiles
    (E) no penis erection

72. The used-car salesman receives both a monthly salary and a commission for every car sold. Which of the following reinforcement schedule elements exist in his pay situation?
    (A) fixed interval, variable ratio
    (B) variable interval, fixed ratio
    (C) fixed interval, fixed ratio
    (D) variable interval, variable ratio
    (E) only fixed interval

73. Which of the following would be true of instrumental conditioning?
    (A) The response is elicited by the presence of the unconditioned stimulus.
    (B) Reinforcement increases the frequency of the response associated with it.
    (C) There is trace presentation of CS and UCS.
    (D) There is delayed presentation of CS and UCS.
    (E) There is simultaneous presentation of CS and UCS.

74. A person who has an IQ score of 60 would be considered
    (A) profoundly retarded   (B) severely retarded   (C) moderately retarded   (D) trainable   (E) mildly retarded

75. Guilford's structure of intellect uses which of the following most prominently?
    (A) semi-interquartile range   (B) rank-order correlation   (C) Duncan's multiple range test   (D) chi square   (E) factor analysis

76. Which of the following is correct?
    (A) The correlation coefficient range is $-.05$ to $+.05$
    (B) $+.40$ is greater correlation than $-.40$.
    (C) Correlation is related to predictability.
    (D) Regression coefficients are essential for factor analysis.
    (E) Analysis of covariance is not related to correlation.

77. Which of the following most commonly expresses central tendency and variability, respectively?
    (A) mode, range   (B) mean, interval   (C) median, range
    (D) median, standard deviation   (E) mean, standard deviation

78. The first two years after birth are critical
    (A) to self-concept formation
    (B) to aptitude formation
    (C) to sensory formation
    (D) to formation of secondary sexual characteristics
    (E) only in the minds of parents

79. The syllogism is a form appropriate to
    (A) deductive thinking   (B) inductive thinking   (C) evaluative thinking   (D) divergent thinking   (E) trial-and-error thinking

80. Which of the following can be anticipated during the first three months after birth?
    (A) shorter periods of wakefulness
    (B) the ability to raise the head slightly to look at something
    (C) a noticeable lack of any effort to attempt an "answer" when an adult talks to the child
    (D) the ability to hold and manipulate a spoon
    (E) masturbation

81. Reinforced for lifting one paw during the presentation of a buzzer, a dog now lifts two paws — a case of
    (A) response generalization
    (B) stimulus generalization
    (C) spread-of-effect
    (D) classical conditioning
    (E) second-order conditioning

82. A conditioned response has been learned to a specific stimulus. When similar stimuli also evoke the conditioned response, the phenomenon is
    (A) stimulus generalization (B) response generalization (C) successive approximation (D) spread-of-effect (E) contiguity

83. Learning how to learn is essentially a process of
    (A) establishing learning sets (B) operant conditioning (C) stimulus generalization (D) imprinting (E) nonreversal shift

Question 84 is based on the information that follows.

Given the list below, complete the vertical arrangement indicated by the words erase and fate, using words from the group and taking erase as the middle word in the column. (Note that not all words on the card need to be used.)

a, gate, no, i, duty, in, cat, ho, ear,
o, travel, erase, both, get, ho, fate.

erase

fate

84. The preceding information and instructions require a person to engage in a process known as
    (A) interpolation (B) extrapolation (C) structuring
    (D) modeling (E) interposition

85. In social-adjustment terms, early maturity has been found
    (A) advantageous among males
    (B) advantageous among females
    (C) detrimental to males
    (D) detrimental to both males and females
    (E) a source of female prestige and male ridicule

86. The period of the embryo spans the time from the end of
    (A) second week to end of second month
    (B) first week to end of second month
    (C) third week to end of second month
    (D) first week to end of first month
    (E) third week to end of third month

87. In contrast to a dissimilar-items list, a similar-items list is
    (A) more difficult to learn
    (B) easier to learn
    (C) learned with equivalent ease
    (D) more susceptible to the serial position effect
    (E) less susceptible to the serial position effect

88. Which of the following is a cell-type distinction?
    (A) nerve and muscle (B) sperm and ova (C) chromosome and gene
    (D) amnion and chorion (E) germ and body

89. Which of the men listed would be most likely to comment that environment is of central importance?
    (A) Leibnitz (B) Wundt (C) Dewey (D) Darwin
    (E) Watson

90. For classical conditioning, it is essential that
    (A) the subject be informed of desired outcome in advance
    (B) the UCS be inherently rewarding
    (C) the UCS be originally neutral
    (D) the CS be originally neutral
    (E) the CR be identical in strength and intensity to the UCR

91. In which of the following situations would the most classical conditioning be expected?
    (A) UCS preceding CS by one-half second
    (B) CS preceding UCS by two seconds
    (C) UCS preceding CS by two seconds
    (D) CS preceding UCS by one-half second
    (E) CS preceding UCS by five seconds

92. Which of the following *cannot* occur during the germinal stage?
    (A) death of the zygote before implantation
    (B) glandular imbalance preventing implantation
    (C) implantation in a Fallopian tube
    (D) cell division
    (E) cell mass differentiation into three distinct layers

93. For a person who has just learned a list of adjectives, the task *least* likely to interfere with this learning would be the learning of
    (A) a list of numbers
    (B) a list of nonsense syllables
    (C) another list of adjectives
    (D) a list of nouns
    (E) a list of synonyms

94. The field theorist emphasizes the role of learning in
    (A) S-R associations   (B) drive reduction   (C) reinforcement
    (D) cognitive processes   (E) sensory processes

95. Among the primary effects of anxiety upon learning, one could expect
    (A) removal of mental blocks
    (B) more interference with familiar material than with new material
    (C) reduced ability to discriminate clearly
    (D) heightened motivation leading to proficiency on virtually any task
    (E) proactive facilitation

96. The von Restorff effect applies to
    (A) serial position   (B) task completion   (C) prepotent stimulus
    (D) meaningfulness of learning material   (E) memory span

97. Which of the following is *not* an experimental approach to recall?
    (A) single-trial, free recall   (B) multi-trial, free recall   (C) split-half, free recall   (D) paired associates   (E) serial presentation

98. Frenkel and Brunswik conclude that the single most important factor distinguishing prejudiced from tolerant adolescents is
    (A) intelligence   (B) aptitude   (C) sexual adjustment
    (D) attitude toward authority   (E) vocational choice

99. Moderate anxiety in a child
  (A) is detrimental to all learning
  (B) may facilitate learning of difficult tasks
  (C) may facilitate learning of simple tasks
  (D) suggests unhealthy defense against Oedipal conflict
  (E) is a function of archetype

100. Which of the following does *not* qualify as a polygenic characteristic?
  (A) intelligence   (B) temperament   (C) schizophrenia
  (D) eye color   (E) violence proneness

101. A man who has normal color vision marries a woman who has normal color vision but who carries a defective color-vision gene. They can expect
  (A) all their offspring to be color-blind
  (B) none of their offspring to be color-blind
  (C) half their sons to be color-blind
  (D) all their daughters and none of their sons to be color-blind
  (E) all their sons and none of their daughters to be color-blind

102. Friends become differentiated from strangers during which of the following young ages
  (A) twelve months   (B) six to seven months   (C) one to two months
  (D) birth   (E) three to four months

103. The psychograph is, in effect, a test
  (A) quartile   (B) booklet   (C) scoring key   (D) profile
  (E) score

104. Which of the following is primarily a verbal test?
  (A) WAIS   (B) Stanford-Binet   (C) WISC   (D) Blacky
  (E) WPPSI

105. Within problem-solving processes, the inductive phase encompasses
  (A) information retrieval from memory
  (B) information storage in memory
  (C) information reception and routing
  (D) idea and hypothesis generation
  (E) systematic memory scanning

106. The heights of kindergarten-aged children are
  (A) negatively correlated with comparative adult heights
  (B) positively correlated with comparative adult heights
  (C) in no way related to comparative adult heights
  (D) most strongly correlated with the heights of their mothers
  (E) most strongly correlated with the heights of their fathers

107. Kendler's experimentation suggests that in child maturation
  (A) mediational processes precede single-unit S-R cognitive mechanisms
  (B) single-unit S-R cognitive mechanisms precede mediational processes
  (C) single-unit S-R cognitive mechanisms and mediational processes occur at the same developmental point
  (D) neither the single-unit S-R cognitive mechanism nor the mediational process occurs until after age six
  (E) single unit S-R cognitive mechamisms never occur

108. In the newborn's second year, the rate of growth
    (A) is faster than that of the first year
    (B) is slower than that of the first year
    (C) parallels that of the first year
    (D) is faster than that of the fetal period
    (E) is faster than that of the embryonic period

109. Of the following, which group contains the most names foreign to imprinting research?
    (A) Hess, Lorenz, Scott   (B) Scott, Hess, Sontag   (C) Lorenz, Hess, Miller   (D) Miller, Hess, Scott   (E) Sontag, Miller, Scott

110. The mouth opens wide and the head turns to the midline in the
    (A) Babinski response   (B) Babkin response   (C) plantar response
    (D) Moro response   (E) push-back response

111. Maleness in the human is determined by the
    (A) Y chromosome   (B) X chromosome   (C) XX zygote
    (D) recessive gene   (E) YY genetic transmission

112. In the Guilford model for problem solving, which of the following occurs first?
    (A) input   (B) filtering   (C) cognition   (D) production
    (E) evaluation

113. The term most closely associated with the work of Tolman is
    (A) perceptual learning   (B) sensory preconditioning   (C) reinforcement learning   (D) place learning   (E) contiguity learning

114. The term *fractional anticipatory goal response* refers to
    (A) backward conditioning   (B) UCR   (C) CR   (D) CS
    (E) Mowrer's Two-Factor Theory

115. In the formula $R = H \times D \times K$, if H is very large, D is very large, and reinforcement is zero
    (A) no response occurs
    (B) a small response occurs
    (C) a response may or may not occur
    (D) if a response occurs, it will not be learned
    (E) if a drive occurs, it will be very small

116. In Piaget's classification system, the child learns language and the logic of classification and numbers during the _____ period.
    (A) sensorimotor   (B) latency   (C) formal operations
    (D) concrete operations   (E) assimilation

117. In Hunter's double alternation response, an animal
    (A) gets shocked for incorrect response
    (B) must turn in a circle prior to making the correct response
    (C) must go down the alley twice before making the appropriate T-maze turn
    (D) must remember which direction it turned on the two preceding trials
    (E) must open a small gate at the sound of a buzzer

118. Studies of sleep learning indicate that
    (A) learning does not occur during deep sleep

(B) simple, rote learning occurs during deep sleep
(C) verbal learning can be achieved during all levels of sleep
(D) eidetic images can be conveyed during all levels of sleep
(E) when the alpha wave is present in the EEG, no learning can occur, but learning occurs during delta wave prevalence

119. In Dollard and Miller's conceptual terms, infant feeding is *not* a setting for learning
(A) future apathy and indifference
(B) sociability
(C) fear
(D) anger-anxiety conflict
(E) overreaction to minor physical discomfort

120. A curve has its most prominent distribution of scores to the left of center and "tails off" to the right. This information would be sufficient to conclude that the curve showed
(A) negative skew   (B) positive skew   (C) normal distribution
(D) bimodal distribution   (E) platikurtic distribution

121. Which of the following most accurately describes negative reinforcement?
(A) onset of an aversive stimulus
(B) cessation of an aversive stimulus
(C) withdrawal of a positive reinforcement
(D) extinction
(E) punishment

122. Performance of an earlier task is interfered with by the learning of a second, more recent task in
(A) proactive facilitation   (B) proactive inhibition   (C) retroactive facilitation   (D) retroactive inhibition   (E) negative transference

123. *Not* an accurate or frequently mentioned distinction between image and percept is that the
(A) visual image is more labile
(B) visual image is less labile
(C) visual image is less vivid
(D) percept is generally more detailed
(E) visual image may become associated with other objects and images

124. Which of the following developed the "overload theory" of crowding?
(A) Lorenz   (B) Schachter   (C) Aronson   (D) Milgram
(E) Ardrey

125. A person is asked to tell a lie for one of the following sums of money. For which sum would the most dissonance be created?
(A) $1   (B) $10   (C) $20   (D) $25   (E) $50

126. Which of the following is *not* characteristic of the Thurstone-type scale?
(A) equal-appearing intervals
(B) a judge expressing his own attitude regarding the statement being judged
(C) an eleven-category scale
(D) a large number of judges
(E) number values assigned to each statement on the scale

127. The most mature view of sex would be evident in which of the following?
  (A) genital stage (B) phallic stage (C) anal stage
  (D) puberty (E) initiative versus guilt

128. "Man's freedom is absolute and it is his own choices which determine what he shall become, since even refusing to choose constitutes a choice." The preceding view is expressed within
  (A) behaviorism (B) psychoanalysis (C) ego analysis
  (D) trait theory (E) existentialism

129. Which of the following is *not* true of attitudes?
  (A) Your own attitudes seem best to you.
  (B) A common defense against differing attitudes is selective attention.
  (C) A common defense against differing attitudes is rationalization.
  (D) Attitudes require an emotional component.
  (E) Attitudes require a stereotype component.

130. A person who judges personality on the basis of facial expression is engaging in
  (A) physiognomy (B) phrenology (C) trait analysis
  (D) syntonomy (E) parataxis

131. In a sequence of measures for creativity, which of the following would be a *least* likely inclusion?
  (A) water jar problems
  (B) Remote Associations Test
  (C) verbal "mind stretchers" such as "What would happen if everyone had three fingers and no thumb?"
  (D) WAIS
  (E) sentence completion

132. An ability that can be expected to continue improving after age thirty-five is
  (A) numerical (B) manual (C) spatial relations
  (D) verbal comprehension (E) associative memory

133. Which of the following personality concepts most accurately describes a boy's intense sexual love for his mother?
  (A) trust versus mistrust
  (B) inferiority feelings versus superiority striving
  (C) Electra complex
  (D) penis envy
  (E) phallic stage

134. Homans' anticipatory socialization refers to
  (A) downward movement in the social system
  (B) upward movement in the social system
  (C) lateral movement in the social system
  (D) preparation for an older age group within one's own social class
  (E) a child's initial preparation for cooperative play

135. Which of the following is unrelated to the 16 PF?
  (A) 16 personality-factor dimensions
  (B) Cattell
  (C) standardization on normal subjects
  (D) Hathaway
  (E) factor analysis

136. A factor analysis approach to personality would be most positively received within which of the following groups?
    (A) Cattell, Eysenck, Goldstein
    (B) Jung, Freud, Horney
    (C) Rogers, Kelly, Allport
    (D) Skinner, Watson, Bandura
    (E) Sullivan, Erikson, Berne

137. Which of the following makes an accurate distinction between the Strong Vocational Interest Blank and the Kuder Preference Record?
    (A) success versus failure
    (B) differences in administration
    (C) occupation emphasis versus broad-area emphasis
    (D) male-female distinctions versus unified format
    (E) an intelligence factor versus an aptitude factor

138. As a corrections officer — other factors being equivalent — which of the following persons would you consider most likely to be rehabilitated successfully?
    (A) person convicted of armed robbery
    (B) person who shot and killed another man found making love to the first man's wife
    (C) person charged with breaking and entering
    (D) person charged with arson
    (E) person who shot and killed another person as part of a profit-making contract

139. Mortimer has worn red shirts for years because he likes them. Now red shirts are the "in" thing with his group and he continues to wear them. In Hollander's terms, he is demonstrating
    (A) conformity   (B) anticonformity   (C) dissonance
    (D) independence   (E) irrelevance

140. In personality theory the most appropriate "home" for the term *motivation* would be within which of the following?
    (A) behaviorism   (B) psychoanalysis   (C) psychodynamics
    (D) trait theory   (E) Gestalt theory

141. "Do you think that you belong to the middle class, upper class, or lower class?" is an example of the _____ approach to class measurement.
    (A) reputational   (B) subjective   (C) objective
    (D) situational   (E) projective

142. The *least* likely treatment procedure, virtually extinct in today's psychiatric facilities, is
    (A) electroconvulsive shock therapy
    (B) chemotherapy
    (C) individual psychotherapy
    (D) encounter group therapy
    (E) prefrontal lobotomy

143. Which of the following was Adler's conceptual substitution for Freud's libido?
    (A) superiority striving   (B) social interest   (C) inferiority feeling
    (D) organ inferiority   (E) pampering

144. Someone well versed in kinesics would be studying
    (A) the meaning of body movements
    (B) personal, territorial space
    (C) mass communication
    (D) brainwashing
    (E) nonzero sum games

145. Jung cites human infant response to mother-closeness and the adult concept of a power beyond himself as examples of
    (A) anima   (B) animus   (C) archetype   (D) prototype
    (E) intuiting

146. Psychoanalytic thought did *not* emphasize
    (A) determinism
    (B) life and death wish conflict
    (C) early childhood experiences
    (D) repression
    (E) ego as a "conflict-free sphere"

147. Which of the following is most firmly supported by experimental evidence?
    (A) psychoanalysis   (B) trait theory   (C) behaviorism
    (D) phenomenology   (E) psychodynamic theory

148. The Generalized Thurstone Scales were developed by
    (A) Likert   (B) Bogardus   (C) Osgood   (D) Remmers
    (E) Aronson

149. A nonzero sum game refers to
    (A) a recent development in sociograms
    (B) a game in which both participants may win
    (C) a game in which both participants must lose
    (D) a game in which one participant ends up with zero
    (E) a game in which one participant may win only if the other participant loses

150. Formulation of dissonance theory was initiated by
    (A) Aronson   (B) Thurstone   (C) Festinger   (D) Heider
    (E) Newcomb

151. A therapeutic technique present in the work of Wolpe and not evident within Skinner's method is
    (A) positive reinforcement
    (B) negative reinforcement
    (C) discriminative stimulus
    (D) logotherapy
    (E) response generalization

152. Transvestism would be classified among
    (A) sociopathic personality disturbances
    (B) character disorder
    (C) personality trait disturbance
    (D) antisocial reaction
    (E) psychosomatic disorder

153. Sixteen different, self-contained personalities within the same individual, manifesting

themselves at different times is a form of
(A) anxiety reaction (B) catatonic schizophrenia (C) paranoid psychosis (D) manic-depressive reaction (E) dissociative reaction

154. In stating his view of neurosis as conditioned maladaptive behavior, Eysenck claims that
    (A) extroverts are most likely to become neurotics
    (B) introverts are most likely to develop conversion reactions
    (C) introverts have greater autonomic reactivity
    (D) phobias persist, once learned, even in the absence of further reinforcement
    (E) parataxic perception must be achieved before therapy can attain significant progress

155. Which of the following distinguishes a sedative from a tranquilizer?
    (A) cost
    (B) drowsiness-inducing characteristics
    (C) speed with which it takes effect
    (D) anxiety-reducing capacity
    (E) mood-elevation properties

156. Which of the following distinguishes anxiety from fear?
    (A) realistic environmental danger
    (B) strength of emotion
    (C) galvanic skin response
    (D) heart rate
    (E) blood pressure

157. A tranquilizer widely used in the treatment of schizophrenia is
    (A) d-tubocurarine (B) chlorpromazine (C) LSD
    (D) mescaline (E) elavil

158. Which one of the following was *not* part of Masserman's experiments?
    (A) conditioned conflict
    (B) air puffs
    (C) electric shock
    (D) rapid increase in room temperature
    (E) sudden lights and sounds

159. Psychotomimetic drugs are associated with which one of the following reactions?
    (A) depressive (B) hypermanic (C) schizophrenic
    (D) psychophysiologic (E) psychosomatic

160. Withdrawal reactions do *not* include which of the following elements?
    (A) repression
    (B) fantasy
    (C) regression
    (D) continual wandering — moves without tangible gain
    (E) paranoia

161. A characteristic of schizophrenia is
    (A) heightened awareness of reality
    (B) eidetic imagery
    (C) withdrawal from interpersonal relationships
    (D) psychological "paralysis" in a portion of the body
    (E) the "phantom limb" experience

162. Constant apprehension and fear make a certain person's life emotionally painful and difficult. Although the individual manages daily tasks reasonably well, the feeling persists, untraceable to any specific object or person. This is a case of
(A) conversion reaction   (B) hypochondriacal reaction   (C) depression reaction   (D) phobic reaction   (E) anxiety reaction

163. The simplest, least sophisticated measure of variability is known as the
(A) range   (B) standard deviation   (C) variance   (D) stanine   (E) quadrant

164. Intense fear of open places is known as
(A) ochlophobia   (B) acrophobia   (C) claustrophobia   (D) triskaidekaphobia   (E) agrophobia

165. Which one of the following is most likely to set fires?
(A) pyromaniac   (B) ochlomaniac   (C) kleptomaniac   (D) aclomaniac   (E) hypomaniac

166. Which of the following is *not* directly related to clinical assessment?
(A) MMPI   (B) 16 PF   (C) Osgood Semantic Differential   (D) Rorschach   (E) TAT

167. Transference and resistance are most common in
(A) psychoanalysis   (B) group therapy   (C) behavior therapy   (D) phenomenological therapy   (E) client-centered therapy

168. Each score in a distribution has been increased by 7 (i.e., 7 has been added to every score). What happens to the standard deviation?
(A) it increases by 7
(B) it remains unchanged from its original value
(C) it triples its current value
(D) it increases by 14
(E) it increases by 3.5

169. Which of the following would *not* be among the dynamics of an anxiety reaction?
(A) a felt threat to status or goals
(B) a threat that dangerous desires may "break through"
(C) fear in decision making
(D) guilt
(E) somnambulism

170. Behavior therapy
(A) treats the disturbed behavior directly
(B) emphasizes early childhood
(C) puts a premium on insight
(D) takes many years
(E) has declined markedly in popularity since the work of Wolpe

171. The procedure of outlining an experimental problem, stating criteria for making observations, describing measuring instruments and their use in observation, and defining procedures to be used in data analysis is
(A) operational definition   (B) hypothetical construct   (C) logical construct   (D) experimental design   (E) hypothesis

172. The function of a theory is to
    (A) prove a hypothesis
    (B) establish a law
    (C) explain and relate observed facts
    (D) develop the steps to be used in experimentation
    (E) establish significance levels

173. For which of the following forms of sexual deviation would treatment be considered most difficult?
    (A) frigidity   (B) impotence   (C) fetishism   (D) pedophilia
    (E) coitus interruptus

174. Depression is severe and includes within it distortions of reality in
    (A) paranoia   (B) neurosis   (C) psychosis   (D) dyssocial reaction   (E) character disorder

175. The life-history method is a
    (A) laboratory method   (B) field-study method   (C) latitudinal method
    (D) longitudinal method   (E) factor-analytical method

176. Michelangelo's frustrated desire for closeness with his mother was expressed in painting. This is an example of
    (A) compensation   (B) rationalization   (C) sublimation
    (D) projection   (E) reaction formation

177. Which one of the following persons would be most likely to study and analyze drawings by schizophrenic children?
    (A) Bandura   (B) Bettelheim   (C) Szasz   (D) Skinner
    (E) Adler

178. For which of the following disorders has effective treatment been most thoroughly developed?
    (A) neurotic depression   (B) dyssocial reaction   (C) antisocial reaction
    (D) catatonic schizophrenia   (E) multiple personality

179. Assuming a mean of 100 and a standard deviation of 15, what percentage of a group of persons selected randomly can be expected to have IQ scores above 130?
    (A) 14 percent   (B) 34 percent   (C) 48 percent   (D) 2 percent
    (E) 1 percent

Questions 180–181 are based on the following situation.

An experimenter plans to study the effects upon comprehension exerted by differences in sex, age, and hair color. His subjects will be equal numbers of males and females, ages twenty-five and forty-five, and either brown-haired or red-haired.

180. His statistical design is
    (A) two-factor   (B) four-factor   (C) one-factor   (D) six-factor
    (E) three-factor

181. Assuming that the experimenter can somehow obtain his data in a single test session with one score for each subject, he could use
    (A) a two-factor factorial design

(B) a three-factor factorial design
(C) a *t*-test for related measures
(D) a *t*-test for unrelated measures
(E) a complex Latin square design

182. *The Psychopathology of Everyday Life* was a prominent work of
(A) Fromm   (B) Rank   (C) Skinner   (D) Freud   (E) Adler

183. The moron-imbecile-idiot classification of the mentally retarded was changed because
(A) the corresponding IQs were inexact
(B) the categories were not sufficiently inclusive
(C) four categories were needed instead of three
(D) unfortunate stereotyping had occurred
(E) five categories were needed instead of three

184. Human engineering control principles indicate that a system is best in which the operation of the controls imposes _____ on the operator consistent with the required degree of accuracy.
(A) below optimum strain
(B) above optimum strain
(C) optimal strain
(D) complete absence of strain
(E) either above optimum or below optimum, depending on the setting

Questions 185–187 are based on the following information.

Two judges ranked five beauty contestants as follows:

Contestant	Judge 1	Judge 2
A	1	5
B	2	4
C	3	3
D	4	2
E	5	1

185. Which of the following can be concluded from the above?
(A) A strong positive correlation exists between the judges.
(B) A strong negative correlation exists between the judges.
(C) There is no correlation between the judges.
(D) A moderately positive correlation exists between the judges.
(E) A moderately negative correlation exists between the judges.

186. Which of the following methods would be used in computation of the above correlation?
(A) Latin Square Design
(B) Spearman Rank-Order Correlation
(C) Point-Biserial Correlation
(D) Simple Analysis of Covariance
(E) Factorial Analysis of Covariance

187. The correlation coefficient that you would be most likely to find would be
(A) +0.5   (B) −0.5   (C) 0.0   (D) −1.0   (E) +1.0

188. In human engineering, the term *shape coding* applies to
(A) visual discriminations

(B) dial calibrations
(C) dial color coding
(D) traffic flow between work positions
(E) knob appearance and contour

189. A situation in which trainees are presented with only the "bare bones" of a managerial situation and are told that participants can get additional information only by asking questions is an example of the
(A) free-association method   (B) case method   (C) incident method
(D) sensitivity-training   (E) role-playing method

190. A company has a screening test that involves responding to letters, memoranda, telephone messages, and other items typical of the contents of an executive's in-basket. This is an example of
(A) an aptitude test   (B) an intelligence test   (C) an achievement test
(D) a sociability measure   (E) an English test

191. Recognizing the difficulty of control in experimental designs, in which of the following could you be assured that variability among subjects has been adequately controlled?
(A) completely randomized design
(B) $2 \times 2 \times 2$ factorial design
(C) point-biserial correlation
(D) test-retest (repeated measures) design
(E) t-test

192. The measure most meaningful to an industry trying to determine the most popular and fastest selling items would be
(A) mean   (B) median   (C) variance   (D) standard deviation
(E) mode

193. In a positively skewed distribution, which of the following will move most noticeably in the direction indicated?
(A) mean, to the right
(B) mode, to the left
(C) mean, to the left
(D) median, to the right
(E) median, to the left

194. Given a very limited time (only a few hours) during which to study for a test, a person's best bet would be
(A) distributed practice
(B) massed practice
(C) a combination of distributed/massed/distributed
(D) a combination of massed/distributed/massed
(E) a combination of massed/massed/distributed

Questions 195–197 are based on the following choices.

(1) t-test for related measures
(2) t-test for two independent means
(3) t-test for sample and population means
(4) chi-square
(5) treatments-by-levels design

195. The experimenter seeks to determine whether one group of eighteen-year-old boys differs significantly in weight from a second group of eighteen-year-old boys. He would use
(A) 1 (B) 2 (C) 3 (D) 4 (E) 5

196. The experimenter wants to test the effect of child rearing upon identical twins — with one of each pair raised in a foster home and the second of each pair raised in an institution. (IQ scores were obtained for analysis when each group member attained age 15.) Which method would he use?
(A) 1 (B) 2 (C) 3 (D) 4 (E) 5

197. The experimenter wishes to determine whether the weight of a specific group of eighteen-year-old boys is significantly different from the national average for boys this age. Which method would he use?
(A) 1 (B) 2 (C) 3 (D) 4 (E) 5

198. Which one of the following could be expected to enhance performance on a vigilance task?
(A) threat of punishment (B) rest periods (C) high pay
(D) coworker interaction (E) background music

199. Most closely associated with the Least Preferred Coworker technique and with task-centered versus people-centered leader distinctions is the work of
(A) Newcomb (B) Asch (C) Rokeach (D) Festinger
(E) Fiedler

200. In McLuhan's framework, television is seen as a
(A) hot medium (B) moderately intense medium (C) cool medium
(D) political medium (E) social medium

Test 2: Answer Comments

1. (B) Hess studied imprinting behavior in mallard ducklings at several different time-after-birth intervals.

2. (C) Witkin found the perceptual phenomenon of tilt least prominent among persons relying on bodily cues.

3. (C) Located below the occipital lobe, the cerebellum functions prominently in muscle-movement coordination.

4. (E) Historically, the European and American approaches to comparative psychology differed in the prominence given to naturalistic observation. It was given a very strong emphasis in the European tradition, but the experimental laboratory method took precedence within the American tradition.

5. (D) The table indicates a higher probability of divergent production in the 120–129 IQ range than in the 110–119 range.

6. (B) Interpretations of table data containing IQ or other test scores must rely heavily upon the assumption that standardized testing and scoring procedures were followed.

7. (C) The 120–129 IQ range shows the greatest statistical likelihood for divergent production.

8. (D) In Brady's "executive monkey" experimentation, those animals that developed ulcers had the capacity to control shock onset.

9. (A) Transfer of excitatory or inhibitory potential between neurons occurs at the synapse.

10. (A) The temporal lobe of the brain receives auditory neural impulses.

11. (C) Pitch is the auditory dimension determined by frequency (number of cycles per second).

12. (A) When a stationary spot of light in a darkened room is perceived as moving, the autokinetic effect has occurred.

13. (B) Alcohol consumption lengthens reaction time — one of the driving hazards mentioned in the public media.

14. (D) The all-or-none law, as its name implies, focuses upon the ungraded-spike potential.

15. (B) The alpha wave has an EEG pattern of approximately ten pulsations per second and occurs when a person is awake.

16. (C) Basing his conclusion on rigorous experimentation, Lashley stated that equipotentiality showed that different parts of the cortex are interchangeable in their roles in learning (a finding critical in cases of brain damage).

17. (D) Apraxia refers to disturbances in the memory of bodily motor movements.

18. (B) Gestalt psychologists have most prominently explored perceptual phenomena.

19. (D) One of the unexpected effects of sensory deprivation has been hallucinations.

20. (E) Sweet, sour, bitter, and salty are the taste primaries.

21. (D) Inability to recognize printed words because of brain damage would be called *alexia*.

22. (A) Such muscle movement following decapitation of a cold-blooded animal occurs because of spinal cord sufficiency for complicated patterns of reflexive behavior.

23. (D) Reciprocal innervation refers to a combination of antagonistic muscle movements such as those present in walking.

24. (E) Sleep interruption during nondreaming periods has no effect upon the incidence of dream attempts in subsequent sleep.

25. (B) The position of the two ears on the head is critical to determinations of sound directionality. Hearing must exist in both ears for the determination of sound direction.

26. (D) The state of consciousness passed through when going from sleeping to waking is called the hypnopompic state.

27. (D) The lowest brain wave frequency is the delta wave, occurring in stage IV (deep) sleep.

28. (A) Broca's area in the frontal lobe of the left cerebral hemisphere is related to speech.

29. (D) The Montreal Foundling Studies indicated that the earliest emotion evident in the newborn is excitement.

30. (E) Although functioning in depth perception, convergence is not a stimulus cue.

31. (C) Tinbergen's fixed-action patterns (e.g., frog's tongue flick when catching flies) are stereotyped action pattens exhibited by all same-sex members of a species and are elicited by simple, specific, external stimuli.

32. (E) The adrenal medulla mobilizes the body by secreting epinephrine in stressful situations.

33. (E) Gustation and olfaction are classified as chemical receptors.

34. (A) Rutherford's frequency theory of audition is best suited to the low frequency range. In the high frequency range, its implementation would be a physical impossibility for the human hearing mechanism.

35. (A) The pituitary gland controls growth and carries responsibilities for stimulating other endocrine glands.

36. (A) Experiments with rats have revealed that sexual behavior survives fairly extensive cortical destruction in males.

37. (C) The study of motivation had its primitive beginnings in the work of Freud and James.

38. (E) Freud did not speak of the manner in which habit combines with drive to express the content of emotion.

39. (C) Thorndike studied animals in puzzle boxes — his major work being *Animal Intelligence*.

40. (B) Consolidation theory expresses Hebb's view that cell assemblies are capable of "self re-exciting" or reverberating to establish memory trace.

41. (E) The quotation most directly constitutes a definition of a species.

42. (D) The normal developmental age range during which a child could be expected to master clock-time concepts would be between five and six years.

43. (C) Reaction time decreases with age up to approximately thirty years, beginning a pattern of increase beyond this age.

44. (D) While ossicles deal with amplification, actual nerve impulse transformation occurs in the cochlea.

45. (B) Brain stem transections in animals reveal that *organization* of intense emotional responses apparently occurs at a level above the midbrain. Rage response, for instance, becomes bits of response that are disorganized.

46. (D) The terminal point for efferent fibers is muscles or glands.

47. (D) Tolman summarized Watson's definition of emotions in terms of stimuli and responses but, of course, took issue with the Watson definition.

48. (B) The term *effectors* collectively describes muscles and glands.

49. (B) The Ames distorted room was designed to test size constancy.

50. (C) Restricting visual input to a specific point on the retina causes gradual and complete stimulus fading. During normal vision, this phenomenon is avoided by small eye movements made without the viewer's conscious awareness.

51. (D) LSD has been found to produce a cognitive experience similar to psychosis.

52. (C) Turtles, fish, monkeys, and humans provide good evidence of color vision, but rodents are deficient in this area.

53. (B) The abrupt, delineated line "block-out" is characteristic of nerve damage — hearing loss evidenced in specific frequency ranges.

54. (A) Ossification is evidenced by hearing loss throughout all frequency ranges.

55. (C) This curve represents far more acuteness than would be true for humans in either the lower or upper frequency ranges.

56. (A) The effects of aging would be equivalent to the ossification hearing loss.

57. (B) Within the temporal lobe lie cerebral responsibilities for audition.

58. (D) Within the occipital lobe lie cerebral responsibilities for vision.

59. (E) The cerebellum is responsible for muscle coordination.

60. (C) In walking from hot sand onto cool grass, the grass provides negative reinforcement — removal of an aversive stimulus.

61. (B) In his work with children, Bandura has found that observation of aggressive models can prompt aggressive behavior by the observer.

62. (C) A verbatim reading of test-taking instructions is indicative of standardization — the effort to be certain that each test taker has an equivalent testing situation.

63. (C) During the third through eighth week of pregnancy, a developing child would be described as being in the embryo stage.

64. (E) Developmental research has found evidence of a relationship between anxiety in the expectant mother and the incidence of crying behavior in the newborn.

65. (E) Cretinism is a mental-physical disorder resulting from thyroid deficiency at an early age. Children with this problem generally have low intelligence.

66. (C) Hopi Indian children — strapped on their mothers' backs with no opportunity to practice walking skills — were found to walk as early as children who had such practice opportunity. The finding suggested that walking was primarily a function of maturation.

67. (E) Retinal disparity and convergence are not among the questions examined with the visual cliff. Primary emphasis rests with questions regarding the innate capacities for depth perception.

68. (C) Children from father-present home settings have the highest incidence or aggressive behavior — perhaps a function of modeling and paternal discipline.

69. (E) Piaget's initial sensorimotor period contains six subdivisions.

70. (E) Given a choice among several stimuli, a newborn prefers pictures of the human face.

71. (B) The newborn demonstrates some irregularities in respiration.

72. (C) Monthly salary is fixed interval and a commission for every car sold is fixed ratio.

73. (B) In operant-instrumental conditioning, reinforcement increases the frequency of the response associated with it.

74. (E) A person with an IQ of 60 is in the mildly retarded classification which spans the 50 to 70 IQ range.

75. (E) Guilford's model is one of the most elaborate examples of the use of factor analysis.

76. (C) Correlation is related to predictability. One indication of this relationship is the predictive validity concept.

77. (E) Mean and standard deviation are the most common expressions of central tendency and variability, respectively.

78. (A) In developmental psychology, the first two years after birth are critical to self-concept formation.

79. (A) The syllogism is a form of deductive thinking.

80. (B) In the first three months after birth, a child can be expected to develop the capacity to raise its head to look at something.

81. (A) The initial response of lifting one paw now has generalized to lifting two paws — response generalization.

82. (A) When stimuli similar to the original CS now elicit the CR, stimulus generalization has occurred.

83. (A) The expression "learning how to learn" refers to the development of learning sets.

84. (B) The task requires extrapolation, that is, inference from known data.

85. (A) Jones's studies find early maturity advantageous among males.

86. (A) The period of the embryo spans the end of the second week to the end of the second month of pregnancy.

87. (A) A similar-items list is more difficult to learn than a dissimilar-items list because distinctions are more difficult to make.

88. (E) One of the major distinctions in cytology is between germ cells and body cells.

89. (E) Watson places primary importance upon environmental influences. He said, in effect, that if you were to give him a child shortly after birth, he would make that child anything you wanted it to be.

90. (D) Classical conditioning requires that the CS have no innate or original reinforcing qualities in its own right.

91. (D) Classical conditioning research has found a half-second interval between CS and UCS onset to be most effective.

92. (E) Cell mass differentiation into three distinct layers occurs during the embryonic period.

93. (A) Learning a list of numbers would be least likely to interfere because of its distinct difference from the initially learned list of adjectives. In all the other choices, either words or letters are involved, promising potential interference.

94. (D) The field theorist emphasizes the role of learning in cognitive processes.

95. (C) One of the primary detrimental effects that anxiety can have upon learning is to reduce a person's ability to discriminate clearly.

96. (C) The von Restorff effect suggests a prepotent stimulus — some distinct quality about a particular stimulus in a series that makes that stimulus stand out from the others (e.g., difference in size, a number in the midst of a word list, a pinup in the midst of a series of automobile pictures, etc.).

97. (C) *Split-half* refers to test reliability and has nothing to do with experimental approaches to recall.

98. (D) Frenkel and Brunswik have found attitudes toward authority to be the single most important factor distinguishing prejudiced from tolerant adolescents.

99. (C) Moderate anxiety in a child may facilitate the learning of simple tasks but will prove detrimental to the learning of difficult tasks.

100. (D) Eye color is a singly determined genetic characteristic.

101. (C) Two of the four possible genetic combinations for male children will produce color blindness. Color blindness is a sex-linked genetic characteristic — females act as carriers, but the characteristic itself, when present, appears in males.

102. (B) A child's differentiation and consequent fear of strangers generally develops in the six-to-seven month age range.

103. (D) *Psychograph* is a term meaning test profile.

104. (B) The Stanford-Binet Intelligence Test relies heavily on the verbal abilities of the test taker.

105. (D) Idea and hypothesis generation are parts of the inductive phase within problem-solving processes.

106. (B) The heights of kindergarten-aged children are positively correlated with comparative adult heights.

107. (B) Kendler's research suggests that single unit S-R cognitive mechanisms precede mediational processes in a child's conceptual development.

108. (B) In the newborn's second year, rate of growth is slower than in the first year.

109. (E) Among this group, only Scott has conducted imprinting research. All the other groups of names contain at least two research names in imprinting.

110. (B) In the Babkin response, a child's mouth opens wide and its head turns to the midline.

111. (A) Male sex determination is accomplished by the Y chromosome.

112. (A) In the Guilford model for problem solving, input occurs first (followed by filtering, cognition, and production — with evaluation available between steps).

113. (D) Tolman's work is associated with purposive behavior and place learning.

114. (C) The term *fractional anticipatory goal response* is a reference to CR.

115. (A) Hull believed that no response could occur without reinforcement (K within the formula, symbolizing response incentive).

116. (D) In Piaget's classification system, the concrete operations period is the point during which the child learns language and the logic of classification.

117. (D) Hunter's double alternation method requires an animal to remember which direction it turned on each of the two preceding trials in order to make the correct current-trial response.

118. (A) Research on learning during sleep indicates that learning does not occur during deep sleep.

119. (D) Dollard and Miller would see anger-anxiety conflict as more likely to occur during the toilet-training period.

120. (B) "Tailing off" to the right would indicate positive skew.

121. (B) Negative reinforcement can be defined as cessation or removal of an aversive stimulus.

122. (D) When earlier learning is interfered with by later learning, the direction is retroactive and the effect is inhibition.

123. (B) Compared with percept, a visual image is more labile, less vivid, less detailed, and holds the potential for becoming associated with other objects and images.

124. (D) Stanley Milgram has developed the theory of "overload" and has outlined its implications for human behavior in the urban environment. Among those implications is a tendency not to speak to other persons on a city street nor to pick up trash or offer to help a pedestrian in distress. Each of these settings threatens to overload the individual's "system" and capacity to cope. To avoid such overload, the individual limits and restricts inputs.

125. (A) The greatest dissonance would be created by the one-dollar payment. It is the smallest amount of money available in this situation and gives a person the least external justification for telling a lie.

126. (B) Judges expressing their own personal responses to the statements themselves would be characteristic of the Likert scale.

127. (A) Freud sees a giving-type relationship within the genital stage. At this point, sexual relationships have moved beyond the selfish narcissism characteristic of the phallic stage.

128. (E) Existentialism sees man as free to make his own choices and, in effect, act as master of his fate.

129. (E) Attitudes contain cognitive, emotional, and behavioral components. A stereotype component does not constitute a general characteristic of attitudes.

130. (A) Judging personality on the basis of facial expression is an example of physiognomy.

131. (D) Wechsler Scales have no direct relationship to creativity. Although creative expression is generally accompanied by above average intelligence, a person's level of intelligence has not been proven to be an accurate predictor of creativity.

132. (D) Verbal comprehension can be expected to continue improving after age thirty-five while other abilities such as associative memory, spatial relations, etc., begin gradual declines.

133. (E) Freud's phallic stage contains the Oedipus complex, which describes a boy's intense sexual love for his mother.

134. (B) Homans' anticipatory socialization refers to a person's adopting social mores characteristic of a higher social level — toward which that person aspires.

135. (D) McKinley and Hathaway developed the MMPI but had no involvement in the development of the 16 PF scale.

136. (A) Cattell, Eysenck, and Goldstein all espouse factor analytic approaches to the study of personality.

137. (C) The Strong interest test makes occupational correlations, and the Kuder preference test puts responses in broad area categories.

138. (B) Persons committing a crime of passion are among those with the least likelihood of committing any subsequent offenses.

139. (D) Mortimer is demonstrating what Hollander calls independence. He wears red shirts when they are both "in" and not "in" — simply because he likes them. Conformity would change systematically in the direction of the "in" style, and anticonformity would change systematically against it.

140. (B) Psychoanalysis functions in terms of underlying, unconscious motivations for behavior.

141. (B) This approach to social-class measurement is subjective; the subject himself is asked to make his own classification.

142. (E) Prefrontal lobotomy — excision or removal of parts of the prefrontal lobes in severe cases of mental disturbance — has long since become extinct in therapeutic practice.

143. (A) Adler replaced Freud's libido concept with his own concept of superiority striving.

144. (A) Kinesics is the study of nonverbal communication within body movements.

145. (C) Jung viewed archetypes as innate concepts being passed from generation to generation within a species. He placed the infant's natural response to mother closeness in this category.

146. (E) Ego-analysis, successor to psychoanalysis, concentrates on the view of ego as a conflict-free sphere — no longer dependent upon id for energy supply, as was true in psychoanalysis.

147. (C) Among personality approaches, behaviorism is supported by the largest body of research evidence.

148. (D) Developed in the same manner as the Thurstone scale, the Remmers Generalized Thurstone Scale contained a standard grouping of statements that could be used for attitude measurement on virtually any topic.

149. (B) In a nonzero sum game, both participants may win or lose simultaneously.

150. (C) Festinger formulated the theory of cognitive dissonance.

151. (B) Wolpe paired removal of an aversive stimulus with an anxiety-reducing word. He theorized that the word would have calming effects even when the aversive stimulus was no longer present.

152. (A) Classified as a sociopathic personality disturbance, transvestism involves sexual gratification obtained from wearing underclothes of the opposite sex.

153. (E) Sybil is said to have manifested sixteen different personalities — a very rare form of dissociative reaction.

154. (C) Eysenck believes introverts have greater autonomic reactivity than extroverts.

155. (B) In contrast to tranquilizers, sedatives have drowsiness-inducing characteristics.

156. (A) Fear relates to realistic environmental danger; anxiety is, in effect, unrealistic fear.

157. (B) Chlorpromazine is a tranquilizer widely used in the treatment of schizophrenia.

158. (D) Room temperature was not an independent variable within Masserman's experimental designs.

159. (C) Psychotomimetic drugs (hallucinogens) are associated with schizophrenic-type reactions.

160. (E) Repression, fantasy, regression, and continual wandering are among withdrawal reactions, but paranoia is not.

161. (C) The schizophrenic exhibits withdrawal from interpersonal relationships.

162. (E) Constant apprehension and fear are characteristic of anxiety reaction.

163. (A) Range is the simplest and least precise measure of variability.

164. (E) Agoraphobia is a neurotic fear of open places.

165. (A) A pyromaniac has an irresistible impulse to set fires.

166. (C) The Osgood Semantic Differential Scale is used primarily in attitude measurement. It is not an instrument for clinical assessment.

167. (A) Transference and resistance are terms commonly used within psychoanalysis.

168. (B) Though each score in the distribution has been changed through the addition of a constant (the number 7), the variability of the distribution itself is unchanged. Therefore, the standard deviation remains unchanged from its original value.

169. (E) Somnambulism is a dissociative reaction characteristic.

170. (A) Behavior therapy treats the immediate, observable behavior problem rather than seeking an underlying motivation or deep-seated cause.

171. (D) An experimental design incorporates all aspects of this item description.

172. (C) Within a specific problem area, a theory carries the function of explaining and relating observed facts.

173. (D) Of the forms of sexual deviation listed, pedophilia (in which an adult desires or engages in sexual relations with a child) is the most difficult to treat.

174. (C) Distortion of reality as an element in depression would be indicative of psychosis.

175. (D) The life-history method is a longitudinal research approach.

176. (C) It could be suggested that Michelangelo's frustrated desire for closeness with his mother was expressed in painting. This would be an example of sublimation — redirection of an unacceptable or ungratified impulse into a higher cultural contribution.

177. (B) Bettelheim works with schizophrenic children and concentrates much effort on study and analysis of their drawings.

178. (A) Of the disorders listed, neurotic depression is the one for which most effective treatment has been developed.

179. (D) The score of 130 is two standard deviations above the mean — a point beyond which only about 2 percent of the scores in a distribution will occur.

180. (E) The experiment has a three-factor design — sex, age, hair color.

181. (B) A three-factor factorial design can be used if only one measure (score) is to be analyzed for each subject. If trials were involved, for instance, a three-factor mixed design with repeated measures on one factor would be needed.

182. (D) Freud wrote *The Psychopathology of Everyday Life* to describe the manner in which apparent accidents, slips of the tongue, and the like betray id impulses.

183. (D) Unfortunate stereotyping became associated with the terms *moron, imbecile,* and *idiot,* prompting a change to the educable-trainable-nontrainable categories.

184. (C) Human engineering control principles indicate that a system is best in which the operation of the controls imposes optimal strain on the operator consistent with the required degree of accuracy. Optimal strain is not to be confused with painful stress; rather it involves the degree of stimulation necessary for alertness and accuracy.

185. (B) The fact that the judges' rankings are completely reversed is indicative of strong (in this case, perfect) negative correlation.

186. (B) The example utilizes rank order and therefore would call upon the Spearman Rank-Order Correlation method for analysis.

187. (D) This correlation coefficient would be -1.0 — a perfect negative correlation.

188. (E) The human engineering term *shape coding* applies to knob appearance and contour — enabling the operator to locate the correct knob by feel, if necessary.

189. (C) Presenting the "bare bones" of a managerial situation and adding that additional information can only be obtained by asking questions is an example of the incident method in managerial training techniques.

190. (A) A company screening test for executive trainees that involved handling, sorting, and dealing with an array of items in a sample executive in-basket would be an aptitude test.

191. (D) A test-retest, repeated-measures design contains impressive subject variability control because the subjects, in effect, act as their own controls. This relieves the experimenter of the problem, or possibility, that the subjects' backgrounds may somehow contribute to any differences found.

192. (E) To spot the fast-moving items in their product line, an industry would concentrate on use of mode — the most frequently occurring score(s).

193. (A) Of the central tendency measures, the mean moves most noticeably in the direction of the skew.

194. (B) With only a few hours allotted for test study, massed practice would be the best approach. Given better study planning, distributed practice would be the more effective method.

195. (B) To determine whether a significant difference in weight exists between two randomly selected groups of eighteen-year-olds, a person would use the *t*-test for independent means.

196. (A) Matched pairing has occurred in the initial grouping — an indication that the design will utilize a *t*-test for related measures.

197. (C) Comparison with the national average of the weight found in the specific groups of eighteen-year-old boys would utilize the *t*-test for sample and population means. In this instance, the national average constitutes the population mean.

198. (B) Researchers have found that rest periods enhance performance on vigilance tasks.

199. (E) One of the most prominent researchers in the area of leadership, Fiedler has used the Least Preferred Coworker technique to identify task-centered and people-centered leaders.

200. (C) McLuhan's framework classifies television as a cool medium — not information intensive, a characteristic required for a hot medium.

Test 2: Evaluating Your Score

Abbreviation Guide

PC	Physiological/Comparative
SnP	Sensation/Perception
LM	Learning/Motivation/Emotion
CHL	Cognition/Complex Human Learning
D	Developmental
PrS	Personality/Social
PyCl	Psychopathology/Clinical
M	Methodology
Ap	Applied

Subject Area Chart

Use this chart to determine the subject matter covered by each question in Test 2.

1.	PC	26.	PC	51.	PC	76.	M	101.	D
2.	SnP	27.	PC	52.	SnP	77.	M	102.	D
3.	PC	28.	PC	53.	SnP	78.	D	103.	CHL
4.	SnP	29.	LM	54.	SnP	79.	CHL	104.	CHL
5.	M	30.	SnP	55.	SnP	80.	D	105.	CHL
6.	M	31.	LM	56.	SnP	81.	LM	106.	D
7.	M	32.	PC	57.	PC	82.	LM	107.	CHL
8.	LM	33.	SnP	58.	PC	83.	LM	108.	D
9.	PC	34.	SnP	59.	PC	84.	CHL	109.	D
10.	PC	35.	PC	60.	LM	85.	D	110.	D
11.	SnP	36.	LM	61.	D	86.	D	111.	D
12.	SnP	37.	LM	62.	M	87.	CHL	112.	CHL
13.	SnP	38.	LM	63.	D	88.	D	113.	LM
14.	PC	39.	LM	64.	D	89.	LM	114.	LM
15.	PC	40.	LM	65.	D	90.	LM	115.	LM
16.	PC	41.	PC	66.	D	91.	LM	116.	CHL
17.	LM	42.	SnP	67.	D	92.	D	117.	CHL
18.	SnP	43.	SnP	68.	D	93.	CHL	118.	CHL
19.	SnP	44.	SnP	69.	CHL	94.	CHL	119.	D
20.	SnP	45.	PC	70.	D	95.	CHL	120.	M
21.	PC	46.	PC	71.	D	96.	CHL	121.	LM
22.	PC	47.	LM	72.	LM	97.	CHL	122.	LM
23.	PC	48.	PC	73.	LM	98.	D	123.	CHL
24.	PC	49.	SnP	74.	CHL	99.	D	124.	PrS
25.	SnP	50.	SnP	75.	CHL	100.	D	125.	PrS

126.	PrS	141.	PrS	156.	PyCl	171.	M	186.	M
127.	PrS	142.	Ap	157.	PyCl	172.	M	187.	M
128.	PrS	143.	PrS	158.	PyCl	173.	PyCl	188.	Ap
129.	PrS	144.	PrS	159.	PyCl	174.	PyCl	189.	Ap
130.	PrS	145.	PrS	160.	PyCl	175.	M	190.	Ap
131.	Ap	146.	PrS	161.	PyCl	176.	PyCl	191.	Ap
132.	Ap	147.	PrS	162.	PyCl	177.	PyCl	192.	Ap
133.	PrS	148.	PrS	163.	M	178.	PyCl	193.	M
134.	PrS	149.	PrS	164.	PyCl	179.	M	194.	Ap
135.	PrS	150.	PrS	165.	PyCl	180.	M	195.	M
136.	PrS	151.	PyCl	166.	PyCl	181.	M	196.	M
137.	PrS	152.	PyCl	167.	PyCl	182.	Ap	197.	M
138.	Ap	153.	PyCl	168.	M	183.	Ap	198.	Ap
139.	PrS	154.	PyCl	169.	PyCl	184.	Ap	199.	Ap
140.	PrS	155.	PyCl	170.	PyCl	185.	M	200.	Ap

Record the number of questions you missed in each subject area.

PC —   CHL —   PyCl —
SnP—   D   —   M   —
LM —   PrS —   Ap   —

Test Score Scale

The first number given is the number of questions in the test in that subject area. The number in parentheses indicates the 75th percentile score. To determine how well you scored in each subject area, subtract the number of questions you missed in a certain area from the total number of questions in that area. Compare the result with the 75th percentile number. If it is lower than 75%, you probably need more review.

PC —24(18)   CHL —20(15)   PyCl —23(17)
SnP —22(17)   D   —26(20)   M   —22(17)
LM —24(18)   PrS —23(17)   Ap   —16(22)

Test 3: Answer Grid

101. A B C D E
102. A B C D E
103. A B C D E
104. A B C D E
105. A B C D E
106. A B C D E
107. A B C D E
108. A B C D E
109. A B C D E
110. A B C D E
111. A B C D E
112. A B C D E
113. A B C D E
114. A B C D E
115. A B C D E
116. A B C D E
117. A B C D E
118. A B C D E
119. A B C D E
120. A B C D E
121. A B C D E
122. A B C D E
123. A B C D E
124. A B C D E
125. A B C D E
126. A B C D E
127. A B C D E
128. A B C D E
129. A B C D E
130. A B C D E
131. A B C D E
132. A B C D E
133. A B C D E
134. A B C D E
135. A B C D E
136. A B C D E
137. A B C D E
138. A B C D E
139. A B C D E
140. A B C D E
141. A B C D E
142. A B C D E
143. A B C D E
144. A B C D E
145. A B C D E
146. A B C D E
147. A B C D E
148. A B C D E
149. A B C D E
150. A B C D E
151. A B C D E
152. A B C D E
153. A B C D E
154. A B C D E
155. A B C D E
156. A B C D E
157. A B C D E
158. A B C D E
159. A B C D E
160. A B C D E
161. A B C D E
162. A B C D E
163. A B C D E
164. A B C D E
165. A B C D E
166. A B C D E
167. A B C D E
168. A B C D E
169. A B C D E
170. A B C D E
171. A B C D E
172. A B C D E
173. A B C D E
174. A B C D E
175. A B C D E
176. A B C D E
177. A B C D E
178. A B C D E
179. A B C D E
180. A B C D E
181. A B C D E
182. A B C D E
183. A B C D E
184. A B C D E
185. A B C D E
186. A B C D E
187. A B C D E
188. A B C D E
189. A B C D E
190. A B C D E
191. A B C D E
192. A B C D E
193. A B C D E
194. A B C D E
195. A B C D E
196. A B C D E
197. A B C D E
198. A B C D E
199. A B C D E
200. A B C D E

Test Three

Time 170 minutes

Directions Each of the following questions contains five possible responses. Read the question carefully and select the response that you feel is most appropriate. Then completely darken the space on your answer grid that corresponds with your choice.

1. Preparing the body "for fight or flight" is the function of the
    (A) pituitary gland (B) parathyroid gland (C) parasympathetic nervous system (D) adrenal medulla (E) pancreas

2. Audition encompasses several of the following stimulus dimensions. The entry which should *not* be included among these is
    (A) intensity (B) duration (C) frequency (D) saturation (E) locus

3. In Miller's classic black-white straight alley
    (A) successive approximation was observed for the first time
    (B) behavior chaining reached complete development
    (C) the strength of the acquired-fear drive was observed
    (D) the response continued only in the presence of the unconditioned stimulus
    (E) positive reinforcement was given for the correct response

4. Which one of the following is a correct statement?
    (A) Whether a neuron is at rest or conducting is determined by the ionic flux of electrically charged particles (ions).
    (B) An important aspect of excitatory potential is the incremental firing principle.
    (C) Excitatory potential is self-propagating.
    (D) Neural impulse transmission is completely chemical in nature.
    (E) IPSP means Inhibitory Presynaptic Potential.

Questions 5–7 are based on the following information.

The subjects were adult males, ages twenty to twenty-five. For this procedure, each subject was attached to GSR monitoring devices, and a shock electrode was placed on each one's left forefinger. Subjects individually received twenty presentations of a tone. In ten of the presentations, the tone was 700 Hz and was followed by electric shock to the left forefinger. In the remaining ten presentations, the tone was 3,500 Hz and was not followed by shock. Presentations were randomized for each subject, making it impossible to predict what tone would be presented on any given trial. GSR to each tonal presentation was recorded, and the results are presented in the following table.

	Amplitude of GSR	
Trial Block	**Tone 1** *700 Hz*	**Tone 2** *3,500 Hz*
1	10	10
2	8	13
3	6	15
4	5	18
5	4	20

5. Between Tone 1 and Tone 2, GSR across trials shows
   (A) strong positive correlation
   (B) weak positive correlation
   (C) strong negative correlation
   (D) weak negative correlation
   (E) no correlation

6. The conditioned stimulus in the experiment was
   (A) shock to left forefinger   (B) GSR   (C) age of subjects
   (D) tone   (E) trials

7. Which of the following phenomena was evident across trial blocks?
   (A) stimulus generalization   (B) stimulus discrimination
   (C) counterconditioning   (D) reciprocal inhibition   (E) extinction

8. Which one of the following is included within the parietal lobe of the human brain?
   (A) motor cortex   (B) reticular activating system   (C) cerebellum
   (D) auditory area   (E) somesthetic cortex

9. Depth perception relies heavily on which one of the following binocular cues?
   (A) accommodation   (B) interposition   (C) phi phenomenon
   (D) convergence   (E) movement

10. Schachter and Singer's work with epinephrine demonstrated
    (A) the prevalence of an anger emotion over emotions of happiness
    (B) the validity of the Yerkes-Dodson law
    (C) the importance of external cues
    (D) the predominance of internal cues
    (E) the validity of the Cannon-Washburn theory

11. In contrast with an emotion, a mood is
    (A) more intense and longer in duration
    (B) less intense and shorter in duration
    (C) more intense and shorter in duration
    (D) less intense and longer in duration
    (E) identical in all respects

12. One of the commonly demonstrated effects in strong support of the trichromatic theory has been the
    (A) phi phenomenon   (B) autokinetic effect   (C) black-white phenomenon   (D) negative after-image   (E) Muller-Lyer phenomenon

13. Depriving a person of stage 1-REM dreaming
    (A) can effectively reduce total sleeping time by 20 percent with no aftereffects
    (B) results in a subsequent increase in REM to compensate for the deficit
    (C) will probably cause death within a week
    (D) causes such deep sleep that waking is almost impossible
    (E) results in subsequent increase in Stage 2 sleep

14. Within the cell body of a neuron, a high concentration of positive ions places the neuron in a state described as
    (A) homeostatic   (B) conducting   (C) efferent   (D) afferent
    (E) innervative

15. Striated muscles
    (A) are synonymous with smooth muscles
    (B) produce stomach contractions
    (C) are prominently involved in voluntary muscle activity
    (D) produce heart-rate change
    (E) supply the viscera

16. An experimenter switches food reinforcement from the right branch to the left branch of a Y-maze, and the rat continues down the nonreinforced branch for several trials following the switch. Spence believes that this occurs because of
    (A) the rat's low level of intelligence
    (B) the need to completely extinguish right-branch response before left-branch can be effectively learned
    (C) counterconditioning
    (D) functional fixedness
    (E) extreme hunger, which causes irrational behavior in the animal

17. The spinal cord does *not*
    (A) relay nerve impulses
    (B) process sensory impulses
    (C) have any function in reflexive behavior
    (D) contain spinal nerves
    (E) control primitive emotions

18. Walter comes to the clinic with a speech impairment resulting from brain damage. One can be reasonably certain that damage has occurred in the
    (A) left cerebral hemisphere   (B) right cerebral hemisphere
    (C) reticular formation   (D) cerebellum   (E) corpus callosum

19. Which of the following is *not* among stimulus-related perceptual phenomena believed to be generally experienced?
    (A) closure   (B) grouping   (C) divergence   (D) contrast
    (E) phi phenomenon

20. GSR measures
    (A) general synaptic response
    (B) specificity of auditory response
    (C) sweat-gland activity
    (D) kinesthetic reflex
    (E) Down's Syndrome

21. Inverted-glasses experiments demonstrate
    (A) the inability of the human visual system to cope with the inversion phenomenon
    (B) the surprising ability of the human visual system to adjust to the inversion phenomenon
    (C) the human visual system's defense of temporary blindness
    (D) exaggerated myopic vision
    (E) exaggerated scotopic vision

22. *Purposive Behavior in Animals and Men* was the major work written by
    (A) Skinner   (B) Thorndike   (C) Pavlov   (D) Tolman
    (E) Woodworth

23. Which one of the following is a function of thyroxin?
    (A) body metabolism-physical growth
    (B) skeletal growth
    (C) sexual arousal
    (D) gamete production
    (E) reticular formation activation

24. Which one of the following would be an example of brightness constancy?
    (A) snow looking white in both sunlight and shadow
    (B) snow and white clothes appearing to be of an identical hue
    (C) cue constancy within the Landolt ring
    (D) red clothes appearing gray at night
    (E) Purkinje effect

25. Accommodation refers to the activity of
    (A) transmitting binaural sound to the oval windows
    (B) the Meissner corpuscle in pilotropism
    (C) echolocation
    (D) change in lens shape to focus on nearby or distant objects
    (E) perception of object constancy regardless of retinal image size

26. The electroencephalogram relies upon
    (A) signals from a single electrode attached to the forehead
    (B) signals from several pairs of electrodes attached to various parts of the scalp
    (C) monitoring of rapid eye movements
    (D) pilograph rhythms
    (E) a frequency rhythm not to exceed six cycles per second

27. In studying bodily reactions to stress, Hans Selye found the initial reaction to be
    (A) resistance   (B) exhaustion   (C) alarm   (D) ulcers
    (E) migraines

28. A subject placed in an elaborate sensory deprivation setting for a remuneration of $20 per day will
    (A) remain in such a setting indefinitely
    (B) usually endure such a setting only one to two weeks
    (C) usually endure such a setting only two to three weeks
    (D) experience motion parallax
    (E) encounter the "phantom limb" phenomenon

29. The adage that a watched pot never boils is given confirmation in the experimental findings that time passage seems
    (A) faster than normal for persons trying hard to complete a task in order to reach a desired goal
    (B) slower than normal for persons trying hard to complete a task in order to reach a desired goal
    (C) faster for younger than for older children
    (D) slower for persons experiencing success than for those experiencing failure
    (E) longer for cooking tasks

30. For success in locating sound directionality, a person depends heavily upon the
    (A) physical location of his two ears
    (B) tracking capability of the pinna
    (C) middle ear capacities for localization

(D) inner ear capacities for localization
(E) intensity of the sound

31. The primaries in subtractive color mixing are
    (A) violet, orange, green
    (B) blue, yellow, red
    (C) blue, green, red
    (D) green, orange, red
    (E) green, yellow, red

32. An involuntary response to stress has just occurred involving the digestive and the circulatory systems. Emphasis would center on which of the following parts of the autonomic nervous system?
    (A) central   (B) peripheral   (C) sympathetic
    (D) parasympathetic   (E) somatic

33. "Any response to a situation will, other things being equal, be more strongly connected with the situation in proportion to the number of times it has been connected with that situation and to the average vigor and duration of the connections." The preceding is a quote from
    (A) Thorndike's Law of Exercise
    (B) Lewin's Field Theory
    (C) Skinner's Law of Reinforcement
    (D) Markel's Law of Diminishing Returns
    (E) Watson's Law of Contiguity

34. A person who is awake but relaxed, with his eyes closed, shows predominantly
    (A) alpha waves
    (B) beta waves
    (C) theta waves
    (D) delta waves
    (E) theta-delta combination of brain-wave activity

35. A young man who wants to return to his native country but fears the legal punishment he may receive from his government is expressing
    (A) approach-approach conflict
    (B) avoidance-avoidance conflict
    (C) approach-avoidance conflict
    (D) double approach-avoidance conflict
    (E) double avoidance-avoidance conflict

36. In animal laboratory experiments relating to food intake, it has been found that
    (A) there is no apparent organismic regulation of meal size
    (B) animals have a tendency to keep their caloric intake constant
    (C) animals made artificially fat by insulin injection will maintain their overweight indefinitely
    (D) there is no relationship between animal food intake and the organism's energy requirements
    (E) there is high negative correlation between the amount of food consumed and water intake

37. The physiological entity commonly referred to as the seat of emotion is the
    (A) thalamus   (B) limbic system   (C) medulla   (D) cerebral cortex   (E) hypothalamus

38. The distinctly male sex hormone is
    (A) estrogen (B) progesterone (C) prolactin (D) androgen
    (E) dextrin

39. Given the task of matching a spot of light to the size of a specific coin
    (A) poor children tended to underestimate the size
    (B) rich children tended to underestimate the size
    (C) poor children tended to overestimate the size
    (D) rich children tended to overestimate the size
    (E) both poor and rich children made accurate size estimates

40. Compared with the use of only a starting gun or command, preparatory instructions such as "On your mark, get set, go!"
    (A) have no effect upon reaction time
    (B) shorten reaction time
    (C) lengthen reaction time
    (D) shorten reaction time for the experienced runner while lengthening it for the less-experienced one
    (E) shorten reaction time for the less-experienced runner while lengthening it for the experienced one

41. Visual and thermal reaction time
    (A) are faster when more sensory space is covered by the stimulus
    (B) are slower when more sensory space is covered by the stimulus
    (C) are not affected by more sensory space being covered by the stimulus
    (D) always occur together
    (E) depend heavily upon circadian rhythm

42. The suggestion that the drive concept be replaced with a concept of optimum level of arousal has been advanced by
    (A) Hess (B) Atkinson (C) Hebb (D) McDougall
    (E) McClelland

43. The group that contains a term *not* mentioned within Murray's list of needs is
    (A) nurturance, autonomy (B) aggression, abasement (C) dominance, affiliation (D) deference, achievement (E) passivity, destruction

44. In trapezoidal window experimentation, Allport and Pettigrew have found that the illusion is
    (A) only present among males
    (B) only present among females
    (C) only present in eastern cultures
    (D) present among all cultures
    (E) present primarily in western cultures

45. Which of the following most clearly distinguishes perception from sensation?
    (A) observation (B) sensation (C) learning (D) sensitivity
    (E) threshold

46. The term *low threshold* refers to
    (A) very few cycles per second
    (B) very low decibel level
    (C) low level of sensitivity to an incoming stimulus

(D) high level of sensitivity to an incoming stimulus
(E) virtual loss of any sensitivity to an incoming stimulus

47. A perfectly homogeneous visual environment is technically known as a
(A) Canfield (B) milieu (C) Ganzfeld (D) Bunson field
(E) Gestalt

48. *Mach bands* refer to
(A) a visual stimulus used on the color wheel
(B) an auditory stimulus used on the sound generator
(C) a measurement band on the reaction-time chronoscope
(D) the distasteful auditory reaction obtained when a sound generator reaches a specific frequency level
(E) a means for cumulative measurement of normal street noise

49. William James's theory of emotional experience held that
(A) emotions are primarily a product of learning
(B) the physical reaction causes the emotional response
(C) all responses are preceded by cognitive awareness
(D) emotional patterns are based upon inherited tendencies
(E) emotional patterns are based upon Gestalt tendencies

50. Existing research suggests that the sight of a pleasurable object causes which one of the following measurable effects?
(A) facial tics (B) blurred vision (C) pupil dilation
(D) lowered heart rate (E) lowered blood pressure

51. A split-brain monkey is taught via his right eye to select triangles but not squares. He is instructed via his left eye to select squares but not triangles. We would expect
(A) complete inability to perform either task
(B) dominance of the right-eye task
(C) dominance of the left-eye task
(D) the equivalence of a short-circuit in motor areas of the brain
(E) in single-eye vision situations, the capacity to perform without confusion the task learned by that eye

52. The concept of instinctive behavior as defined by Lorenz and Tinbergen does *not* refer to behavior patterns that
(A) are innate or develop through maturation
(B) are species-specific, that is, generally found in all members of a species and therefore characteristic of the species
(C) include young-bird experience in learning to fly
(D) include bird nestbuilding and migration
(E) are released by certain patterns of stimulation

53. The rod-and-frame test is designed to study
(A) the horizontal-vertical illusion
(B) the Ganzfeld illusion
(C) the Holzman illusion
(D) susceptibility to contextual cues
(E) the Wapner effect

54. Cannabis sativa is most commonly known as
(A) LSD (B) heroin (C) opium (D) marijuana
(E) milkweed

Questions 55–56 are based on the following diagram.

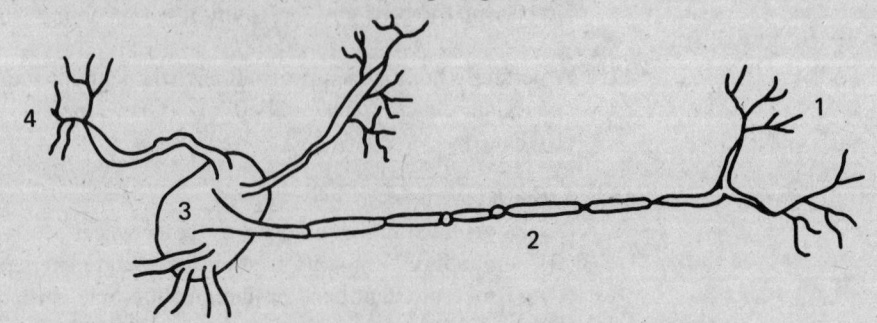

55. The dendrite-to-cell-body connection is correctly represented by which of the following?
    (A) 3–2   (B) 2–1   (C) 1–2   (D) 2–3   (E) 4–3

56. The myelin sheath would be in evidence at
    (A) 1   (B) 4   (C) 3   (D) 2   (E) 4 to 3 connecting point

57. To study and record spike activity within a specific individual fiber, researchers use
    (A) a microelectrode   (B) a trace-type chemical substance
    (C) an oscilloscope   (D) an amplifier   (E) a sonar wave

58. A person performing calculus computations has attained which one of the following stages of cognitive development?
    (A) sensori-motor operations   (B) formal operations
    (C) preoperational   (D) concrete operations   (E) abstract operations

59. Which one of the following terms is *not* generally used to describe the developmental period from ages two to six?
    (A) pregang age
    (B) age of dominance
    (C) exploration age
    (D) preschool age
    (E) age of solitary, parallel, and associative play

60. Primary work in the area of reversal and nonreversal shift has been conducted by
    (A) Miller   (B) Mowrer   (C) Kagan   (D) Kaplan
    (E) Kendler and Kendler

61. Which one of the following characteristics does an item need to be eligible for inclusion in the Stanford-Binet?
    (A) The percentage of test takers getting the item correct is positively correlated with test-taker age.
    (B) The percentage of test takers getting the item correct is negatively correlated with test-taker age.
    (C) The percentage of test takers getting the item correct is constant across all age levels.
    (D) The item has a standard deviation of less than 1.
    (E) No child below age six can answer the item correctly.

62. A change in the structure of a gene that leads to minor or major changes in an organism's physical constitution is
    (A) mitosis   (B) meiosis   (C) mastation   (D) parthenogenesis
    (E) mutation

63. According to the tenets of family constellation, which one of the following would be most eager for physical demonstrations of attention?
    (A) first-born children   (B) middle children   (C) identical twins
    (D) youngest children   (E) fraternal twins

64. Research among institutional children has revealed
    (A) strong, normal capacities for deep emotional relationships
    (B) lack of normal capacities for deep emotional relationships
    (C) easygoing, healthy personalities
    (D) a strong sense of responsibility for their actions
    (E) strong leadership tendencies

65. Tulving finds that, in a high-priority word list, the
    (A) words immediately following the high-priority word are forgotten
    (B) words immediately preceding the high-priority word are forgotten
    (C) words at the beginning of the list are forgotten
    (D) words at the end of the list are forgotten
    (E) high-priority word is forgotten

66. In the Skinner-box experiments, it has been found that, compared with animals receiving normal extinction trials, animals receiving punishment during extinction trials exhibit
    (A) fewer total responses prior to complete extinction
    (B) more total responses prior to complete extinction
    (C) the same total number of responses prior to extinction
    (D) retroactive inhibition
    (E) proactive inhibition

67. The relationship between a child's intellectual development and the age at which he first walks is
    (A) strong
    (B) moderate
    (C) nonexistent
    (D) the subject of current investigation which will probably form the basis for an established theory
    (E) believed by Wechsler to be important

68. Which one of the following would be most concerned with the development of imagery and verbal systems in the infant and how they are interwoven?
    (A) Skinner   (B) Bruner   (C) Miller   (D) Brown
    (E) McCandless

69. Acknowledging that some materials are more difficult to learn than others, which of the following would constitute an easy-to-hard spectrum?
    (A) meaningful poetry, nonsense syllables, meaningful prose, digits
    (B) nonsense syllables, meaningful poetry, digits, meaningful prose
    (C) meaningful prose, meaningful poetry, nonsense syllables, digits
    (D) meaningful poetry, meaningful prose, digits, nonsense syllables
    (E) digits, meaningful poetry, meaningful prose, nonsense syllables

70. The dog that was classically conditioned to a bell now makes the same response in the presence of a buzzer — an incidence of
    (A) response generalization   (B) stimulus generalization   (C) negative transfer   (D) reminiscence   (E) spontaneous recovery

71. The brain of the newborn
    (A) is the least-developed aspect of the child's body
    (B) is fully developed
    (C) will continue to grow in size
    (D) will continue to add brain cells, increasing its total number of cells
    (E) will not permit any reflex activity immediately after birth

72. Which one of the following would most directly affect the development of intelligence?
    (A) diet deficiency in the expectant mother
    (B) smoking by the expectant mother
    (C) premature birth
    (D) Rh factor
    (E) alcoholic beverage intake by the expectant mother

73. The square root of the sum of squared deviations from the mean, divided by the number of scores, provides
    (A) variance   (B) standard deviation   (C) z-score   (D) t-score
    (E) F-score

74. The closer the soldier gets to the bull's-eye, the more encouragement he is given by his rifle coach — an example of
    (A) stimulus discrimination and shaping
    (B) latency and feedback
    (C) stimulus generalization and feedback
    (D) retroactive facilitation and shaping
    (E) retroactive facilitation and stimulus discrimination

75. Which one of the following is most likely to enhance learner performance?
    (A) massed practice   (B) distributed practice   (C) nonsense syllables   (D) functional fixedness   (E) feedback

76. Which of the following types of learning is measured by a matching item on a test?
    (A) savings   (B) relearning   (C) recognition   (D) recall
    (E) reconstruction

77. Which one of the following is characteristic of the fetal period?
    (A) initial indications of sensitivity to stimulation
    (B) human-like physical characteristics beginning to take shape
    (C) highest susceptibility to diseases
    (D) greatest susceptibility to the effects of thalidomide
    (E) initiation of heartbeat

78. Extreme scores in a distribution most prominently affect the
    (A) mean   (B) median   (C) mode   (D) semi-interquartile range
    (E) negative skew

79. Throughout the first three months after birth, there is
    (A) an increase in day sleep and a decrease in night sleep
    (B) a decrease in day sleep and an increase in night sleep
    (C) no change in sleeping schedule
    (D) erratic sleep without identifiable pattern
    (E) increased day sleep for boys, decreased day sleep for girls

80. Menarche refers to the _____ and occurs around _____ years of age.
    (A) appearance of pubic hair; twelve
    (B) acquisition of one's final height; eighteen
    (C) ability to become pregnant; fourteen
    (D) first menstrual period; thirteen
    (E) first incidence of secondary sexual characteristics; eleven

81. Which one of the following is most characteristic of learning?
    (A) response change as a function of maturation
    (B) response change as a function of extinction
    (C) response change as a function of experience
    (D) functional fixedness
    (E) reflex action

82. Which of the following could you legitimately predict for a person with an IQ of 50?
    (A) fifth-grade level of learning
    (B) entire life spent in an institution
    (C) need for constant supervision
    (D) high-school graduation if given special instruction
    (E) no control over basic bodily functions

83. In experiments where adult subjects have been asked whether a given slide was among up to 2,500 slides viewed previously, recognition
    (A) was very poor
    (B) was virtually nonexistent
    (C) was moderately good
    (D) was extremely good
    (E) compared unfavorably with that for a similar number of words

84. Which of the following deficiencies in a pregnant mother would have the most direct and marked effect on brain metabolism and development of learning ability in her newborn?
    (A) vitamin A   (B) vitamin B   (C) vitamin C   (D) vitamin D
    (E) cholesterol

85. Newborns
    (A) cannot discriminate differences in tonal pitch
    (B) have good eye-muscle coordination
    (C) have prominent sphincter-muscle control
    (D) can detect color and shape
    (E) have keen sensitivity to pain

86. Severe anoxia at birth most likely will result in damage to the
    (A) brain   (B) lungs   (C) heart   (D) kidneys   (E) liver

87. In Mowrer's two-factor theory, avoidance responses continue when no shock is presented because
    (A) functional autonomy is operating
    (B) fear is reduced by cessation of the CS
    (C) fear is reduced by cessation of the UCS
    (D) animal drive is sufficiently high to motivate the animal in the absence of any reinforcement
    (E) higher-order conditioning has occurred

88. A continuity theory of learning suggests that learning
    (A) is on an all-or-nothing basis
    (B) is sudden
    (C) is a gradual process
    (D) continues throughout one's life
    (E) begins at birth

89. *Animal Intelligence* was a major work written by
    (A) Hull (B) Thorndike (C) Guthrie (D) Skinner
    (E) Watson

90. One boy has brown eyes. His twin brother has blue eyes. This information enables a person to conclude that the two
    (A) are identical twins
    (B) are fraternal twins
    (C) exhibit sex-linked hereditary characteristics
    (D) are monozygotic
    (E) have blue-eyed parents

91. Developmentally, which of the following refers to reduction division?
    (A) mitosis (B) heterosis (C) parthenogenesis
    (D) morphosis (E) meiosis

92. Which of the following is a correct developmental sequence?
    (A) Ovum-sperm, blastocyst, zygote
    (B) Blastocyst, ovum-sperm, zygote
    (C) Blastocyst, zygote, ovum-sperm
    (D) Ovum-sperm, zygote, blastocyst
    (E) Ovum-sperm, placenta, blastocyst

93. Among the following, the most rigorous type of validity is
    (A) face (B) split-half (C) content (D) test-retest
    (E) predictive

94. Assuming that the correlation between length of eyelashes and number of dates is +.74, which of the following would apply to the process through which the experimenter seeks to determine the number of dates for a specific girl having a given eyelash length?
    (A) correlation (B) regression (C) significance level
    (D) sampling (E) hypothesis testing

95. "Period of adolescent sterility" refers to
    (A) prepubescence in boys
    (B) the time immediately before menarche in girls
    (C) the time immediately after menarche in girls
    (D) an adolescent male's temporary sterility immediately following the attainment of sexual maturity
    (E) the postpubescent period in boys

96. Which of the following tests might ask a child what to do upon discovering a stamped, addressed, sealed envelope on the sidewalk?
    (A) Allport-Vernon-Lindzey
    (B) Tennessee Self-Concept Scale

(C) MMPI
(D) Stanford-Binet
(E) Wechsler

97. The smallest meaningful units of a language are
    (A) tacts   (B) morphologies   (C) phonemes   (D) mands
    (E) morphemes

98. During a child's first two years, his weight concept is
    (A) highly accurate
    (B) based entirely on stimulus brightness
    (C) based entirely on stimulus shape
    (D) based entirely on stimulus size
    (E) based entirely on stimulus color

99. Which one of the following instruments is most familiar to paired associates learning experiments?
    (A) pursuit rotor   (B) Skinner box   (C) visual cliff
    (D) memory drum   (E) memory slides

100. Information theory is concerned primarily with
     (A) communication   (B) extrapolation   (C) interpolation
     (D) decision making   (E) gaming

101. Which one of the following is found in newborns?
     (A) identical sleep-wakefulness time proportions
     (B) almost immediate emotional response to their mothers
     (C) fear of strangers
     (D) babbling
     (E) partial taste sensitivity

102. At what point could a newborn be expected to have the capacity for visually tracking a moving object?
     (A) immediately after birth
     (B) within a few days after birth
     (C) during the second week after birth
     (D) at the end of the first month after birth
     (E) only shortly before walking occurs

103. In Bandura's experimental work with children, he has demonstrated that
     (A) imitation learning occurs through observation
     (B) mimicking occurs through reinforcement
     (C) toilet training occurs through modeling
     (D) toilet training occurs through judicious use of punishment
     (E) aggression does not appear to be learned

104. Which of the following did Hunter find in his double alternation maze experiments?
     (A) no suggestion of imagery anywhere in the phylogenetic scale below humans
     (B) no suggestion of memory for complex events anywhere in the phylogenetic scale below humans
     (C) distinct signs of imagery and memory for complex events among rats
     (D) distinct signs of imagery and memory for complex events among raccoons
     (E) signs of imagery but no memory for complex events among rats

105. Human recall can be expected to be strongest when concerned with material that is
    (A) related to very painful experiences
    (B) opposed to one's own viewpoint
    (C) slightly pleasant
    (D) in agreement with one's own attitudes and values
    (E) slightly unpleasant

106. Eidetic imagery is
    (A) déjà vu
    (B) a step in mathematical thought
    (C) most prominent among elderly persons
    (D) highly correlated with general intelligence
    (E) a clear visual memory

107. Research on infant feeding practices indicates that
    (A) there is a clear advantage for breast-fed babies
    (B) mothers who breast feed actually tend to be rather tense about sexual matters
    (C) most women who try breast feeding soon stop for psychological reasons
    (D) the particular methods matter relatively little if the mother is sincere and comfortable with the method
    (E) there is a lower incidence of smoking among adults who were breast-fed as infants than among their bottle-fed counterparts

108. A ten-year-old child with a mental age of twelve would have an IQ of
    (A) 110   (B) 100   (C) 83   (D) 125   (E) 120

109. Which one of the following statements about IQ scores is true?
    (A) There is a strong correlation of IQ test scores throughout the entire life span.
    (B) The highest validity is found in early IQ test scores.
    (C) There is a negative correlation between early and later test scores.
    (D) The highest reliability and lowest validity are found in early test scores.
    (E) There is virtually no predictive validity between scores obtained prior to age two and those obtained at a later age.

110. At certain points in the Guilford model for problem solving, exit is indicated. An exit following production would indicate
    (A) rejection of the problem
    (B) erroneous solution
    (C) that the problem is insoluble
    (D) that the person has given up
    (E) sequence termination

111. Which one of the following is *not* specifically an aid to retention?
    (A) chunking
    (B) overlearning
    (C) meaningfulness
    (D) knowledge of results
    (E) associating a mental picture or scene with the verbal material

112. In which one of the following areas does an older person have the greatest likelihood of demonstrating increases in intelligence?
    (A) digit span   (B) pursuit rotor   (C) block design   (D) spatial relations   (E) vocabulary

113. Research evidence suggests that in the final aspects of the fetal stage
    (A) extreme pain sensitivity is present
    (B) capability exists only for reflex movements
    (C) capability exists for learning simple responses
    (D) a "quiet period" sets in during which detectable motor movements are very rare
    (E) the basics of newborn vocal sound can be detected

114. Which of the following is *not* part of a computer instructional program?
    (A) sequential steps
    (B) immediate knowledge of results
    (C) supplementary questions prompted by wrong answers
    (D) "branching"
    (E) interlocution

115. Childhood accidents are
    (A) more prevalent in the second year than in the first year
    (B) more prevalent in the first year than in the second year
    (C) prevalent with equal incidence in both the first and second years
    (D) more frequent among girls than among boys
    (E) more prevalent in the first six months after birth than thereafter

116. Which one of the following elements would invariably be present in Type I error?
    (A) rejection of a null hypothesis
    (B) acceptance of a null hypothesis
    (C) one-tailed test
    (D) two-tailed test
    (E) establishment of a significance level below .05

Questions 117–120 are based on the following diagrams.

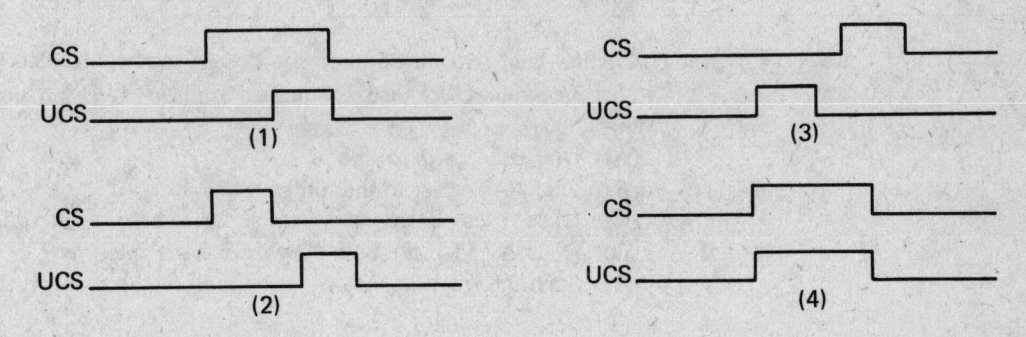

Note: Onset is indicated at the point where the CS and UCS lines move upward from their baselines.

117. The most efficient conditioning paradigm is _____.
    (A) 1   (B) 2   (C) 3   (D) 4   (E) 5

118. The least efficient conditioning paradigm is _____.
    (A) 1   (B) 2   (C) 3   (D) 4   (E) 5

119. The trace conditioning method is _____.
    (A) 1   (B) 2   (C) 3   (D) 4   (E) 5

120. The delayed conditioning method is _____.
    (A) 1   (B) 2   (C) 3   (D) 4   (E) 5

121. On a five-item Guttman Scale, a person has a score of 3. To fulfill unidimensionality requirements, this person would be in agreement with items
    (A) 1, 3, 5   (B) 1, 3, 4   (C) 1, 2, 3   (D) 2, 4, 5
    (E) 1, 4, 5

122. Correctional institutions are finding which one of the following to be the most effective rehabilitative device?
    (A) punishment
    (B) isolation
    (C) positive reinforcement
    (D) negative reinforcement
    (E) threat of the electric chair or gas chamber

123. Goldstein's organismic theory is *not* characterized by
    (A) a unified view of the organism
    (B) a nomothetic approach
    (C) the idea of man striving to reach his inherent potential
    (D) development being seen as the unfolding of inherited potential
    (E) Leibnitzian emphasis

124. Erikson's trust-versus-mistrust stage occurs during
    (A) middle childhood   (B) early adulthood   (C) infancy
    (D) early childhood   (E) middle adulthood

125. The most broadly used personality assessment instrument among the following is the
    (A) TAT   (B) MMPI   (C) Rorschach   (D) Draw-a-Man
    (E) Allport-Vernon-Lindzey

126. Circular Dial A contains three equidistant sections labeled *hot, safe, cold;* Circular Dial B contains clockwise calibrations from zero to 500. Human engineering suggests that
    (A) Dial B is easier to interpret
    (B) Dial A is easier to interpret
    (C) Dials A and B are equivalent as far as ease of interpretation
    (D) Dials A and B are both very difficult to interpret
    (E) Such information should not be presented on circular dials

127. Which one of the following criteria would be utilized to differentiate "hot" from "cool" media in McLuhan's definitional framework?
    (A) verbal message combined with pictures
    (B) capacity to present pictures in motion
    (C) amount of information conveyed
    (D) shock potential of the medium
    (E) political potential of the medium

128. Freud believed that dreams are caused by
    (A) sexual-aggressive forces, unacceptable to waking consciousness
    (B) rapid eye movements
    (C) the continuation of waking thoughts
    (D) conscious effort
    (E) anxiety-laden events of the current day

129. Which one of the following pairs contains *unrelated* terms?
    (A) thanatos – eros
    (B) script – contract
    (C) endomorph – ectomorph
    (D) propium – functional autonomy
    (E) parapraxes – anima

130. Which one of the following would be most likely to use the term *ergs* in discussing personality concepts?
    (A) Eysenck   (B) Cattell   (C) Jung   (D) Rogers
    (E) Goldstein

131. When the government first began citing statistics correlating lung cancer with cigarette smoking, which of the following statements was a frequent answer from the cigarette manufacturers?
    (A) The tests were biased.
    (B) Representative samples had not been selected.
    (C) The research lacked a control group.
    (D) Correlation does not mean causation.
    (E) Research was performed only on males.

132. A correct sequential or developmental order is represented by
    (A) ego, superego, id
    (B) anal, oral, phallic
    (C) inferiority feeling, superiority striving
    (D) autonomy versus shame and doubt; trust versus mistrust
    (E) parataxic, prototaxic, syntaxic

133. In a communications diagram, noise is
    (A) any variation in the message received, not predictable at its source
    (B) any variation in the message received, predictable at its source
    (C) only possible at the transmitter
    (D) only possible in channel
    (E) only possible within the receiver

134. Wolfgang takes the position that within American society
    (A) violence has been legitimized
    (B) TV violence has had a wholesome effect on children
    (C) watching football games provides catharsis
    (D) general observance of violence reduces one's likelihood of performing it
    (E) the mental health field has been very progressive in its acceptance of violence-related programming

Questions 135–138 are based on the following questionnaire excerpt.

Under some conditions, war is necessary to maintain justice. (7.5)
The benefits of war rarely pay for its losses even for the victor. (3.5)
War brings out the best qualities in men. (9.7)
There is no conceivable justification for war. (.2)

135. The above items along with their numbers and decimals are part of a (an)
    (A) Likert Scale   (B) Thurstone Scale   (D) Osgood Scale
    (D) Bogardus Scale   (E) Remmers Scale

136. A subject obtaining a high score on a scale of this type (in comparison with a low-scoring subject) would be
    (A) much more prowar
    (B) much less in favor of war
    (C) essentially the same in war viewpoint
    (D) strongly antiwar
    (E) moderately antiwar

137. To be selected for inclusion in this scale, a statement must meet the criterion of
    (A) high standard deviation in judge ratings
    (B) moderate standard deviation in judge ratings
    (C) low standard deviation in judge ratings
    (D) high mean rating among judges
    (E) low mean rating among judges

138. The numbers in parentheses
    (A) represent the mean of ratings assigned to this statement by a large number of judges
    (B) represent the mode of ratings assigned to this statement by a large number of judges
    (C) represent the average rating assigned to similar statements by a large number of judges
    (D) are determined and assigned by the experimenter
    (E) are determined and assigned by the subject

139. Which one of the following combinations would, by definition, be necessary to have an attitude?
    (A) enduring system, feeling component
    (B) temporary system, cognitive component
    (C) stereotype system, action component
    (D) modification system, behavioral component
    (E) action system, temporary component

140. According to the findings of Lewin, Lippitt, and White, which of the following leadership styles would create the highest group productivity when the leader is absent?
    (A) autocratic
    (B) democratic
    (C) laissez-faire
    (D) laissez-faire or autocratic (equally productive)
    (E) laissez-faire or democratic (equally productive)

141. When two people play nonzero sum games, there is a tendency for
    (A) cooperation
    (B) competition
    (C) high level of trust
    (D) matrices renovation
    (E) threat potential to enhance cooperation

142. In Sheldon's classification system, the slender, nervous person who is extremely sensitive to pain would come within the category of
    (A) endomorph   (B) mesomorph   (C) ectomorph
    (D) somatomorph   (E) neuromorph

143. Person A has lied for a $1 payoff while Person B told a similar lie for $20. Person B is
    (A) less likely to believe the lie
    (B) more likely to believe the lie
    (C) equivalent to Person A in belief likelihood
    (D) experiencing more cognitive dissonance
    (E) experiencing more cognitive irrelevance

144. When pilots must learn to fly a new type of passenger plane, their transfer to the new set of controls is facilitated most when the new panel
    (A) is similar to but has subtle functional differences from the old panel
    (B) is distinctly different from the old panel in all respects
    (C) looks identical but has some functions that are the exact reverse of what they were in the previous setting
    (D) is an exact right-left reverse of the previous panel
    (E) is an exact copy of the previous panel except that all dial calibrations are reversed

145. Which one of the following lists does *not* contain a name associated with need in personality theory?
    (A) Murray, McClelland, Bandura
    (B) Jung, Murray, Eysenck
    (C) Eysenck, Maslow, Jung
    (D) Maslow, Freud, Bandura
    (E) Freud, Bandura, Jung

146. Which one of the following statements would *not* be a firmly based criticism of psychoanalysis?
    (A) It is heavily based upon subjective, clinical observation.
    (B) It places an overemphasis upon instinctual behavior.
    (C) It places heavy emphasis upon abnormal behavior.
    (D) It stresses intrapsychic, nonobservable emotions.
    (E) It places primary emphasis upon changing the current problem behavior.

147. Which one of the following pairs is incorrect?
    (A) Mowrer – two-factor theory
    (B) Rogers – contract
    (C) Jung – shadow
    (D) Adler – superiority striving
    (E) Sullivan – interpersonal relationships

148. As viewed by phenomenologists, which of the following does *not* affect personality in any tangible way?
    (A) past perceptions
    (B) the length of time a person has been exposed to a given perceptual environment
    (C) the person's perceptual outlook brought to the experiencing of external events
    (D) early childhood relationships to family
    (E) archetypal continuities

149. In Newcomb's theoretical model, which one of the following statements is correct?
    (A) An even number of negative signs indicates balance.
    (B) An odd number of negative signs indicates balance.
    (C) Three negative signs indicate balance.
    (D) Four negative signs indicate balance.
    (E) Two positive signs indicate balance.

150. Emotional problems are treated through role-playing techniques in
(A) psychodrama (B) client-centered therapy (C) implosive therapy
(D) logotherapy (E) psychoanalysis

151. Kallmann finds the highest incidence of schizophrenia
(A) between fraternal twins (B) between identical twins (C) between siblings (D) in the southeastern United States (E) in urban areas

152. Which one of the following name sequences contains *no* mental hospital reformers?
(A) Clifford Beers, Sigmund Freud
(B) Eric Fromm, Carl Rogers
(C) William Tuke, Hans Hartmann
(D) Dorothea Dix, Alfred Adler
(E) George Miller, Dorothea Dix

153. Relaxation followed by successive approximation to objects formerly feared is
(A) aversive conditioning (B) fear conditioning (C) systematic desensitization (D) implosive therapy (E) environmental shock therapy

154. A form of group therapy in which the therapist lectures and leads discussions is
(A) inspirational (B) release (C) didactic (D) nondirective
(E) abreaction

155. Long-term follow-up studies of patients treated through behavior modification techniques indicate
(A) high rates of relapse among practically all patients
(B) high rates of relapse among neurotic patients
(C) high rates of relapse among hypochondriacal patients
(D) few relapses
(E) a low, marginal level of effective life functioning

156. Which one of the following constitutes a distinction between conversion reaction and psychosomatic disorder?
(A) detectable physiological problems (B) learning disability
(C) brain damage (D) illusions (E) delusions

157. A process has just been completed in which items were sorted into groups on the basis of color. This sorting process is known as
(A) qualitative classification (B) quantitative classification
(C) paired comparisons (D) rank-order correlation (E) matching

Questions 158–159 are based on the following statistical information.

95% — use a z-score of 1.96
99% — use a z-score of 2.58

158. For one hundred scores on a given test, the mean is 74 and the standard deviation, 8. The 95 percent confidence interval for the mean of the population is
(A) 72.4 to 75.6 (B) 71.8 to 75 (C) 70.5 to 73.7
(D) 71 to 74.2 (E) 70 to 73.2

159. The 99 percent confidence interval for the mean of the population is
(A) 69.8 to 74 (B) 70 to 74.2 (C) 71.9 to 76.1
(D) 72.5 to 76.7 (E) 73 to 77.2

160. A researcher sits beside a playground, carefully observing a small group of children. The method being utilized is
  (A) life-history (B) case-history (C) laboratory (D) survey
  (E) field-study

161. A therapist working with a patient suffering from multiple personality will
  (A) use electroconvulsive shock therapy to rid the person of all memories of these personalities
  (B) often resort to LSD
  (C) treat each personality as distinct and separate
  (D) seek, through psychotherapy, to eliminate all personalities and build a new one
  (E) resort to implosive therapy

162. Which one of the following would probably *not* be part of the treatment program for someone diagnosed as having an affective psychotic reaction?
  (A) tranquilizing drugs
  (B) electroconvulsive shock
  (C) attendant protection against self-inflicted wounds
  (D) recreational therapy
  (E) LSD therapy

163. Which one of the following reactions would *not* be considered psychoneurotic?
  (A) asthenic (B) affective (C) phobic (D) conversion
  (E) dissociative

164. Functional mental disorders are prompted by
  (A) brain-wave malfunctioning
  (B) abnormal blood supplies to the brain
  (C) organic brain damage
  (D) malnutrition
  (E) unknown causes

165. Which one of the following has *not* been categorized among psychophysiologic disorders?
  (A) stomach ulcers (B) asthma (C) migraines
  (D) neurodermatitis (E) skin cancer

166. Which one of the following findings has been voiced in the past few years by notable mental health professionals?
  (A) Lack of warm social approval is in no way related to disease susceptibility.
  (B) Disease prevention is not dependent on diet.
  (C) Disease prevention is not dependent on exercise.
  (D) Married men have a higher death-rate incidence than their divorced male counterparts.
  (E) Geographical locations with the highest heart disease rate also have the highest rates of cancer incidence.

167. A person expressing functional blindness could be experiencing a
  (A) dissociative reaction (B) conversion reaction (C) paranoid reaction (D) depression reaction (E) psychosomatic reaction

168. Behaviorists would *not* consider counterconditioning an appropriate therapeutic technique for
  (A) anxiety reactions (B) chronic tensions (C) inhibitions
  (D) transvestism (E) phobias

169. Which one of the following is the *least* likely cause of homosexuality?
    (A) lack of opportunity for heterosexual relationships
    (B) homosexual seduction
    (C) fear of the opposite sex
    (D) impotence
    (E) gratifying homosexual experience in middle childhood

170. A thirsty cat approaches his milk and receives a noxious blast of air — most likely an experiment by
    (A) Harlow   (B) Scott   (C) Hess   (D) Webb
    (E) Masserman

171. Which of the following would *not* characterize any form of sociopathic personality disturbance?
    (A) emotional shallowness   (B) antisocial behavior   (C) dyssocial behavior   (D) depression   (E) rebellion against society

172. Repression : suppression ::
    (A) classical : instrumental
    (B) semiautomatic : automatic
    (C) fixation : regression
    (D) frustration : conflict
    (E) involuntary : voluntary

173. Which of the following is the *most* common psychoneurotic disorder?
    (A) anxiety reaction   (B) conversion reaction   (C) asthenic reaction
    (D) conversion hysteria   (E) depression reaction

174. Raker's analysis of reaction to a civilian catastrophe does *not* contain which of the following stages?
    (A) shock   (B) suggestible   (C) recovery   (D) possible delayed traumatic neurosis   (E) panic

175. Which of the following would be considered the *least* important factor in a therapist's success rate?
    (A) personality theory orientation   (B) amount of experience
    (C) capacity for empathy   (D) genuineness   (E) warmth

176. When told, "Your father has died," an institutionalized child, even though she loved her father very much, responded by giggling — a characteristic of
    (A) affective reaction   (B) hebephrenic schizophrenia   (C) catatonic schizophrenia   (D) paranoid schizophrenia   (E) simple schizophrenia

177. In a positively skewed distribution, the median is
    (A) larger than the mean   (B) equal to the mean   (C) equal to the mode
    (D) larger than the mode   (E) actually negatively skewed

178. Given limited funds and a limited time period, which of the following methods might be recommended for dealing with a phobic reaction?
    (A) psychoanalysis   (B) transcendental meditation   (C) systematic desensitization   (D) logotherapy   (E) ego analysis

179. As the industrial psychologist deals with physical conditions relating to the work setting, which of the following is of *least* significance?
    (A) illumination (B) heat and humidity (C) noise (D) space arrangements (E) coffee-break intervals

180. In the classic Hawthorne plant study at Western Electric, results pointed to the critical importance of
    (A) supervisor dominance
    (B) employer's concern toward workers
    (C) timing and frequency of coffee breaks
    (D) employing only females for work in the plant
    (E) employing only highly skilled workers

181. The mean of a group of scores is 50 and the standard deviation, 10. What percentage of the people taking this test will score between 10 and 60?
    (A) 16 percent (B) 50 percent (C) 64 percent
    (D) 84 percent (E) 98 percent

Questions 182–183 are based on the following percentile ranks in a normal distribution.

    (1) 2nd
    (2) 16th
    (3) 84th
    (4) 98th
    (5) none of the above

182. Which one of the above percentile ranks would correspond to a z-score of -1.0?
    (A) 1 (B) 2 (C) 3 (D) 4 (E) 5

183. Which one of the above percentile ranks would correspond to a z-score of $+3.0$?
    (A) 1 (B) 2 (C) 3 (D) 4 (E) 5

184. To predict vocational interest you would be well advised to turn to which of the following?
    (A) 16 PF (B) MMPI (C) Rorschach (D) Strong
    (E) Pintner-Patterson

185. A test score which has *not* been converted into a form permitting comparison with scores from other tests is known as a
    (A) stanine score (B) percentile score (C) raw score
    (D) z-score (E) quartile score

186. Which one of the following has *not* been used as an industrial method at the supervisor-management levels?
    (A) case method (B) incident method (C) sensitivity-training method
    (D) free-association method (E) role-playing method

187. Human engineers estimate that the best room temperature for moderately heavy work extending over two to four hours to be in range of
    (A) 55–60 degrees (B) 80–90 degrees (C) 90–95 degrees
    (D) 65–70 degrees (E) 75–80 degrees

188. The most reliable public opinion polling is that which
  (A) accompanies census bureau statistics
  (B) was done for the Kinsey report
  (C) private firms conduct prior to a political election
  (D) detergent firms conduct concerning product satisfaction
  (E) gasoline companies conduct to learn about driving habits

189. If the double alternation experimentation is representative of comparative experiments in the learning area, it would be fair to say that
  (A) animals cannot think
  (B) most lower animals can think
  (C) only humans have thought-type mental capacities
  (D) some animals high on the phylogenetic scale demonstrate thought-type mental capacities
  (E) rats have strong capacities for thought-type processes

190. To make a green costume stand out most vividly on stage, which one of the following colors would be the most appropriate for lighting?
  (A) orange   (B) red   (C) violet   (D) pink   (E) blue

191. The members of the training group each read several pages of description dealing with a managerial dilemma and the way in which it was dealt with by an individual. The method being used with the group is
  (A) case   (B) incident   (C) role playing   (D) sensitivity training
  (E) free association

192. Which one of the following persons could be expected to have the most lasting command of examination material (assuming equal study time and ability)?
  (A) one who engaged solely in rote memory
  (B) one who studied the material in one massed session
  (C) one who studied all the material silently
  (D) one who recited portions of the material periodically
  (E) one who listened to the material on a cassette recorder

193. One of the first steps for a psychologist assigned to develop selection procedures for a specific job would be to
  (A) develop an intelligence test
  (B) develop a test for creativity
  (C) develop a test for musical aptitude
  (D) examine a test for manual dexterity
  (E) examine the tasks of that specific job

194. Human engineering principles indicate that the best type of cockpit display panel
  (A) makes minimum use of shape
  (B) makes minimum use of color
  (C) maximally uses both shape and color
  (D) maximally uses only size, minimizing shape and color
  (E) maximally uses only position, minimizing shape and color

195. To determine the values of a specific group, the best procedure among the following would be the
  (A) Stanford-Binet   (B) Wechsler   (C) Otis
  (D) Allport-Vernon-Lindzey   (E) Doll

196. A company wishes to market a new product and has the natural desire to get large consumer subscription to it. The cognitive dissonance research results of Doob et al. recommend which of the following pricing approaches?
(A) price initially below the eventual price
(B) price initially well above the eventual price
(C) price initially at the eventual price level
(D) price identically with the largest competitors, regardless of their existing prices
(E) price regionally rather than nationally set

197. In a randomly selected sample, the following distribution was obtained:

Sex	Democrat	Republican
Male	65	35
Female	30	20

To test the hypothesis that the two discrete variables (sex, political party) are independent in the population that yielded the sample, we should use
(A) a t-test   (B) regression statistics   (C) a z-test
(D) chi-square   (E) Duncan's multiple-range test

198. Assuming that a multitude of equal-sized, random samples are gathered from the same infinite population, the mean of each sample is computed, and the means of the different samples are put together to form a new distribution; which one of the following statements about the new distribution is true?
(A) The mean would be greater than the median or the mode.
(B) The distribution would be normal.
(C) The distribution would be positively skewed.
(D) The standard deviation would equal 1.0.
(E) The distribution would be negatively skewed.

199. "The mean of the squared differences from the mean of the distribution" is a definition of
(A) mode   (B) platikurtic   (C) chi-square   (D) variance
(E) t-distribution

200. According to the research of Janis, Kaye, et al., which one of the following activities would be most likely to establish persuasiveness in a written communication?
(A) reading while in a very relaxed position
(B) reading while watching TV
(C) eating while reading
(D) talking while reading
(E) listening to music while reading

Test 3: Answer Comments

1. (D) The adrenal medulla has this emergency preparatory function for the human body.

2. (D) Saturation is a descriptive term specifically related to color.

3. (C) After shock had been discontinued, rats placed on the former shock side would demonstrate escape behavior indefinitely.

4. (A) Neuron rest or conduction is determined by the ionic flux of electrically charged ions.

5. (C) As the amplitude of GSR increases across trial blocks for tone 2, a corresponding pattern of response decrease across trial blocks is evident for tone 1 — events indicative of strong negative correlation.

6. (D) The conditioned stimulus in the experiment was tone.

7. (B) Stimulus discrimination was evident across trial blocks. The pattern described in the explanation accompanying question 5 gives strong indication that the subjects were making prominent discrimination between the two tones.

8. (E) Within the parietal lobe, the somesthetic cortex is responsible for the skin and kinesthetic senses.

9. (D) Convergence is a very slight crossing of the eyes as they focus upon an object. This focus on the object from two slightly different locations provides depth perception cues.

10. (C) These epinephrine studies vividly demonstrated the potential effects of external suggestion upon experienced emotion.

11. (D) As distinguished from emotions, moods last longer and are less intense.

12. (D) Negative after-image is the visual experience of a color complementary to the one that a person has just experienced. It suggests, in trichromatic theory terms, that the color-specific cones not activated during initial color viewing have now become active.

13. (B) Subsequent sleep exhibits a marked tendency toward increased stage 1-REM dreaming as if to make up for prior deprivation.

14. (B) A high concentration of positive ions in the cell body of a neuron places the neuron in a conducting state.

15. (C) Striated muscles provide skeletal movement. The other two types are smooth muscles (associated with visceral response) and the heart muscle.

16. (B) This is one of the behavioral phenomena in rats for which Spence is best known. There appears to be a need for the rat to completely extinguish his initial response before the second (alternate) response can be learned effectively.

17. (E) Primitive emotion control rests in the hypothalamus.

18. (A) Speech-related functions are localized in the left cerebral hemisphere.

19. (C) While closure, grouping, contrast, and phi phenomenon are stimulus-related perceptual phenomena, divergence is a "clunker" inserted to trip the uninformed.

20. (C) The letters GSR mean Galvanic Skin Response, a measure of change in the electrical resistance of the skin (a change produced by sweat-gland activity).

21. (B) Pioneering, classic experiments by Stratton in 1897 demonstrated the human visual system's surprising capacity to adapt (in effect, reinvert the perceptual field) when a person wears inversion goggles for a period of several days.

22. (D) *Purposive Behavior in Animals and Men* is Tolman's major work.

23. (A) Secreted by the thyroid gland, thyroxin is integral to the functions of body metabolism and physical growth.

24. (A) Snow seen as white in both sunlight and shadow is a demonstration of brightness constancy. The visual stimuli themselves are not uniformly and equivalently white.

25. (D) Muscles stretch the lens for distant-object vision and allow the lens to get "fatter" for near-object vision; this is accommodation.

26. (B) The EEG is a brain wave pattern obtained from electrodes attached to various parts of the scalp.

27. (C) Selye developed the concept of the general adaptation syndrome. The body's reaction under stress occurs in the three major stages — alarm reaction, resistance, and exhaustion.

28. (C) The absence of stimulation has produced within subjects an inability to endure the setting despite appealing remuneration.

29. (B) In contrast with time perception where no significant effort is being devoted to task completion, time passage seems much slower where significant effort is being devoted to a completion goal.

30. (A) The physical location of the human ears, on opposite sides of the head, is critical to the determination of sound directionality.

31. (B) Primaries in subtractive (pigment) color mixing are blue, yellow, and red. For additive (light) color mixing, the primaries are blue, green, and red.

32. (C) The sympathetic nervous system controls bodily response to emergency situations.

33. (A) The number of stimulus-response connections is a concept of Thorndike's Law of Exercise.

34. (A) Relaxation with wakefulness but closed eyes should produce a predominance of alpha waves.

35. (C) The same behavior (return to his native country) has within it both reinforcing and punishing aspects — approach-avoidance conflict.

36. (B) Animal experiments (Teitelbaum et al.) reveal that animals have a tendency to keep their caloric intake constant.

37. (E) The hypothalamus is commonly referred to as the seat of emotion.

38. (D) Among the hormones listed, the distinctly male sex hormone is androgen.

39. (C) In the classic Bruner and Postman study, poor children overestimated the size of specific coins — apparently demonstrating that these children perceived them as being more valuable than rich children did.

40. (B) Preparatory instruction serves to shorten reaction time.

41. (A) Visual and thermal reaction times prove faster when more sensory space is covered by the stimulus.

42. (C) It is Hebb's desire to replace the drive concept with an optimum-level-of-arousal concept.

43. (E) Murray does not speak of a destruction need.

44. (E) The trapezoidal window illusion has been most evident in western cultures — perhaps a function of a "carpentered" perceptual world.

45. (C) Perception relates the present sensation to prior perceptual experience.

46. (D) Low threshold suggests a high level of sensitivity to an incoming stimulus.

47. (C) *Ganzfeld* is a perceptual term describing a perfectly homogenous visual environment.

48. (A) The *Mach band* is a three-pointed black stimulus on a white background. When spinning, it produces the perceptual effect of a dark ring midway between the center and the periphery of a disc.

49. (B) The James-Lange theory expresses the view that physical reaction prompts emotional response rather than vice versa.

50. (C) Pupil dilation is a prominent current measure of pleasurable object perception.

51. (E) Whereas two-eye vision can cause performance confusion, single-eye vision preserves the separation necessary to perform without confusion.

52. (C) Lorenz and Tinbergen's concept of instinctive behavior does not include behaviors that are primarily learned.

53. (D) The frame can give a false impression of horizontal-vertical, hindering contextual, cue-dependent persons from accurate vertical rod judgment.

54. (D) Cannabis sativa is a technical name for marijuana.

55. (E) 4–3 on the drawing represents the dendrite-to-cell-body connection.

56. (D) The myelin sheath would be in evidence at the axon (2 on the drawing).

57. (A) For research in neuronal physiology, experimenters use microelectrodes to study and record spike activity within a specific individual fiber.

58. (B) In Piaget's system, calculus computations have the cognitive complexity of formal operations.

59. (B) Although the period from ages two to six has been called pregang, preschool, exploration, and the time of solitary-parallel-associative-play sequence, it has not been called a period of dominance.

60. (E) Kendler and Kendler has been the most prominent research team in the investigation of reversal and nonreversal shift.

61. (A) For inclusion in the Stanford-Binet, the percentage of correct responses to a test item must be positively correlated with the ages of the test takers.

62. (E) Gene mutation can produce either minor or major changes in the organism's physical characteristics.

63. (B) In family constellation aspects of personality theory, the middle child is often described as the forgotten child (an Adler concept), therefore the prime candidate for receptiveness to physical demonstrations of attention.

64. (B) Research among institutional children has revealed a lack of normal capacity for deep emotional relationships. Although this finding does not characterize all institutions, it is disturbingly frequent.

65. (B) In his retrograde amnesia work, Tulving finds that words immediately preceding the high-priority word are forgotten.

66. (C) Skinner has found that punishment during extinction trials produces the same total number of responses as are found in extinction trials without punishment — evidence of an immediate but not long-range deterrent effect.

67. (C) The age of initial walking in no way relates to a child's intelligence.

68. (B) Bruner is prominently concerned with the development of imagery and verbal systems in the young child, having equal concern for their developmental relationships.

69. (D) As revealed in a pioneering experiment by Lyon, the most meaningful item is the easiest to learn: meaningful poetry, meaningful prose, digits, nonsense syllables.

70. (B) Response now being made to a stimulus similar to that present during original conditioning is an example of stimulus generalization.

71. (C) Though it will not gain brain cells, the brain of the newborn will continue to grow in size after birth.

72. (A) Maternal diet deficiency during the embryonic period could be critically detrimental to the development of intelligence.

73. (B) A standard deviation is obtained by taking the square root of the sum of squared deviations from the mean and dividing by the number of scores.

74. (A) By encouraging the soldier when he approximates the bull's-eye, the coach gives the soldier critical feedback about his approach to the desired stimulus (stimulus discrimination) and the appropriate response (shaping).

75. (E) Learner performance is most enhanced by immediate knowledge of results (feedback).

76. (E) The matching test item deals with ability to reconstruct an association (reconstruction-type learning).

77. (A) Researchers have found indications of sensitivity to stimulation during the fetal period.

78. (A) The mean is most dramatically affected by extreme scores because it is, in effect, an average.

79. (B) During the first three months after birth, the newborn shows a noticeable increase in night sleep and a decrease in day sleep.

80. (D) Menarche refers to the first menstrual period; occurring generally during the thirteenth year.

81. (C) Learning encompasses the elements of response change as a function of experience.

82. (A) A person with an IQ of 50 (mildly retarded) could be expected to complete a fifth-grade level of learning by adulthood.

83. (D) Experiments demonstrate that recognition ability for pictures is extremely strong.

84. (B) Several B vitamins serve as coenzymes in brain metabolism; vitamin B deficiencies in pregnant women have been found to impair the learning abilities of their children.

85. (D) Stimulus discrimination research with newborns suggests that the infants can detect both color and shape.

86. (A) Severe anoxia at birth (interruption of oxygen supply) could result in brain damage.

87. (B) Fear reduction functions as a negative reinforcement, perpetuating the avoidance response.

88. (C) Continuity theory (in contrast to all-or-none views) suggests that learning is a gradual process. Differences between recognition and recall learning support this position.

89. (B) *Animal Intelligence* was Thorndike's major work.

90. (B) Only two separate zygotes could produce one brown-eyed and one blue-eyed twin (fraternal twins).

91. (E) Meiosis refers to reduction division in which chromosome pairs separate, with one set going to one new cell and the remaining set to the other.

92. (D) Ovum-sperm, zygote, blastocyst is a correct developmental sequence.

93. (E) Predictive validity is the most rigorous form of validity. It is because the GRE has predictive validity that you and your "ancestors" have had to take it.

94. (B) Regression would deal with establishing the best prediction for an individual case based on a known general correlation.

95. (C) Immediately after menarche, a girl is incapable of conception — the time period known as adolescent sterility.

96. (D) The general comprehension section of the Stanford-Binet contains this item.

97. (E) The smallest meaningful units of a language are called morphemes.

98. (D) During the first two years of development, a child bases his weight concept on stimulus size. A large box, therefore, is seen as heavier than a small box.

99. (D) The memory drum is an integral part of paired-associates experimentation.

100. (A) Information theory relates directly to processes involved in verbal communication.

101. (E) Newborns have a partially developed taste sensitivity and corresponding taste preferences that will change as their sensitivity develops further.

102. (B) The capacity for visually tracking a moving object appears in the newborn a few days after birth.

103. (A) Bandura's research has centered upon observational learning and points to the strength of imitation learning achieved by children through the observation process.

104. (D) Although no evidence of imagery or memory for complex events was found among rats, Hunter found significant suggestions of its presence among raccoons. The double alternation maze requires an animal to remember what response it has made on the preceding two trials.

105. (D) A person's selective memory is weighted most heavily toward material that is in agreement with his own attitudes and values.

106. (E) Eidetic imagery refers to a clear visual memory. In its most extreme form it would be demonstrated by the person described as having a photographic memory.

107. (D) The mother's sincerity and warmth in the child relationship overshadows the feeding method in importance.

108. (E) MA/CA is 12/10, which is then multiplied by 100 to produce 120.

109. (E) Scores obtained prior to age two are most aptly called the Developmental Quotient, which bears no predictive validity for the later Intelligence Quotient.

110. (E) In the Guilford model for problem solving, the production step signals termination of a sequence.

111. (D) Knowledge of results is an aid to learning acquisition rather than to retention.

112. (E) The vocabulary or verbal information areas offer the greatest possibility for an older person to demonstrate increases in intelligence.

113. (C) Classical conditioning has been achieved late in the fetal stage, demonstrating that the fetus has a capacity for learning simple responses.

114. (E) Computer instructional programs include sequential steps, immediate knowledge of results, supplementary questions when wrong answers are given, and "branching." Interlocution is a "clunker" for the unsuspecting.

115. (A) Childhood accidents are more prevalent in the second year than in the first — which is at least partially attributable to the youngsters' increased mobility.

116. (A) Type I error would be mistaken rejection of a null hypothesis. Type II error is mistaken acceptance of a null hypothesis.

117. (A) Diagram 1 is delayed conditioning, the most efficient classical conditioning method.

118. (C) Diagram 3 is backwards conditioning, totally inefficient.

119. (B) Diagram 2 is the trace conditioning method, next in efficiency to delayed conditioning but having the disadvantage of requiring memory of CS onset.

120. (A) As explained in question 117.

121. (C) Guttman's concept of unidimensionality would require a score of 3 to reflect agreement with items 1, 2, and 3.

122. (C) Positive reinforcement has proved most effective in attaining desired long-range behavioral change. Punishment has been ineffective in attaining this goal.

123. (B) The nomothetic approach involves establishing personality elements (such as id impulse) that are then applied uniformly to all individuals. Goldstein's emphasis on the inherited potential of the organism does not take the nomothetic approach.

124. (C) Erikson's trust versus mistrust stage occurs in the earliest mother-child social interaction related to feeding.

125. (B) The MMPI (Minnesota Multiphasic Personality Inventory) is the most rigorously objective of these personality assessment instruments and the most widely used among them.

126. (B) Human engineers consider a three-section circular dial easier to interpret than the strictly numerical circular dial.

127. (C) The amount of information conveyed distinguishes "hot" from "cool" media in McLuhan's definitional framework. Books and articles are considered "hot" media, but TV is a "cool" medium.

128. (A) Freud believed that sexual-aggressive forces could be expressed within dreams because the relaxed state of sleep lowered the defenses against these forces that normally existed within the wakeful state.

129. (E) *Parapraxes* is a Freudian term relating to slips of the tongue, and *anima* is a Jungian term describing man's bisexual nature.

130. (B) Cattell speaks of instincts and needs in terms of *ergs* and *sentiments*.

131. (D) It was in the cigarette manufacturers' best interests to suggest that correlation does not mean causation but, rather, only shows a relationship between two observed events.

132. (C) Adler believed that inferiority feelings develop early in life through interaction with adults. Superiority striving is the consequence.

133. (A) Generally occurring within channel, *noise* is a communications term referring to any variation in the message received, not predictable at its source.

134. (A) A prominent sociologist and former head of a presidential commission to study the problem of violence, Wolfgang takes the position that violence has been legitimized in American society.

135. (B) These statements are part of a Thurstone Scale designed to measure attitudes toward war.

136. (A) A high-scoring subject would be more prowar than a low-scoring subject.

137. (C) To be acceptable for inclusion in a Thurstone Scale, an item must have low variability (low standard deviation) in judge ratings.

138. (A) The numbers in parentheses reflect the mean of all judge ratings of this statement.

139. (A) Attitudes are enduring systems that contain both cognitive (knowledge) and affective (feeling) components manifested in behavior.

140. (B) Democratic leadership groups proved most productive in a leader-absent setting.

141. (B) In the nonzero sum game, where both persons can experience simultaneous gains or losses, there is a tendency for competition to develop.

142. (C) Sheldon's system contains three body-type-related entries: endomorph (plump), mesomorph (athletic), ectomorph (very slender).

143. (A) The person receiving $20 is less likely to believe the lie because he has more external justification ($20) for telling it — and consequently, less cognitive dissonance than a person receiving only $1.

144. (B) In contrast to a similar panel with subtle functional differences or identical controls with exact reversal in function, a pilot would experience more success and less interference in learning a new panel that was distinctly different from the old panel in all respects.

145. (E) Murray and Maslow both speak of needs in personality theory. The name grouping of Freud-Bandura-Jung was the only one in which one of those two names did not appear.

146. (E) Psychoanalysis focuses upon the early childhood bases underlying personality problems rather than the current behavioral symptoms.

147. (B) Rogers does not speak of a contract. This term is associated with Berne's transactional analysis.

148. (E) Only Jung speaks of archetypal continuities, and the concept is totally foreign to phenomenologists.

149. (A) In Newcomb's model, an even number of negative signs indicates balance. I dislike cigarettes, my dad dislikes cigarettes, and I like my dad (two negatives and in balance).

150. (A) Treating emotional problems through role playing is a primary aspect of psychodrama.

151. (B) In Kallmann's studies, the highest incidence of schizophrenia was found in identical twins — evidence frequently cited to prove the disorder's hereditary characteristics.

152. (B) Dorothea Dix, Clifford Beers, and William Tuke were prominent persons dedicated to the reform of mental hospitals.

153. (C) Systematic desensitization in the Wolpe approach involves substituting a relaxation response for fear in the presence of a formerly feared object.

154. (C) Group therapy in which the therapist lectures and leads discussions is classified as didactic.

155. (D) In follow-up studies of patients treated through behavior modification techniques, few relapses to problem behavior have been found.

156. (A) Detectable physiological problems are present in the psychosomatic disorder but not in conversion reaction.

157. (A) Sorting items on a dimension such as color is an example of qualitative classification.

158. (A) A basic confidence interval formula determines the lower limit by subtracting the (z-score times the standard deviation/the square root of N) from the mean of the distribution. The upper limit is obtained by adding the same quantity expressed in parentheses to the mean.

159. (C) See question 158.

160. (E) Such observation of a natural setting is characteristic of the field-study method.

161. (C) In working with a person suffering from multiple personality, a therapist must treat each personality as a distinct and separate entity. Long range, the therapist may attempt to make the most wholesome personality the dominant one.

162. (E) Tranquilizing drugs, electroconvulsive shock, protection against self-inflicted wounds, and recreational therapy would be likely treatments for an affective psychotic reaction, but LSD therapy would not be.

163. (B) The affective reaction is psychotic.

164. (E) A major characteristic of functional mental disorders is an inability to trace them to physiological bases.

165. (E) While stomach ulcers, asthma, migraines, and neurodermatitis have psychophysiologic characteristics, skin cancer does not.

166. (E) Mental health professionals find that the geographical locations with the highest heart-disease rates also have the highest rates of cancer incidence.

167. (B) Functional blindness — not traceable to a physiological cause — could be a conversion reaction.

168. (D) The pleasure obtained from the problem act itself — transvestism — is too great for counterconditioning to be an effective method for treatment.

169. (D) Lack of opportunity for heterosexual relationships, homosexual seduction, fear of the opposite sex, and a gratifying homosexual experience during middle childhood are seen as likely bases for homosexuality.

170. (E) Masserman uses this type of method to achieve conditioned neurotic behavior in cats.

171. (D) While sociopathic personality disturbance encompasses emotional shallowness, antisocial behavior, dyssocial behavior, and rebellion against society, it does not include depression.

172. (E) In Freudian theory, repression constitutes a kind of involuntary absence from consciousness; suppression, on the other hand, involves a voluntary act of removal from consciousness. ("I'm not going to think about that anymore!")

173. (A) Anxiety reaction is the most commonly found psychoneurotic disorder, and multiple personality is among the most rare.

174. (E) Raker speaks of the stage sequence of reaction to a civilian catastrophe as shock, suggestible, recovery, and possible delayed traumatic neurosis.

175. (A) The therapist's personal qualities and experience are considered far more important factors in therapeutic success than his personality theory orientation.

176. (B) The emotion is strikingly inappropriate to the situation — an element characterizing hebephrenic schizophrenia.

177. (D) In a skewed distribution, the median moves in the direction of the skew, and the mode occurs at the distribution's high point. The mean moves more exaggeratedly in the tail direction than does the median.

178. (C) Systematic desensitization is the method in this listing used for directly treating problem behavior without concern for its underlying cause.

179. (E) Industrial psychologists find that physical aspects of the work setting itself (noise, illumination, etc.) are more critical than the number of coffee breaks.

180. (B) The Hawthorne plant study at Western Electric launched the human relations movement in American industry. It pointed convincingly to the relationship between supervisory attention and concern for workers and resulting work output.

181. (D) Being four standard deviations below the mean encompasses virtually all scores on that side of the distribution (50 percent). The score of 60 is one standard deviation above the mean (approximately an additional 34 percent), resulting in a combined 84 percent.

182. (B) Approximately 16 percent of the scores in a distribution would occur beyond a point that is one standard deviation below the mean.

183. (E) For all practical purposes, this point (three standard deviations above the mean) would encompass all distribution scores — essentially a 100th percentile, which is not among your answer choices.

184. (D) A prominent vocational interest test is the Strong Vocational Interest Blank.

185. (C) Raw scores are not in a form that permits comparison with performance on other test measures.

186. (D) Although common in psychoanalysis, the free-association method is not used in supervisor-management training within industry.

187. (D) Human engineers have found that 65 – 70 degrees is the best working temperature for moderately heavy work extending over a two-to-four hour period.

188. (C) The most reliable public opinion polling is that of private organizations conducted prior to a political election. Such firms are heavily staffed for such polling because they know there will be a "day of reckoning" when their findings will be confirmed or disproved.

189. (D) In Hunter's double alternation experimentation, some animals high on the phylogenetic scale have demonstrated thought-type mental capacities.

190. (E) In the subtractive color wheel, green is "next door" to blue. With the probable existence of an "impure" green in the costume, the blue light would best reflect and accentuate the outfit.

191. (A) Having participants read several pages of description relating the problems and dilemmas of a specific manager would be an example of using the case method.

192. (D) Recitation — in effect, an active participation in the material — aids retention.

193. (E) A psychologist assigned to do the screening for a given job must first examine the tasks of that specific job, seeking to approximate their required skills within the testing instrument.

194. (C) Human engineering most firmly underwrites the cockpit display panel that makes maximal use of both shape and color.

195. (D) Among the test groupings presented, the Allport-Vernon-Lindzey Scale would enable you to study the values of a specific group.

196. (C) Research studies indicate that the product should be priced initially at the eventual price level rather than at a discount price. In systematic studies, this recommendation has been born out repeatedly.

197. (D) Determining that two discrete variables are independent within a population on the basis of the sample data would be a mission of chi-square.

198. (B) The distribution of sample means would be a normal distribution.

199. (D) Variance is defined as the average/mean of the squared differences from the mean of the distribution.

200. (C) Eating while reading was found to enhance the persuasiveness of the material being read. Thus, a salesman taking a client to lunch is right on target.

Test 3: Evaluating Your Score

Abbreviation Guide

PC	Physiological/Comparative
SnP	Sensation/Perception
LM	Learning/Motivation/Emotion
CHL	Cognition/Complex Human Learning
D	Developmental
PrS	Personality/Social
PyCl	Psychopathology/Clinical
M	Methodology
Ap	Applied

Subject Area Chart

Use this chart to determine the subject matter covered by each question in Test 3.

1.	PC	11.	LM	21.	SnP	31.	SnP	41.	SnP
2.	PC	12.	SnP	22.	LM	32.	PC	42.	LM
3.	LM	13.	PC	23.	PC	33.	LM	43.	LM
4.	PC	14.	PC	24.	SnP	34.	PC	44.	SnP
5.	M	15.	PC	25.	SnP	35.	LM	45.	SnP
6.	M	16.	LM	26.	PC	36.	PC	46.	SnP
7.	M	17.	PC	27.	LM	37.	PC	47.	SnP
8.	PC	18.	PC	28.	SnP	38.	PC	48.	SnP
9.	SnP	19.	SnP	29.	SnP	39.	SnP	49.	LM
10.	LM	20.	SnP	30.	SnP	40.	SnP	50.	LM

51.	PC	81.	CHL	111.	CHL	141.	PrS	171.	PyCl
52.	PC	82.	CHL	112.	D	142.	PrS	172.	PyCl
53.	SnP	83.	CHL	113.	D	143.	PrS	173.	PyCl
54.	PC	84.	D	114.	CHL	144.	Ap	174.	PyCl
55.	PC	85.	D	115.	D	145.	PrS	175.	PyCl
56.	PC	86.	D	116.	M	146.	PrS	176.	PyCl
57.	PC	87.	LM	117.	LM	147.	PrS	177.	M
58.	LM	88.	LM	118.	LM	148.	PrS	178.	Ap
59.	D	89.	LM	119.	LM	149.	PrS	179.	Ap
60.	CHL	90.	D	120.	LM	150.	PyCl	180.	Ap
61.	CHL	91.	D	121.	PrS	151.	PyCl	181.	M
62.	D	92.	D	122.	Ap	152.	PyCl	182.	M
63.	D	93.	M	123.	PrS	153.	PyCl	183.	M
64.	D	94.	M	124.	PrS	154.	PyCl	184.	Ap
65.	CHL	95.	D	125.	PrS	155.	PyCl	185.	M
66.	LM	96.	CHL	126.	Ap	156.	PyCl	186.	Ap
67.	D	97.	CHL	127.	Ap	157.	M	187.	Ap
68.	CHL	98.	CHL	128.	PrS	158.	M	188.	Ap
69.	CHL	99.	CHL	129.	PrS	159.	M	189.	Ap
70.	LM	100.	CHL	130.	PrS	160.	M	190.	Ap
71.	D	101.	D	131.	Ap	161.	PyCl	191.	Ap
72.	D	102.	D	132.	PrS	162.	PyCl	192.	Ap
73.	M	103.	D	133.	PrS	163.	PyCl	193.	Ap
74.	LM	104.	CHL	134.	PrS	164.	PyCl	194.	Ap
75.	LM	105.	CHL	135.	PrS	165.	PyCl	195.	Ap
76.	LM	106.	CHL	136.	PrS	166.	PyCl	196.	Ap
77.	D	107.	D	137.	PrS	167.	PyCl	197.	M
78.	M	108.	CHL	138.	PrS	168.	PyCl	198.	M
79.	D	109.	CHL	139.	PrS	169.	PyCl	199.	M
80.	D	110.	CHL	140.	PrS	170.	PyCl	200.	Ap

Record the number of questions you missed in each subject area.

PC —   CHL —   PyCl —
SnP —   D   —   M   —
LM —   PrS —   Ap —

Test Score Scale

The first number given is the number of questions in the test in that subject area. The number in parentheses indicates the 75th percentile score. To determine how well you scored in each subject area, subtract the number of questions you missed in a certain area from the total number of questions in that area. Compare the result with the 75th percentile number. If it is lower than 75%, you probably need more review.

PC —22(17)   CHL —21(16)   PyCl —23(17)
SnP —20(15)   D   —24(18)   M   —20(15)
LM —25(19)   PrS —24(18)   Ap   —21(16)

Test 4: Answer Grid

1. A B C D E	21. A B C D E	41. A B C D E	61. A B C D E	81. A B C D E
2. A B C D E	22. A B C D E	42. A B C D E	62. A B C D E	82. A B C D E
3. A B C D E	23. A B C D E	43. A B C D E	63. A B C D E	83. A B C D E
4. A B C D E	24. A B C D E	44. A B C D E	64. A B C D E	84. A B C D E
5. A B C D E	25. A B C D E	45. A B C D E	65. A B C D E	85. A B C D E
6. A B C D E	26. A B C D E	46. A B C D E	66. A B C D E	86. A B C D E
7. A B C D E	27. A B C D E	47. A B C D E	67. A B C D E	87. A B C D E
8. A B C D E	28. A B C D E	48. A B C D E	68. A B C D E	88. A B C D E
9. A B C D E	29. A B C D E	49. A B C D E	69. A B C D E	89. A B C D E
10. A B C D E	30. A B C D E	50. A B C D E	70. A B C D E	90. A B C D E
11. A B C D E	31. A B C D E	51. A B C D E	71. A B C D E	91. A B C D E
12. A B C D E	32. A B C D E	52. A B C D E	72. A B C D E	92. A B C D E
13. A B C D E	33. A B C D E	53. A B C D E	73. A B C D E	93. A B C D E
14. A B C D E	34. A B C D E	54. A B C D E	74. A B C D E	94. A B C D E
15. A B C D E	35. A B C D E	55. A B C D E	75. A B C D E	95. A B C D E
16. A B C D E	36. A B C D E	56. A B C D E	76. A B C D E	96. A B C D E
17. A B C D E	37. A B C D E	57. A B C D E	77. A B C D E	97. A B C D E
18. A B C D E	38. A B C D E	58. A B C D E	78. A B C D E	98. A B C D E
19. A B C D E	39. A B C D E	59. A B C D E	79. A B C D E	99. A B C D E
20. A B C D E	40. A B C D E	60. A B C D E	80. A B C D E	100. A B C D E

101. A B C D E	121. A B C D E	141. A B C D E	161. A B C D E	181. A B C D E
102. A B C D E	122. A B C D E	142. A B C D E	162. A B C D E	182. A B C D E
103. A B C D E	123. A B C D E	143. A B C D E	163. A B C D E	183. A B C D E
104. A B C D E	124. A B C D E	144. A B C D E	164. A B C D E	184. A B C D E
105. A B C D E	125. A B C D E	145. A B C D E	165. A B C D E	185. A B C D E
106. A B C D E	126. A B C D E	146. A B C D E	166. A B C D E	186. A B C D E
107. A B C D E	127. A B C D E	147. A B C D E	167. A B C D E	187. A B C D E
108. A B C D E	128. A B C D E	148. A B C D E	168. A B C D E	188. A B C D E
109. A B C D E	129. A B C D E	149. A B C D E	169. A B C D E	189. A B C D E
110. A B C D E	130. A B C D E	150. A B C D E	170. A B C D E	190. A B C D E
111. A B C D E	131. A B C D E	151. A B C D E	171. A B C D E	191. A B C D E
112. A B C D E	132. A B C D E	152. A B C D E	172. A B C D E	192. A B C D E
113. A B C D E	133. A B C D E	153. A B C D E	173. A B C D E	193. A B C D E
114. A B C D E	134. A B C D E	154. A B C D E	174. A B C D E	194. A B C D E
115. A B C D E	135. A B C D E	155. A B C D E	175. A B C D E	195. A B C D E
116. A B C D E	136. A B C D E	156. A B C D E	176. A B C D E	196. A B C D E
117. A B C D E	137. A B C D E	157. A B C D E	177. A B C D E	197. A B C D E
118. A B C D E	138. A B C D E	158. A B C D E	178. A B C D E	198. A B C D E
119. A B C D E	139. A B C D E	159. A B C D E	179. A B C D E	199. A B C D E
120. A B C D E	140. A B C D E	160. A B C D E	180. A B C D E	200. A B C D E

Test Four

Time 170 minutes

Directions Each of the following questions contains five possible responses. Read the question carefully and select the response that you feel is most appropriate. Then completely darken the space on your answer grid that corresponds with your choice.

1. The motion picture depends for its perceptual success upon
   (A) the physiological limitations of the human visual apparatus
   (B) synesthesia
   (C) motion parallax
   (D) the unique capacities of the optic chiasm
   (E) the closure phenomenon

2. Which one of the following statements is *incorrect*?
   (A) Bekesy has done significant research work in the area of audition.
   (B) Olfactory receptors are located within the turbinate bones.
   (C) The work of Hubel and Weisel has been of central importance in the area of visual receptive fields.
   (D) In terms of cortex location, taste and facial somatic functions are closely related.
   (E) Microelectrode techniques have been used in taste research.

3. The area between the eardrum and the oval window is occupied by the
   (A) cochlea   (B) Organ of Corti   (C) cilia   (D) ossicles
   (E) round window

4. Feedback regarding internal organs of the body is obtained through the
   (A) skin senses   (B) somesthetic senses   (C) labyrinthine senses
   (D) visceral senses   (E) striated senses

5. The phenomenon whereby four closely contiguous lines are perceived as a square demonstrates the principle of
   (A) contiguity   (B) closure   (C) continuation   (D) similarity
   (E) contrast

6. In contrast to children who were low in achievement need, McClelland found that children with high achievement need had a
   (A) stronger preference for intermediate-risk tasks
   (B) weaker preference for intermediate-risk tasks
   (C) stronger preference for low-risk tasks
   (D) stronger preference for high-risk tasks
   (E) stronger preference for tasks at all risk levels

7. Given a choice of tasks for which a person can anticipate equal probabilities of success, Atkinson has found that a key factor in determining the strength of the response is the
   (A) size of the achievement
   (B) prepotency of the stimulus
   (C) value that the subject places on the achievement
   (D) value that the experimenter places on the achievement
   (E) UCS nature of the reinforcement

8. Experimental work in perception received its earliest beginnings with
   (A) Restle (B) Weber (C) Wertheimer (D) Kohler
   (E) Koffka

9. Which of the following illusions involves two lines with arrow heads on both ends?
   (A) Vertical-horizontal (B) Ames room (C) trapezoidal window
   (D) Muller-Lyer (E) Landolt-C

10. On the basis of existing research, which one of the following influences is found in the childhood backgrounds of adults with a high achievement need?
    (A) encouragement of curiosity
    (B) encouragement of creativity
    (C) encouragement of independence
    (D) frequent frustration
    (E) encouragement of aggression

11. As Joan walks along the beach, one set of muscles operates antagonistically to another set in achieving the coordination necessary for walking. Coordination of this antagonistic muscle activity is described as
    (A) reciprocal inhibition
    (B) reciprocal innervation
    (C) retroactive innervation
    (D) proprioception
    (E) somatoception

12. Striated muscles are
    (A) known as involuntary
    (B) synonymous with smooth muscles
    (C) the type that produce stomach contractions
    (D) responsible for producing skeletal movement
    (E) responsible for labyrinthine sensitivity

13. Wernicke's center in the brain relates to
    (A) speech
    (B) understanding spoken language
    (C) handedness
    (D) coordination necessary in walking
    (E) sexual arousal

14. Prominent among monocular depth cues is
    (A) accommodation
    (B) texture-density gradient
    (C) retinal disparity
    (D) reciprocal innervation
    (E) retinal polarity

15. Which one of the following statements about the area of vigilance is true?
    (A) The probability of operator detection declines with the amount of vigilance time.
    (B) The probability of operator detection increases with the amount of vigilance time.
    (C) Performance worsens when the operator receives feedback.
    (D) Performance is worsened by the introduction of brief rest periods.
    (E) Performance decline is faster than normal if the position and timing of signals is uncertain.

16. In reaction time settings
    (A) at levels close to threshold, increasing the strength of a stimulus shortens reaction time
    (B) at levels close to threshold, decreasing duration of a stimulus shortens reaction time
    (C) at levels close to threshold, decreasing the strength of a stimulus shortens reaction time
    (D) kinesthesis is generally the sensory modality utilized
    (E) pain sensitivity is generally the sensory modality utilized

17. When two sense organs are stimulated simultaneously, reaction time is
    (A) faster than when only one is stimulated
    (B) slower than when only one is stimulated
    (C) retarded in the second sensory modality being stimulated
    (D) retarded in the first sensory modality being stimulated
    (E) equivalent to reaction time when only one sense organ is being stimulated

18. Perceptually, to "wait till Christmas" would be the longest wait for the
    (A) preschool child   (B) elementary school child   (C) teenager
    (D) college-age adult   (E) middle-age adult

19. Between which one of the following pairs of men could basic, conceptual agreement be anticipated?
    (A) Tolman and Lewin   (B) Lewin and Freud   (C) Lewin and Skinner
    (D) Tolman and Thorndike   (E) Tolman and Pavlov

20. Among the following, the most important name in achievement motivation research is
    (A) Miller   (B) Bandura   (C) Mowrer   (D) Atkinson
    (E) Murray

21. Watson identified the three distinct emotional responses in the human infant as
    (A) love, rage, fear
    (B) love, rage, surprise
    (C) surprise, rage, fear
    (D) love, surprise, fear
    (E) love, rage, distress

22. Near the turn of the century, a psychologist named Stratton wore goggles that inverted the retinal image. Which of the following did he experience?
    (A) The world looked upside down while he wore the goggles.
    (B) The world appeared upside down at first, then later became perceptually normal.
    (C) The world looked perceptually normal throughout the time he wore the glasses.
    (D) The world looked perceptually normal immediately after he removed the glasses.
    (E) He was affected by temporary blindness.

23. One of the familiar criticisms leveled at the work of McGinnies has been his
    (A) failure to distinguish recognition threshold from the act of reporting
    (B) failure to select words equivalent in the extent of their normal usage
    (C) use of schizophrenic subjects
    (D) use of the memory drum apparatus
    (E) failure to select taboo words equivalent in their inhibitory effects

24. The familiar face-vase picture seen in most introductory and perception sources is an example of
    (A) parallax (B) closure (C) figure reversibility
    (D) size constancy (E) shape constancy

25. The Pacinian corpuscle is related to
    (A) audition (B) vision (C) pressure (D) taste (E) smell

26. Which one of the following statements is *not* true of dreaming?
    (A) It is usually accompanied by erection of the penis in males.
    (B) It is reported by about 80 percent of the subjects awakened during REM periods.
    (C) It occurs in a rhythmic cycle about every ninety minutes.
    (D) It always occurs during beta wave activity.
    (E) It occurs during stage 1-REM.

27. The Gestalt school of psychology subscribes to the basic principle that
    (A) only overt behavior can be studied scientifically
    (B) behavior or experience equals more than the sum of its parts
    (C) psychology must concern itself only with studying man's adjustment to his environment
    (D) thanatos-eros forms the primary conflict to be studied within psychology
    (E) conscious experience cannot be a legitimate area for scientific investigation

28. Misperception of a stimulus : illusion :: _____ : hallucination.
    (A) delusion
    (B) autokinesis
    (C) response in the absence of external stimulus
    (D) accurate perception of an external stimulus
    (E) alpha wave

29. The "moon illusion" relates to the tendency to perceive
    (A) a quarter moon as a half moon
    (B) a three-quarter moon as a full moon
    (C) the moon in the sky as larger than the moon on the horizon
    (D) the moon on the horizon as larger than the moon in the sky
    (E) the milky way as a "shadow moon"

30. In the midst of deep sleep, the dominant brain wave is
    (A) alpha (B) beta (C) theta (D) gamma (E) delta

31. The basilar membrane plays an important role in
    (A) vision (B) hearing (C) olfaction (D) taste
    (E) kinesthetic sensation

32. William McDougall
    (A) criticized the stimulus-response mode of thought
    (B) criticized the notion of purposive behavior
    (C) aligned himself with the arguments of Thorndike
    (D) initiated the work that eventually led to Pavlov's theories
    (E) differed with the positive valence theory but promoted the views relating to negative valence

33. Tinbergen outlines four major areas of study in animal behavior. *Not* among them is
    (A) development (B) mechanisms (C) function (D) habits
    (E) evolution

34. "The only determinants of behavior at a given time are the properties of the person and his psychological environment at that time." This a quote from
    (A) Lewin (B) Skinner (C) Watson (D) Atkinson
    (E) McClelland

35. In James's view, habit
    (A) is purely instinctive
    (B) involves instinct in combination with experience
    (C) involves learning in combination with experience
    (D) involves only learning
    (E) is purely emotion-centered

36. Duplicity Theory applies to
    (A) sympathetic and parasympathetic nervous systems
    (B) reciprocal innervation
    (C) bone and nerve conductant elements in audition
    (D) rod-cone vision
    (E) overlapping functions of taste and olfaction

37. The specific-energy-of-nerves concept is directly attributable to
    (A) Mowrer (B) Magoun (C) Sherrington (D) Meissner
    (E) Muller

38. Critical flicker frequency is the rate of light fluctuation
    (A) above which flicker is reported
    (B) above which fusion occurs
    (C) below which fusion occurs
    (D) above which both flicker and fusion occur
    (E) below which both flicker and fusion occur

39. The suggestion that *all* nerves fire constantly and repeatedly to produce the reception of pitch would be an expression of the
    (A) place theory (B) frequency theory (C) volley theory
    (D) decibel theory (E) amplitude theory

40. Among corpus callosum functions is
    (A) transferral of messages between brain hemispheres
    (B) division of the brain hemispheres
    (C) the sending of the right side of the human visual field to the right hemisphere of the brain
    (D) the sending of the right side of the human visual field to the left hemisphere of the brain
    (E) the inhibition of hemisphere interaction within the brain

41. Perceptual constancies are primarily a function of
    (A) reflex (B) tropism (C) instinct (D) learning
    (E) convergence

42. A person has just sustained a severe blow on the back of the head. It is most likely that which one of the following senses would be impaired?
    (A) speech (B) associative memory (C) hearing
    (D) olfaction (E) vision

43. The fact that, during neural transmission, an impulse is sent to the end of the axon without fading or weakening is known as
    (A) stimulus constancy
    (B) absolute threshold retention
    (C) nondecremental property
    (D) all-or-none property
    (E) activation constancy

44. The alpha wave has a frequency of approximately how many cycles per second?
    (A) five (B) twenty (C) thirty (D) ten (E) two

45. According to the Montreal Studies, the original infant emotion upon which all others are based is
    (A) fear (B) excitement (C) love (D) distress (E) delight

46. Very high anger arousal causes which one of the following bodily responses?
    (A) lowered blood pressure
    (B) dilation of blood vessels near the skin
    (C) heightened visual acuity
    (D) lowered activity among the striated muscles
    (E) lowered blood sugar

47. Which of the following persons located pleasure centers in the brain via rat experimentation?
    (A) Sperry (B) Krech (C) Meissner (D) Olds
    (E) Delgado

48. Assuming the analogy of a doorbell, which aspect of the neuron would most closely approximate the button that a visitor would push?
    (A) terminal endings (B) axon (C) cell body
    (D) myelin sheath (E) dendrites

49. Which one of the following statements can be concluded from dream research?
    (A) Dreaming apparently serves a basic organismic need.
    (B) Dreaming is dispensable and unnecessary.
    (C) Most persons do not dream.
    (D) Dreaming drops markedly in frequency among the elderly.
    (E) No activity suggesting dreaming can be found in the infant.

50. Which one of the following is an apparent bodily response to the emotions of resentment and hostility?
    (A) lower heart rate
    (B) lower blood pressure
    (C) heightened auditory sensitivity
    (D) lower breathing rate
    (E) increased stomach acidity

51. The Cannon-Bard theory deals with the
    (A) Islets of Langerhans
    (B) thalamus and hypothalamus
    (C) corpus callosum
    (D) adrenal cortex
    (E) pineal gland

52. Which one of the following is responsible for nerve impulse travel from a cell body to other neurons?
    (A) axon   (B) dendrite   (C) cell membrane   (D) prototaxon
    (E) Meissner response

53. The most appropriate example of the difference-limen method among the following is
    (A) a single tone varied systematically in decibels
    (B) a spot of light continuously presented as a fixed stimulus
    (C) a sequence of light stimuli at different fixed intensities above and below threshold
    (D) two different intensities of light presented simultaneously
    (E) two different decibel levels of tone presented sequentially

54. Which of the following is the formula for Weber's Law?
    (A) Delta $I/K = I$
    (B) Delta $I/I = K$
    (C) $K/I =$ Delta I
    (D) $I/K =$ Delta I
    (E) $K/$Delta $I = I$

55. The neural connection pattern between the eyes and the brain
    (A) presents special problems and considerations in split-brain research
    (B) is identical to the auditory pattern
    (C) bears close resemblance to the labyrinthine sensory pattern
    (D) perpetuates the Duplicity Theory concept
    (E) relies heavily on the cerebellum

Questions 56–59 are based on the following drawing.

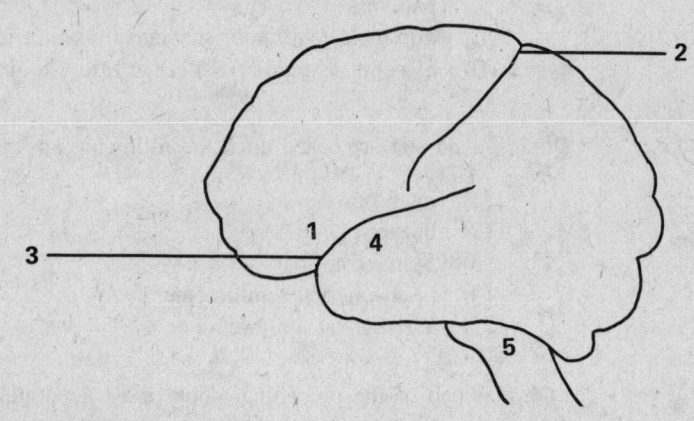

Indicate by the appropriate number:

56. Broca's area
    (A) 1   (B) 2   (C) 3   (D) 4   (E) 5

57. Wernicke's center
    (A) 1   (B) 2   (C) 3   (D) 4   (E) 5

58. Sylvian fissure
    (A) 1   (B) 2   (C) 3   (D) 4   (E) 5

59. Reticular formation
    (A) 1   (B) 2   (C) 3   (D) 4   (E) 5

60. A primary difference between escape and avoidance conditioning is that
    (A) in escape conditioning, the aversive stimulus is always received by the subject
    (B) in escape conditioning, the aversive stimulus is not received by the subject
    (C) in escape conditioning, successive approximation is used
    (D) in escape conditioning, successive approximation is not used
    (E) escape conditioning utilizes response chaining

61. Which of the following is a memory storage distinction espoused by many psychologists?
    (A) minimal and maximal
    (B) subsequent and consequent
    (C) perceptual and motor
    (D) short-term and long-term
    (E) informational and motivational

62. The principal value of punishment lies in its capacity to
    (A) weaken existing conditioned responses
    (B) prevent neurosis by suppressing undesirable responses
    (C) serve as a cue
    (D) force the learning of a new response
    (E) change behavior

63. Which one of the following pairs is *incorrect*?
    (A) ectoderm—contains basis for development of skin, sensory cells, and nervous system
    (B) mesoderm—contains basis for development of muscles, skeleton, and circulatory organs
    (C) endoderm—contains basis for development of thyroid glands, liver, lungs, and pancreas
    (D) trophoblast—a major substance within the endoderm
    (E) placenta—extends from embryo to the uterus-chorion juncture

Questions 64–65 are based upon the following answer choices.

(1) meat powder
(2) buzzer
(3) Skinner box
(4) fixed-interval reinforcement
(5) variable-ratio reinforcement

64. Which of the preceding would most accurately characterize the horse-race betting situation?
    (A) 1   (B) 2   (C) 3   (D) 4   (E) 5

65. Which of the above qualifies as an unconditioned stimulus?
    (A) 1   (B) 2   (C) 3   (D) 4   (E) 5

66. Concurrent validity is demonstrated by which one of the following?
    (A) examining of test content by a panel of experts
    (B) correlating scores with a test taker's general performance in other areas
    (C) correlating a current score with a test taker's earlier score on the same instrument
    (D) correlating scores on two halves of the same test
    (E) correlating a given test with other established tests in the field

67. Retention is highest for
    (A) poetry (B) meaningful material (C) specific dates
    (D) motor tasks (E) concepts and principles

68. *Not* among terms utilized by Guilford is
    (A) operations (B) contents (C) products (D) syntax
    (E) transformations

69. In higher-order conditioning, a former
    (A) UCS serves as a CS
    (B) UCR serves as a CR
    (C) CR serves as a UCS
    (D) CR serves as a UCR
    (E) CS serves as a UCS

70. Which one of the following significance levels is most rigorous?
    (A) .05 (B) .02 (C) .01 (D) .005 (E) .1

71. Which one of the following would *not* be expected in the newborn?
    (A) well-developed temperature sensitivity
    (B) Moro reflex
    (C) Babinski response
    (D) well-developed grasping reflex
    (E) well-developed pain sensitivity

72. Within normal communications, noise
    (A) is nonexistent
    (B) will occur only at the source
    (C) will occur only in encoding
    (D) can occur at any point in the communication process
    (E) occurs only in radio-wave-type transmission

73. In contrast to adolescent gangs, children's gangs
    (A) are formed as a result of social rejection
    (B) are formed on the basis of inferiority feelings
    (C) are not formed with a "get-even" purpose in mind
    (D) are formed on the basis of family similarities
    (E) are formed on the basis of birth order

74. Which one of the following is a mnemonic strategy?
    (A) learning music lines and spaces by developing a word such as FACE
    (B) frequently repeating rhyming words
    (C) grouping digits in a series into larger and smaller numbers
    (D) visualizing a picture on a printed page
    (E) moving from specific information to general conclusions

75. Which one of the following is *not* related closely to the term *sickle cell*?
    (A) abnormal form of hemoglobin
    (B) possibility of dangerous clotting
    (C) specific race prominence
    (D) a form of cancer
    (E) a form of anemia

76. Tom is blue-eyed (homozygous) and Mary is brown-eyed (heterozygous). Their chances for brown-eyed offspring are
    (A) 2 in 4   (B) 1 in 4   (C) 3 in 4   (D) 4 in 4   (E) 0 in 4

77. *Least* likely to succeed in obtaining a balanced diet through self-selection would be a
    (A) rat   (B) cat   (C) rabbit   (D) human infant
    (E) human adult

78. Genotype : phenotype ::
    (A) aptitude : performance
    (B) identical : fraternal
    (C) recessive : dominant
    (D) prenatal : postnatal
    (E) heredity : appearance

79. The critical-periods concept of intelligence as it relates to environmental stimulation during early childhood is being challenged by the experimental work of
    (A) Scott   (B) Harlow   (C) Kagan   (D) Mussen
    (E) McCandless

80. Which one of the following is the Moro response?
    (A) sucking
    (B) rooting
    (C) toes curling upward and outward
    (D) grasping reflex
    (E) arms and legs stretched outward suddenly

81. In gamete development, the fact that each mature egg or sperm contains only one chromosome from each pair is attributable to a process known as
    (A) fertilization   (B) immunization   (C) reduction division
    (D) zygotic division   (E) monozygotic division

82. A memory aid is best if it
    (A) increases negative transfer
    (B) makes material meaningful
    (C) increases spontaneous recovery
    (D) accentuates competing responses
    (E) reduces positive transfer

83. In Harlow's experiments, the surrogate-reared infant monkeys were *least* fearful in the presence of
    (A) the surrogate mother to which the sucking response had been directed
    (B) the surrogate mother to which the clinging response had been directed
    (C) their siblings
    (D) their natural father
    (E) playmates

84. Which of the following is an *incorrect* pairing?
    (A) duct glands—secretions emptied into body cavities
    (B) ductless glands—secretions made directly into the bloodstream
    (C) gray matter—indicative of cell bodies
    (D) white matter—indicative of myelinated fibers
    (E) cardiac muscle—a nonstriated (smooth) muscle

85. Positive transfer is greatest when a person performs
    (A) new responses to similar stimuli
    (B) old responses to different stimuli
    (C) new responses to different stimuli
    (D) old responses to similar stimuli
    (E) new responses to new stimuli

86. Tulving's primary experimental concern is
    (A) processes underlying information reception, retention, and recall
    (B) processes underlying schizophrenia
    (C) processes underlying the cognitive stages of the child
    (D) processes underlying the eros-thanatos conflict
    (E) the effects of nutrition upon brain-cell formation

87. In Bruner's terms, the three modes of developing a mental world model are
    (A) motor, emotional, cognitive
    (B) enactive, iconic, symbolic
    (C) physical, physiological, psychophysical
    (D) conscious, subconscious, unconscious
    (E) parataxic, prototaxic, syntaxic

88. According to certain learning theories, introduction of a rest interval after massed practice of a motor skill will most likely produce
    (A) spontaneous recovery   (B) reminiscence   (C) proactive inhibition
    (D) retroactive inhibition   (E) chunking

89. Jones's study of early and late maturers indicates that
    (A) early maturation is an advantage for males but a disadvantage for females
    (B) psychological differences between the early and late maturing males disappear when the individuals are in their thirties
    (C) by the late teens, differences in personality traits between early and late maturing girls are at the maximum
    (D) early maturation is advantageous for both sexes
    (E) early maturation is an advantage for girls but a disadvantage for boys

90. A single list of nonsense syllables is presented sequentially in the
    (A) serial-position method
    (B) paired-associates method
    (C) serial-anticipation method
    (D) paired-anticipation method
    (E) von Restorff method

91. The most severe conflict situation is likely to be produced by the classification known as
    (A) approach-approach
    (B) simple approach-avoidance
    (C) approach-avoidance
    (D) double approach-approach
    (E) avoidance-avoidance

92. Teaching machines require children to choose one of four suggested alternative answers to each situation presented. The method utilizes a
    (A) recall design   (B) recognition design   (C) savings design
    (D) relearning design   (E) reconstruction design

93. Which one of the following is *not* one of Dollard and Miller's requirements for learning?
    (A) drive (B) cue (C) transfer (D) response
    (E) reinforcement

Questions 94–96 are based on the following answer choices.

(1) pressing the palms of child's hands while he is lying on his back
(2) stroking the sole of the neonate's foot
(3) a loud handclap
(4) having the baby lie prone with the bottoms of his feet against a vertical surface
(5) stimulating the baby's palms or fingers

94. Which one of the above stimuli is used to obtain the grasping reflex?
    (A) 1 (B) 2 (C) 3 (D) 4 (E) 5

95. The Babkin response is obtained by using which one of the above stimuli?
    (A) 1 (B) 2 (C) 3 (D) 4 (E) 5

96. Which one of the above stimuli is used to obtain a Babinski response?
    (A) 1 (B) 2 (C) 3 (D) 4 (E) 5

97. That the upper part of the body develops earlier than the lower part is termed
    (A) proximodistal (B) cephalocaudal (C) corticodistal
    (D) general to specific (E) sensorimotor

98. Mitosis refers to
    (A) union of sperm and ovum
    (B) cell division and multiplication
    (C) skeletal muscle tissue development
    (D) nerve tissue development
    (E) intrauterine metabolism

99. Lovaas utilizes behavior modification techniques in the treatment of
    (A) autism (B) aphasia (C) acute depression
    (D) alcoholism (E) drug addiction

100. Which of the following is an *incorrect* pairing?
    (A) Lorenz–aggression
    (B) Bandura–modeling
    (C) Scott–imprinting
    (D) Kagan–intelligence
    (E) Harlow–psycholinguistics

101. In contrast to the Stanford-Binet Scale, the Wechsler Scale
    (A) was developed through trial and error
    (B) was developed through intensive child interviews
    (C) separates verbal from performance IQ
    (D) has a different standard deviation for each age group
    (E) utilizes the MA/CA-type computational formula

102. Adjustment to postnatal environment is accomplished
    (A) more quickly among males than females
    (B) more quickly among females than males

(C) with equal speed and ease by both males and females
(D) more quickly among blacks than whites
(E) more quickly among whites than blacks

103. The term *sham feeding* refers to experiments in which
    (A) food is introduced directly into the stomach
    (B) a brain operation is performed prior to the experiment
    (C) food is eaten in the normal way, without surgical alteration to any portion of the organism
    (D) nonnutritive bulk is fed to the animal
    (E) food is "eaten" and "swallowed" but does not reach the stomach

104. Chomsky includes which one of the following in his explanation of grammar acquisition in children?
    (A) "programmed" nervous system
    (B) learned concept of human language
    (C) learned concept of language specific to one's culture
    (D) archetypal communication
    (E) ITA system

105. Intelligence tests for infants
    (A) correlate with adult tests at +.85 and above
    (B) sample the same abilities tested at later ages
    (C) provide initial information relating to aptitudes
    (D) require no standardization
    (E) are not accurate predictors of later IQ

106. In Piaget's theoretical view, a cognitive operation has both
    (A) assimilation and accommodation
    (B) externalized action and convertibility
    (C) internalized action and reversibility
    (D) internalized action and convertibility
    (E) externalized action and reversibility

107. The term *congenital* means
    (A) genetic   (B) embryonic   (C) recessive characteristic
    (D) present at birth   (E) dominant characteristic

108. Which one of the following statements is true of learning and performance?
    (A) Learning and performance are identical.
    (B) Learning is behavior-linked.
    (C) Performance implies a potentiality.
    (D) Learning implies a potentiality.
    (E) Performance is theoretical and learning is action-oriented.

109. Which one of the following groups is *not* sequentially correct?
    (A) idiot, imbecile, moron
    (B) trainable, educable, nontrainable
    (C) profoundly, severely, moderately (retarded)
    (D) severely, moderately, mildly (retarded)
    (E) moderately retarded, mildly retarded, dull normal

110. On the basis of Kendler and Kendler's general research findings, one would expect reversal shifts to be accomplished most easily and most rapidly within which one of the following groups?
(A) rats (B) dogs (C) two-year-old children (D) seven-year-old children (E) ten-year-old children

111. Given a Bartlett interpolation sequence such as 2, 4, 6, _, _, 12 and a subsequent word sequence such as: a, by, cow, _____, horrible; which one of the following series of words could constitute a correct word sequence?
(A) gate, no, i, duty
(B) dog, eagle, from, goat
(C) ho, get, fate, erase
(D) drop, event, friend, Germans
(E) event, friend, drop, Germans

112. If we assume a mean of 100 and a standard deviation of 25, a score of 140 would provide a z-score of
(A) +1.25 (B) +1.50 (C) +1.60 (D) −1.60 (E) −1.50

113. Among characteristics evident in creative children is a
(A) strong fear of failure
(B) complex system of learning sets
(C) frequent philosophical reflection
(D) willingness to risk a seemingly "kooky" idea
(E) low frustration tolerance

114. Sears's work suggests that a child who has been parentally punished for aggression will demonstrate
(A) strong prosocial aggression
(B) strong antisocial aggression
(C) low anxiety about aggression
(D) no aggressive behavior
(E) self-actualization

115. Proactive facilitation involves
(A) practice on an earlier task making a subsequent task more difficult
(B) practice on an earlier task making a subsequent task seem simpler
(C) practice on a subsequent task making an earlier task more difficult
(D) practice on a subsequent task making an earlier task easier
(E) no relationship between earlier and subsequent tasks

116. If a person has a z-score of +2, he has scored at approximately the _____ percentile within that specific distribution.
(A) 75th (B) 84th (C) 50th (D) 98th (E) 40th

117. A frequency distribution that has two distinct concentrations of scores is
(A) negatively skewed (B) positively skewed (C) normal
(D) bimodal (E) bimedial

118. A cryptarithmetic problem widely used in the study of human problem solving has been
(A) $A + B = C$
(B) Alpha + Beta = Kappa
(C) DONALD + GERALD = ROBERT
(D) MARY + SUSAN = ELIZABETH
(E) Alpha = Gamma + Beta

119. In the Freudian system, defense mechanisms protect against which one of the following?
(A) ego   (B) repression   (C) superego   (D) id   (E) archetype

120. On the basis of Schachter's research, one might conclude that
(A) misery loves any kind of company
(B) misery loves any kind of miserable company
(C) misery loves only miserable company in the same situational circumstances
(D) familiarity breeds prejudicial contempt
(E) likes attract, opposites repel

121. In Rogers's view, through interaction with one's environment, a portion of the phenomenal field becomes differentiated and known as the
(A) archetype   (B) script   (C) superego   (D) frame of orientation   (E) self-concept

Questions 122–123 are based on the following answer choices.
(1) same race
(2) same attitudes
(3) same sex
(4) same family-type background
(5) same age

122. In the work of Rokeach and Newcomb, which of the above would seem most critical to social attraction?
(A) 1   (B) 2   (C) 3   (D) 4   (E) 5

123. Rokeach and Mezei's studies combined the most influential social attraction variable with that of _____.
(A) 1   (B) 2   (C) 3   (D) 4   (E) 5

124. When the performance of an individual is enhanced by the mere presence of others, the phenomenon is called
(A) reactive facilitation   (B) cognitive dissonance   (C) conformity
(D) social facilitation   (E) complementarity

125. Learning theory views of neurotic conflicts suggest that such conflicts are
(A) a function of competition encountered by the child in the early school years
(B) learned early in childhood as a function of parent-created learning conditions
(C) transmitted from parent to child genetically
(D) capable of being extinguished with systematic, programmed punishment
(E) a result of sibling rivalry

126. The basic thesis of Newcomb's theory is that
(A) persons with similar orientations are attracted to each other
(B) persons with widely differing backgrounds are attracted to each other
(C) complementarity is essentially predominant except in courtship and marital relationships
(D) cognitive dissonance prevails in interpersonal attraction
(E) the rewards and costs of social exchange are the predominant factors within every interaction

127. "Brotherliness versus incest" is a concern of
(A) Adler   (B) Freud   (C) Jung   (D) Berne   (E) Fromm

128. Sublimation and displacement
    (A) are synonymous
    (B) differ only in the cultural value of the behavior
    (C) refer specifically to the mechanical details of reaction formation
    (D) are both identical to projection
    (E) speak to the phenomenon of mental compartmentalization

129. Which one of the following combinations is included in Allport's psychodynamic view of prejudice?
    (A) instinctive, scapegoating
    (B) frustration, regression
    (C) regression, aggression
    (D) aggression, exploitation
    (E) reputation, situational response

130. In the psychoanalytic view, childhood negativism can be expected during which one of the following stages?
    (A) oral   (B) anal   (C) phallic   (D) latent   (E) genital

131. After having been away from the following tasks for several years, a person could be expected to return to which one with least practice?
    (A) a list of nonsense syllables
    (B) a list of digit spans
    (C) verbatim recollection of a story
    (D) tightrope walking
    (E) bicycle riding

132. In Freudian theory, which one of the following is reality-oriented?
    (A) id   (B) ego   (C) superego   (D) repression
    (E) reaction formation

133. Which one of the following does *not* refer to attitudes?
    (A) predispositions to respond   (B) relatively stable   (C) an emotional component   (D) unconditioned   (E) a cognitive component

134. One of the leading researchers in the leadership area has been
    (A) Deutsch   (B) Janis   (C) Dember   (D) Harlow
    (E) Fiedler

135. In psychoanalysis, the castration fear appears
    (A) among pubescent girls
    (B) within both sexes during the genital stage
    (C) among boys during the genital stage
    (D) among girls during the anal sadistic stage
    (E) among boys during the phallic stage

136. Aggression displacement suggests that the farther removed an object or person is from the source of frustration
    (A) the lower the frustration
    (B) the lower the cooperation
    (C) the higher the inhibition
    (D) the greater the cooperation
    (E) the greater the likelihood of aggressive actions

Questions 137–139 refer to the following experiment.

Fifty children, ages nine and ten, were randomly assigned to two groups, twenty-five children per group. Using a pencil and paper, each subject was given the task of tracing a path around a geometric figure of a star. Normal cues were removed by using a shield between the subject's line of vision and the work area. It was impossible for the subjects to see their hands at work, but they could watch the hands in a mirror that was mounted on the table in front of the immediate work area. A trial began after the subject had been comfortably seated and given the signal to begin work; it concluded when the subject had completed the star-tracing task. A stopwatch monitored the time required for a subject to complete a given trial. Group 1 received one trial per day for seven days; Group 2 received seven trials during a single test session. Comparative tracing time per trial is outlined in the following table.

Trial	Tracing Time (seconds) Group 1	Group 2
1	200	200
2	170	190
3	140	170
4	100	165
5	60	150
6	50	130
7	45	120

137. Important to interpretation of the table data would be a determination that the children in the two groups were equivalent in
    (A) verbal IQ   (B) motor ability   (C) art proficiency
    (D) mechanical aptitude   (E) degree of introversion

138. The mirror serves to
    (A) help the child work more quickly than he could if he were directly observing his work
    (B) provide immediate, helpful feedback and knowledge of results
    (C) promote stimulus generalization
    (D) reorient and move the child beyond familiar habits in eye-hand coordination
    (E) provide proactive facilitation

139. The results support the statement that
    (A) massed practice proved more effective than spaced practice
    (B) spaced practice proved more effective than massed practice
    (C) practice had no appreciable effect on performance
    (D) spaced practice prompted subjects to encounter the effects of forgetting
    (E) retroactive aversion operates in star-tracing experiments

140. On the basis of Bryan and Test's experiments, we could expect a person to offer help more readily in which one of the following situations?
    (A) where he has just seen a situation in which someone was giving help to a person in distress
    (B) where he comes upon the person in distress without having had any prior example of helping
    (C) where the person in distress is injured
    (D) where the person in distress is elderly
    (E) where several other people are observing the person needing help

141. Adorno's work concludes that
    (A) attitudes have no effect on any other aspect of one's personality
    (B) no generalizations can be made on the basis of existing research in anti-Semitism
    (C) there is slight, low correlation between authoritarian attitudes and distinct personality characteristics
    (D) home background has virtually no effect upon the later development of authoritarian attitudes
    (E) there is strong correlation between authoritarian attitudes and distinct personality characteristics

142. Phrenology encompasses
    (A) free association
    (B) systematic behavioral observation
    (C) introspection
    (D) a primitive, "bumps-on-the-head" approach to personality determination
    (E) desensitization

143. A concept *not* associated with Rogers is
    (A) ideal self   (B) nondirective therapy   (C) phenomenal field
    (D) functional fictionalism   (E) self-actualization

144. Superstition would be most evident within which of the following personality terms?
    (A) prototaxic   (B) intuiting mode   (C) syntaxic
    (D) thinking mode   (E) parataxic

145. Witkin's personality experimentation has contrasted
    (A) introversion and extroversion
    (B) field dependence and field independence
    (C) inferiority and superiority
    (D) displacement and sublimation
    (E) trust and mistrust

146. In Sherif's experimentation on autokinetic effect, individual judgments
    (A) remained unchanged in the face of group judgment
    (B) changed significantly toward group judgment
    (C) changed slightly, but not significantly, toward group judgment
    (D) changed slightly in a nonconforming direction
    (E) changed dramatically in a nonconforming direction

147. Peptic ulcers are an example of
    (A) character disorder
    (B) hypochondriacal disorder
    (C) psychosomatic disorder
    (D) psychotic disorder
    (E) neurasthenic disorder

148. Which one of the following is an accurate statement about most sexual offenders?
    (A) They are typically homicidal sex fiends.
    (B) They progress to more serious types of sex crimes.
    (C) They are oversexed.
    (D) They are among the least likely to be second offenders.
    (E) They suffer from glandular imbalance.

149. On the basis of existing research, which one of the following is an *incorrect* statement relating to suicide?
    (A) There is a higher incidence of suicide among churchgoers.
    (B) The suicide's family frequently attempts to conceal the cause of death.
    (C) The lowest likelihood of suicide is among persons who talk about doing it.
    (D) There is a higher incidence of suicide among divorced persons and persons living alone.
    (E) There is a higher incidence of suicide among persons believing in life after death.

150. The psychoanalyst becomes the recipient of affection that the patient felt earlier in her life toward her father in
    (A) transference (B) connotation (C) reaction formation
    (D) Oedipus complex (E) castration fear

151. A person has scored 30 on a test that has a mean of 50 and a standard deviation of 10. The person's score ranks at which of the following percentiles?
    (A) 16th (B) 50th (C) 2nd (D) 68th (E) 84th

152. The general prognosis for most psychoneurotic disorders is
    (A) good
    (B) the same as that for schizophrenia
    (C) poor
    (D) very poor
    (E) that behavior change is virtually impossible

153. In Coleman's framework, which one of the following events affects the most body systems?
    (A) home looted at age three
    (B) discord between parents at age ten
    (C) marriage at age twenty-seven
    (D) divorce at age forty-three
    (E) remarriage at age fifty

154. In Roger Brown's terminology, a culture that places great emphasis on the caste system is utilizing which of the following status determinations?
    (A) anticipatory socialization (B) achieved status (C) ascribed status
    (D) status equilibration (E) role status

155. Electroconvulsive shock therapy has been most effective in the treatment of
    (A) paranoia (B) schizophrenia (C) conversion reactions
    (D) hypomania (E) depression

156. Which of the following has *not* been used in the treatment of alcoholism?
    (A) hospital setting (B) chlorpromazine (C) Synanon
    (D) Alcoholics Anonymous (E) family support

157. Which one of the following disorders is most likely to lead a person to cover a sizable amount of geographical territory?
    (A) amnesia (B) multiple personality (C) schizophrenia
    (D) somnambulism (E) fugue

158. A therapeutic technique in which the patient enacts a life situation or experience demonstrating his conflict is called
   (A) psychodrama   (B) sociodrama   (C) release therapy
   (D) nondirective therapy   (E) Gestalt therapy

159. An experimenter wishes to determine the effects of different shock intensities on GSR. He believes, however, that it will be essential to counterbalance the shock intensities by having one group receive high intensity first, a second group receive medium intensity first, etc. The statistical design within which he has organized his experiment is
   (A) Two Factor Mixed   (B) Pearson Product Moment   (C) t-test
   (D) point-biserial correlation   (E) Latin Square

160. Hollingshead and Redlich found psychosis most prominent in which of the following social classes?
   (A) upper   (B) middle   (C) lower   (D) professional
   (E) white-collar

161. Which of the following does *not* express a dissociative reaction?
   (A) somnambulism   (B) fugue   (C) amnesia
   (D) multiple personality   (E) conversion

162. The term *psychosomatic disorder* refers to
   (A) the imagined discomforts of hypochondriacs
   (B) the unique symptoms displayed by psychotics
   (C) a continuous emergency reaction and the resulting tissue damage
   (D) a physical disorder complicated by a neurosis
   (E) malfunction in the Islets of Langerhans

163. Among the following, the most serious phase of alcoholism is
   (A) crucial   (B) occasional   (C) prodromal   (D) critical
   (E) chronic

164. In a psychiatric team, which one of the following would be the exclusive responsibility of the psychiatrist?
   (A) insight therapy   (B) group therapy   (C) psychodiagnosis
   (D) behavior modification   (E) electroconvulsive shock therapy

165. "Driver attention as a function of car radio sound" is a phrase in which the driver attention aspect represents the
   (A) intervening variable   (B) independent variable   (C) dependent variable   (D) irrelevant variable   (E) divergent variable

166. As one compares the backgrounds of normal and psychotic children, which one of the following is *not* significantly different between the two groups?
   (A) prenatal stress   (B) abnormal siblings   (C) destitute home environment   (D) foster home settings   (E) difficulty during delivery

167. X and Y are perfectly positively correlated. It is possible to conclude that
   (A) A caused Y
   (B) Y caused X
   (C) X and Y are caused by still a third variable
   (D) a strong, systematic relationship exists between them
   (E) very little relationship exists between the two

168. Which of the following has *not* been used in the treatment of alcoholism?
(A) filming the patient's drinking behavior for later viewing by the patient himself
(B) drinking rules that include taking sips
(C) drinking rules that include making each drink last at least twenty minutes
(D) placing electrodes on the patient's drinking hand
(E) chemoconvulsive shock therapy

169. Which of the following techniques places greatest emphasis upon the goal of making a client aware of the totality of his behavior?
(A) implosive therapy   (B) logotherapy   (C) client-centered therapy
(D) Gestalt therapy   (E) ego analysis

170. In electroconvulsive shock therapy
(A) a muscle relaxant is used to reduce the dangers of the seizure
(B) a very low voltage current of five to ten volts is applied for ten to twenty seconds
(C) the resultant seizure lasts for five to ten minutes
(D) consciousness is retained throughout
(E) LSD is often administered

171. The sociopath is marked by
(A) hallucinations
(B) delusions
(C) illusions
(D) an abnormal social environment
(E) sexual deviation

172. *Not* characteristic of psychosis is
(A) time, place, or person disorientation
(B) that it is more severe than neurosis
(C) the absence of apparent anxiety
(D) the ability to distinguish reality from fantasy
(E) hallucination

173. From a therapeutic and prognostic standpoint, which of the following would be considered the most serious?
(A) paranoid states   (B) paranoia   (C) conversion reaction
(D) obsessive compulsion   (E) anxiety reaction

174. Believing that the CIA and the attorney general are out to get him, a man comes out of his apartment only at night after painstaking efforts to be certain he is not being followed. This is a case of
(A) paranoid schizophrenia
(B) paranoid reaction
(C) dissociative reaction
(D) anxiety reaction
(E) obsessive-compulsive reaction

175. An IQ of 40 is associated with the classification known as
(A) educable   (B) nontrainable   (C) mildly retarded
(D) severely retarded   (E) moderately retarded

176. Industrial screening procedures for given positions rely heavily on
    (A) the intelligence factor
    (B) the creativity factor
    (C) factors correlating with past success in the specific positions
    (D) manual dexterity
    (E) identifiable factors correlating with future success in the specific positions

177. In human engineering, the best display panel
    (A) maximizes operator interpretation and integration of data from several sources
    (B) minimizes operator interpretation and integration of data from several sources
    (C) maximizes time delay between the receipt of information and the behavioral response
    (D) functions adequately in a limited number of ambient conditions
    (E) keeps operator interpretation and integration of data from several sources at an intermediate level

Questions 178–180 are based on the following instructions and answer choices. For each of the following, determine the best definition among the subsequent items.

   (1) mean
   (2) median
   (3) chi-square
   (4) z-score
   (5) mode

178. The average of the scores in a distribution.
    (A) 1   (B) 2   (C) 3   (D) 4   (E) 5

179. The score that functions as the midpoint dividing line, i.e., the 50th percentile in a distribution.
    (A) 1   (B) 2   (C) 3   (D) 4   (E) 5

180. The most frequently occurring score in a distribution.
    (A) 1   (B) 2   (C) 3   (D) 4   (E) 5

181. To utilize the Purkinje effect on a night reconnaissance mission, which of the following should pilots wear in the lighted briefing session just prior to night takeoff?
    (A) green goggles   (B) blue goggles   (C) red goggles
    (D) yellow goggles   (E) violet goggles

Questions 182–186 are based on the following answer choices. For each of the following situations, determine the most appropriate design among the subsequent items.

   (1) *t*-test: related measures
   (2) treatments-by-subjects design
   (3) completely randomized design
   (4) Latin Square design
   (5) treatments-by-treatments-by-subjects design

182. Reaction time as a function of distraction level. Group 1 — no distraction; group 2 — low distraction; group 3 — moderate distraction; group 4 — high distraction. Equal number of subjects in each group and one score per subject.
    (A) 1   (B) 2   (C) 3   (D) 4   (E) 5

183. Children matched initially on the basis of sex and equivalent IQ score. One child in

each pair will be assigned to a group that will receive no special instruction. Score recorded for analysis will be IQ score on a second test administered to each group at the end of the instructional period.
(A) 1   (B) 2   (C) 3   (D) 4   (E) 5

184. The effect of drug administration upon learning lists of varying difficulty. Within the drug and no-drug groups, there will be three subdivisions, counterbalancing for order of list learning (e.g., one subgroup — hard, med., easy; a second subgroup — easy, hard, med.; a third subgroup — med., easy, hard). One score for each list learned.
(A) 1   (B) 2   (C) 3   (D) 4   (E) 5

185. Experimental investigation of short-term and long-term retention of (1) digits and (2) nonsense syllables in a single group of subjects.
(A) 1   (B) 2   (C) 3   (D) 4   (E) 5

186. An experiment to study the IQ performance of the same group at four different ages.
(A) 1   (B) 2   (C) 3   (D) 4   (E) 5

187. Human engineering experiments that have involved the comparison of performance by persons who could breathe only warm, "stale" air while their bodies were appropriately cooled with that by persons who breathed cool, dry air while their bodies were exposed to warm, moist air found that the critical factor prompting excellence in performance was
(A) breathing warm, "stale" air
(B) breathing cool, dry air
(C) appropriate exterior body cooling
(D) body exposure to warm, moist air
(E) the combination of breathing cool air and having the body exposed to warm, moist air

188. During the past thirty years, industrial psychology has evolved toward
(A) less reliance on standardized instruments
(B) more emphasis on human relations
(C) more emphasis on hierarchy
(D) more emphasis on organizational structure
(E) less emphasis on communication

189. In most social settings, the theory of social attraction of which one of the following appears most applicable?
(A) Newcomb   (B) Winch   (C) Webster   (D) Finch
(E) Zajonc

190. In which one of the following test setting types might a person be asked to respond to the statement "I would accept him as a close friend"?
(A) Thurstone   (B) Osgood   (C) Bogardus   (D) Remmers
(E) Likert

191. If every score in a distribution has been divided by 7, the standard deviation
(A) decreases by 7
(B) decreases by 14
(C) decreases to the quotient obtained when the original standard deviation value is divided by 7
(D) remains unchanged
(E) increases to 7 times the original standard deviation value

192. Which test gauges the probability of occupational success by comparing a subject's interests with those reported by persons successfully engaged in various occupational fields?
    (A) Kuder (B) 16 PF (C) Allport-Vernon-Lindzey
    (D) WAIS (E) Strong Vocational Interest Blank

193. In designing and arranging work space, human engineering personnel seek to
    (A) build in unnecessary worker movement to reduce boredom
    (B) eliminate all unnecessary movement
    (C) keep workers within close talking distance of each other
    (D) place the most important functions just above the worker's head
    (E) keep as many work settings as possible adjacent to the lounge area

194. Research with industrial workers has found which one of the following to be the most effective motivator?
    (A) money (B) prestige (C) opportunity for advancement
    (D) frequency of coffee breaks (E) laissez-faire supervision

195. The problem encountered with one form of the Stanford-Binet was that
    (A) standard deviations for one age group were not consistent for other age groups
    (B) means for one age group were not consistent for other age groups
    (C) modes for one age group were not consistent for other age groups
    (D) tasks in the test had not been standardized
    (E) no cross-cultural standardization procedures had been used

196. The statistic that deals most prominently with the terms *observed frequency*, *expected frequency*, and *contingency tables* is
    (A) t (B) z (C) chi-square (D) analysis of covariance
    (E) point-biserial correlation

197. In equipment design, human engineering recommends that the *least* important and *least* frequent tasks on a console be placed
    (A) immediately in front of the person
    (B) immediately above the person
    (C) approximately forty-five degrees to the right of center
    (D) approximately forty-five degrees to the left of center
    (E) approximately ninety to one hundred degrees to the right or left of center

198. Knowledge that two people obtained test scores of 85 in an introductory psychology class is
    (A) sufficient to determine their test performance
    (B) meaningless without knowledge of the mean
    (C) meaningless without knowledge of both the mean and the standard deviation
    (D) meaningless without knowledge of the mode
    (E) meaningless without knowledge of the distribution skew

199. A decision to study bright children intermittently over a period of several years is a decision to conduct a
    (A) cross-cultural study (B) latitudinal study (C) longitudinal study
    (D) laboratory study (E) field study

200. When an election is being held almost immediately (within a day or two) after a political gathering, and a political candidate can choose his spot on the program, which one of the following positions would be his best choice?
(A) first speaker
(B) middle speaker
(C) last speaker
(D) either first or last speaker
(E) any of the three speaking slots

Test 4: Answer Comments

1. (A) The physiological limitations of the human visual apparatus enable the motion picture principle to function effectively. The human eye does not have the capacity to detect individual frames when presented in rapid succession.

2. (B) Olfaction occurs in the roof of the nasal cavity above the turbinate bones.

3. (D) The ossicles — hammer, anvil, and stirrup — occupy the area between the eardrum and the oval window.

4. (D) The visceral senses provide feedback relating to the internal organs of the body.

5. (B) When four closely contiguous lines are perceived as a square, closure (gap fill-in) has occurred.

6. (A) McClelland has found that children with high achievement need seem to demonstrate a preference for intermediate risk tasks.

7. (C) In a situation where winning probabilities are equivalent, Atkinson has found that response strength is also dependent upon the value that the subject places on the achievement.

8. (C) Experimental work in perception was pioneered by Wertheimer, founder of the Gestalt school and approach.

9. (D) Draw two lines of equal length. At either end of one line draw an arrowhead. At either end of the other, draw an inverted arrowhead. You now have the basic ingredients of the Muller-Lyer illusion — which *seems* to show that the two lines are not equal in length.

10. (C) Encouragement of independence has been found in the childhood backgrounds of persons with high achievement need.

11. (B) The term describing coordination of antagonistic muscle activity is *reciprocal innervation*.

12. (D) Striated muscles have skeletal movement responsibility.

13. (B) Wernicke's center, in the left temporal lobe just below the auditory area, relates to the understanding of spoken language.

14. (B) A prominent monocular depth cue is the texture-density gradient.

15. (A) The longer the vigilance time, the lower the likelihood of operator detection.

16. (A) At levels close to threshold, increasing the strength of a stimulus shortens reaction time.

17. (A) When two sense organs are stimulated simultaneously, reaction time is faster than when only one is stimulated.

18. (A) A unit of time (day, month, etc.) seems longest when it is being perceived by a young child.

19. (A) Tolman and Lewin held similar views relating to purposive behavior and field theory.

20. (D) Atkinson's work is among the most important in achievement motivation research.

21. (A) Watson categorized human infant emotional responses as love, rage, and fear.

22. (B) Stratton's "goggle world" was upside-down at first, but within a matter of days surprising visual adaptation occurred, and the world was perceptually normal again, despite the goggles.

23. (A) Critics argued initially that McGinnies's subjects had perceived taboo words but had failed to report them.

24. (C) The familiar face-vase picture is one of the most prominent demonstrations of figure reversibility.

25. (C) The Pacinian corpuscle is related to pressure sensation. Distributed widely in the body, these corpuscles are associated with deep pressure sensitivity.

26. (D) Dreaming occurs in Stage I, rapid-eye-movement sleep, which is characterized by a low-amplitude, fast, irregular rhythm (similar in EEG pattern to that of an active, walking person).

27. (B) A basic Gestalt tenet is that behavior is more than the sum of its parts.

28. (C) Misperception of a stimulus is the definition of illusion, and a response in the absence of an external stimulus defines a basic characteristic of hallucination.

29. (D) In Restle's "moon illusion," the moon on the horizon is perceived as larger than the moon overhead.

30. (E) Deep sleep, Stage IV, is characterized by the delta wave.

31. (B) The basilar membrane is central to the neural transmission aspect of hearing.

32. (A) McDougall was an early, strong proponent of the belief that behavior must be viewed in molar, purposive terms, not in mechanistic S-R terms.

33. (D) Tinbergen considers development, mechanisms, function, and evolution to be the four major areas of study in animal behavior.

34. (A) In his field theory, Lewin expressed the belief that a person responds on the basis of his psychological environment at the moment of action.

35. (B) James expressed the view that habit involves instinct in combination with experience.

36. (D) Duplicity theory relates to rod-cone vision. Early theorists went so far as to postulate a "double retina," later modifying and correcting this theory in terms of rod-cone.

37. (E) Muller's famous "specific energies of nerves" position continues to have a far-reaching effect in sensory theory.

38. (B) Critical flicker frequency is the rate of light fluctuation above which fusion occurs.

39. (B) The suggestion that all auditory nerves fire constantly and repeatedly to produce reception of a given pitch would be the crux of the basic frequency theory.

40. (A) One of the major corpus callosum functions is message transference between cerebral hemispheres of the brain.

41. (D) Perceptual constancies are primarily attributable to learning. A person must learn, for instance, that the train on the distant horizon is a large machine and not a tiny dot.

42. (E) Because of the location of the occipital lobe, a severe blow on the back of the head would endanger vision.

43. (C) The nondecremental property refers to the neural transmission finding that an impulse is sent to the end of the axon without fading or weakening.

44. (D) Alpha wave frequency is approximately ten cycles per second.

45. (B) The Montreal Studies indicated that the original infant emotion was excitement.

46. (B) Very high anger arousal causes dilation of blood vessels near the skin.

47. (D) By electrical stimulation, Olds located pleasure centers in the rat brain.

48. (E) In comparing the neuron to a doorbell system, the dendrites most closely approximate the button that a visitor would push. They are located at the receiving end of the neuron.

49. (A) Because there is strong evidence of compensation for instances of dream deprivation, it appears that dreaming serves a basic organismic need.

50. (E) There appears to be a relationship between increased stomach acids and the presence of resentment-hostility emotions within a person.

51. (B) The Cannon-Bard theory relates to the thalamus and hypothalamus. Disputing the James-Lange theory of emotion, Cannon and Bard pointed out that different emotions are accompanied by the same visceral state.

52. (A) The axon governs nerve-impulse travel from a cell body to other neurons.

53. (D) Two different intensities of light presented to a subject simultaneously would be an implementation of the difference-limen method in psychophysics experimentation.

54. (B) Weber's Law is expressed in the formula: $(\Delta I)/I = K$. The formula suggests a constant ratio. If, for a weight of twenty-five pounds, you require the addition of five pounds before you can detect that weight has been added, Weber would say that for a fifty-pound weight a ten-pound addition would be required for detection.

55. (A) The left part of each retina is connected to the left occipital lobe, and the right part of each retina is connected to the right occipital lobe — a neural phenomenon creating obvious problems in split-brain research. It is for this reason that split-brain research must be preceded by surgery to the optic chiasm.

56. (A) Broca's area is in the frontal lobe of the left cerebral hemisphere, just above the fissure of Sylvius. It is responsible for speech.

57. (D) Wernicke's center, responsible for understanding spoken language, is an area in the left temporal lobe, just below the auditory area and curving around the end of the fissure of Sylvius.

58. (C) In each cerebral hemisphere, the fissure of Sylvius separates the temporal from the frontal and parietal lobes.

59. (E) Reticular formation refers to neural fibers in the brain stem that have an important telephone-switchboard-type selective arousal function.

60. (A) In escape conditioning, the aversive stimulus (e.g., shock) is always received by the subject. This distinguishes escape conditioning from avoidance conditioning.

61. (D) A common memory storage distinction is short-term and long-term.

62. (C) While punishment is generally ineffective in weakening existing conditioned responses and changing long-range behavior patterns, it can have cue value.

63. (D) Trophoblast refers to a group of cells surrounding the blastocyst cavity — cells that will later become the placenta and chorion.

64. (E) A horse-race betting situation illustrates the variable ratio reinforcement setting.

65. (A) Meat powder qualifies as a UCS because of its inherent reinforcing qualities.

66. (E) Concurrent validity is obtained by correlating performances on a new test with the same test taker's performances on an established test in the field.

67. (D) Retention for motor tasks is much higher than retention for verbal or conceptual material.

68. (D) While the Guilford model did use the terms *operations*, *contents*, *products*, and *transformations*, it did not use the term *syntax*.

69. (E) In higher-order conditioning, a former CS functions as a UCS for further conditioning. The method has limited applicability.

70. (D) The lower the decimal figure, the higher the significance level. In this instance, the lowest figure is .005.

71. (E) The newborn does not have well-developed pain sensitivity, as is evidenced by circumstances that have occurred without anesthesia.

72. (D) One cannot predict at what point in the communication process noise will occur. It has the potential for occurring at virtually any point.

73. (C) While adolescent gangs frequently are formed with "get-even" purposes, children's gangs are not.

74. (A) Mnemonic strategies facilitate remembering by adding meaningfulness to the material. Forming a word from the notations for the treble clef exemplifies such a strategy.

75. (D) While sickle cell is a race-prominent form of anemia that involves an abnormal form of hemoglobin and the possibility of dangerous clotting, it is not a form of cancer.

76. (A) Half the possible combinations could yield brown-eyed children.

77. (E) Balanced diet through self-selection functions most effectively in the absence of learned tastes. The human adult's development of learned taste preferences seriously reduces prospects for success in obtaining a balanced diet via self-selection.

78. (E) A genotype-phenotype relationship is analogous to heredity-appearance.

79. (C) The critical-periods concept of cognitive-intellectual development is being called into question by the research work of Kagan.

80. (E) Moro response is an infantile startle response caused by any sudden, intense stimulus such as a loud noise. The response itself involves the sudden outstretching of arms and legs.

81. (C) The fact that each mature egg or sperm contains only one chromosome from each pair is attributable to the process known as reduction division.

82. (B) Memory aids that add meaningfulness to material are most effective.

83. (B) In Harlow's experiments, the surrogate-reared infant monkeys were least fearful in the presence of the surrogate mother to which clinging responses had been directed during early development.

84. (E) The cardiac muscle is a special kind of striated muscle. All striated muscles share the quality of having a striped appearance that is evident through microscopic examination. With the exception of the cardiac muscle, striated muscles have skeletal-movement functions.

85. (D) Positive transfer (proactive facilitation) is greatest where the person is asked to perform an old response to similar stimuli.

86. (A) Tulving's research concentrates upon the processes underlying the reception, retention, and recall of information.

87. (B) Bruner's terms expressing the three modes of developing a mental world model are *enactive*, *iconic*, and *symbolic*.

88. (B) The rest interval following practice will produce reminiscence — opportunity to "consolidate" — resulting in subsequent performance with an absence of intervening practice.

89. (A) Jones's studies of adolescents indicate that early maturation is an advantage for males but a disadvantage for females.

90. (C) In the serial-anticipation method of verbal learning, a single list of nonsense syllables is presented sequentially.

91. (E) The most severe conflict situation is likely to be that of avoidance-avoidance — prompting organismic flight from the conflict situation.

92. (B) The multiple-choice format in teaching machine instruction is a recognition design.

93. (C) Dollard and Miller state the basic requirements for learning to be drive, cue, response, and reinforcement.

94. (E) The grasping reflex in the newborn is obtained by stimulating the palms or fingers.

95. (A) The Babkin response is obtained by pressing the palms of the child's hands while he is lying on his back. The response itself involves head return to midline.

96. (B) Babinski response is obtained by stroking the sole of the neonate's foot. The toes now fan outward, but later in life they will curl inward when such stroking occurs.

97. (B) The term *cephalocaudal* refers to the fact that the upper part of a young child's body develops earlier than the lower part.

98. (B) The developmental term *mitosis* refers to cell division and multiplication. A natural confusion occurs with the term *meiosis*, meaning reduction division.

99. (A) Lovaas has conducted some of the most influential, pioneering behavior modification work with autistic children.

100. (E) Harlow's best-known work deals with primate research relating to emotional development and learning sets. He is not involved in psycholinguistics research.

101. (C) The Wechsler Scale provides separate IQ scores for the verbal and performance sections.

102. (B) In research comparison with male newborns, females have demonstrated more rapid adjustment to the postnatal environment.

103. (E) Sham feeding is an experimental technique of "eating" and "swallowing" food that does not reach the stomach.

104. (A) In Chomsky's explanation of grammar acquisition in children, he speaks of a "programmed" nervous system.

105. (E) Infant intelligence tests are not accurate predictors of later IQ. Instead, they tend to measure DQ (developmental quotient).

106. (C) Piaget's theoretical view holds the position that a cognitive operation has both internalized action and reversibility.

107. (D) Congenital refers to presence at birth.

108. (D) Learning implies a potentiality, while performance is action-oriented.

109. (B) A correct sequence would be nontrainable, trainable, educable.

110. (E) Kendler and Kendler have found that reversal shifts are performed more quickly and more easily among older children than among younger children or animals. The well-known Kendler studies have investigated the phenomenon systematically with children of different ages as well as with laboratory animals.

111. (D) Each subsequent word must both advance by one letter in the alphabetical sequence and increase its total number of letters by one.

112. (C) The score is above the mean by $1^3/_5$ standard deviations, making $+1.60$ the corresponding z-score.

113. (D) Research has found among creative children a willingness to risk a seemingly "kooky" idea.

114. (A) In his child studies, Sears has found a strong relationship between a child's receiving parental punishment for aggression and that child's expressing strong prosocial aggression.

115. (B) In proactive facilitation, practice on an earlier task facilitates learning and performance of a subsequent task.

116. (D) Two standard deviations above the mean of a normal distribution is a point at which approximately 98 percent of scores are less than or equal to that point — the 98th percentile.

117. (D) Two distinct concentrations of scores in a frequency distribution means that the distribution is bimodal. It would be possible for such a distribution to be symmetrical, having neither positive nor negative skew.

118. (C) Attributable to Bartlett in England, this cryptarithmetic problem has found wide usage in the study of human problem solving both in this country and abroad.

119. (D) Freudian defense mechanisms carry the function of relieving anxiety associated with the threat of the emergence of the id impulse.

120. (C) Schachter found that persons experiencing fear of an upcoming event preferred the company of others having a similar fear based on their scheduling to experience the same threatening event. If given a choice of associating with other persons not scheduled to experience the event, they preferred to be alone.

121. (E) Rogers emphasizes the self-concept — differentiation of a portion of one's phenomenal field.

122. (B) Similarity in attitudes has proved most critical to social attraction in the work of Rokeach and Newcomb.

123. (A) Rokeach and Mezei found that same attitudes, combined with the same-different race variable, continued to be the most critical variables in social attraction.

124. (D) Social facilitation refers to performance enhancement prompted by the mere presence of others (e.g., "I play better with an audience.").

125. (B) Dollard and Miller's learning-theory approach to neurotic conflict suggests that such conflicts are learned early in childhood as a function of parent-created learning settings.

126. (A) Newcomb espouses similarity as the basic factor in attraction.

127. (E) Fromm speaks of brotherliness versus incest in his sociopsychoanalytic approach to personality theory.

128. (B) Association with higher cultural value or cultural contribution is related to sublimation.

129. (A) Within his discussion of the psychodynamic view of prejudice, Allport includes the instinctive and scapegoating processes.

130. (B) In psychoanalysis, the anal stage of psychosexual development is seen as carrying a strong likelihood of child negativism.

131. (E) Motor tasks have the strongest long-term retention.

132. (B) In Freud's divisions of the psyche, the ego is the reality-oriented entry. Id operates on the instinctual, pleasure principle, and superego functions on the social, morality principle.

133. (D) Attitudes are learned, not unconditioned.

134. (E) Fiedler has been one of the leading researchers in the area of leadership.

135. (E) Occurring with the Oedipus complex, the castration fear is experienced by male children and is directed toward the father.

136. (E) With greater distance from the source of frustration comes lower inhibition and, consequently, greater likelihood of aggressive actions.

137. (B) It would be essential for the two groups to be equivalent in motor ability. Otherwise, differences in performance would be meaningless.

138. (D) The child's access only to a mirror to monitor his tracing movements means that his feedback is reversed from that which he normally would receive through direct observation. Therefore, he must reorient himself and move beyond familiar habits in eye-hand coordination.

139. (B) Group 1 tracing time per trial dropped much more rapidly across trials than tracing time in group 2 — a factor in support of spaced practice as more effective than massed practice in this experimental setting.

140. (A) Models of helping occurring prior to a given potential helping setting increase the likelihood that a person in the latter setting will render help.

141. (E) Adorno and his associates conclude that there is a strong correlation between authoritarian attitudes and distinct personality characteristics.

142. (D) Phrenology is the primitive, "bumps-on-the-head" approach to personality determination.

143. (D) *Functional fictionalism* was a term used by Adler in referring to an individual's perception and interpretation of his environment.

144. (E) Sullivan's parataxic category — casually associating events occurring in proximity to each other — is tailor-made for superstition.

145. (B) Utilizing rod-and-frame and associated methods, Witkin has focused attention on field dependence and field independence.

146. (B) Sherif's observed change in individual judgments toward group judgments reflected the strength of group influence upon the judgments of individual members.

147. (C) Peptic ulcers are classified as psychosomatic disorders — that is, emotionally initiated physiological disorders.

148. (D) Most sexual offenders are among the persons least likely to be second offenders.

149. (C) At one time, talking about suicide was believed to indicate low likelihood of its occurrence. On the basis of research, such a belief is no longer held.

150. (A) Expressing in the psychotherapy setting a strong emotion once held toward a close relative would be transference.

151. (C) The second percentile, two standard deviations below the mean of the distribution — 2 percent of total scores being lower than or equal to this score.

152. (A) The general prognosis for psychoneurotic disorders is good. They can be treated on an outpatient basis while the patient remains functional in his environment.

153. (D) Of the choices indicated, Coleman's framework would indicate that divorce at age forty-three would affect the most body systems.

154. (C) Ascribed status is a function of birth; achieved status is a function of learning and performance. Caste emphasizes the former.

155. (E) Electroconvulsive shock therapy has proven most effective in the treatment of depression.

156. (C) Synanon is a treatment center for drug addicts — based on the same treatment philosophy employed by Alcoholics Anonymous.

157. (E) The fugue dissociative reaction includes physical flight from the conflict setting.

158. (A) Taking roles and enacting conflict-ridden life situations is characteristic of psychodrama.

159. (E) The Latin Square experimental design sets up controls for the order in which treatments are received.

160. (C) Hollingshead and Redlich found that psychosis was most prominent in the lower social class.

161. (E) Sleepwalking, fugue, amnesia, and multiple personality are all expressions of dissociative reaction; conversion is not.

162. (C) *Psychosomatic disorder* suggests the presence of a continuous bodily emergency reaction and resulting tissue damage.

163. (E) The most serious phase of alcoholism is the chronic phase — the phase a person generally must reach before being receptive to meaningful rehabilitation efforts.

164. (E) The psychiatrist, as a physician, must take responsibility for the administration of electroconvulsive shock therapy.

165. (C) In this description, car radio sound is the independent variable and driver attention is the dependent variable.

166. (E) Between normal and psychotic children, research has revealed no detectable difference in prevalence of difficulty during delivery.

167. (D) Perfect positive correlation is indicative of the strongest possible systematic relationship between two variables.

168. (E) Chemoconvulsive shock therapy is not used in the treatment of alcoholism.

169. (D) Client awareness of the totality of his behavior is a central emphasis within Gestalt therapy.

170. (A) In electroconvulsive shock therapy, a muscle relaxant is administered to reduce the dangers of the seizure.

171. (D) An abnormal social environment is central to the sociopathic disorder.

172. (D) The psychotic lacks the capability of distinguishing between reality and fantasy.

173. (B) Paranoia is a long-term, defensive reaction to stress; it often proves very resistant to therapy.

174. (B) The setting vividly describes a paranoid reaction.

175. (E) An IQ of 40 comes in the moderately retarded range, which covers the 30-to-50 span.

176. (C) Industrial screening procedures for a given position rely heavily on factors correlating with past success in that position.

177. (B) In human engineering, the best display is the one that minimizes operator interpretation and integration of data from several sources.

178. (A) The mean is the average of the scores in a distribution.

179. (B) The median functions as the midpoint dividing line for high and low scores in a distribution.

180. (E) The mode is the most frequently occurring score in a distribution.

181. (C) Red goggles would protect the rods so that they could function as soon as the pilot moved out of the briefing room into the darkness.

182. (C) The presence of only one independent variable (distraction level) and one measure (score) per subject suggests a completely randomized design.

183. (A) Initial matching of subjects, with assignment of one member in each pair to the second group and comparison of scores on the same testing instrument, suggests the t-test for related measures (in this case, the related-measure aspect was the initial matching).

184. (D) The built-in control for the order of presentation suggests the Latin Square design.

185. (E) Two treatments for the same group of subjects suggests the treatments-by-treatments-by-subjects design.

186. (B) The same group being tested at four different intervals suggests the treatments-by-subjects design.

187. (C) Human engineering has found performance efficiency more directly related to appropriate exterior body cooling than to breathing cool, dry air.

188. (B) During the past thirty years, industrial psychology has evolved toward more emphasis on human relations, that is, expressed concern for the worker himself.

189. (A) Newcomb's similarity-in-social-attraction position has proved applicable to the broadest range of settings.

190. (C) The Bogardus-type scale uses several social-distance statements of this kind.

191. (C) Standard deviation will be affected in the same manner as every score in the distribution — in this instance, it will be divided by 7.

192. (E) Comparisons of subjects' interests with the interests of persons successfully engaged in various occupational fields is the basic structure of the Strong Vocational Interest Blank.

193. (B) In any given work setting, human engineering seeks to eliminate all unnecessary movement.

194. (C) Among the answer choices, opportunity for advancement has been found to be the most effective work incentive. Contrary to popular belief, money is not the leading work incentive.

195. (A) In the 1937 form, standard deviations were not consistent throughout age ranges. The problem was corrected in the 1960 form.

196. (C) *Observed frequency, expected frequency,* and *contingency tables* are terms relating to the chi-square statistic.

197. (E) Human engineering recommends placing the least important and least frequent tasks approximately ninety to one hundred degrees to the right or left of center on a console. Ideally, the most important and frequent tasks should be placed directly in front of the person.

198. (C) Knowledge that two people have obtained a given score is meaningless unless we know both the mean and the standard deviation of the score distribution.

199. (C) The study of bright children intermittently over a period of years would be a longitudinal study.

200. (C) Because of the nearness to the election, his best choice would be the position of last speaker on the program.

Test 4: Evaluating Your Score

Abbreviation Guide

PC	Physiological/Comparative
SnP	Sensation/Perception
LM	Learning/Motivation/Emotion
CHL	Cognition/Complex Human Learning
D	Developmental
PrS	Personality/Social
PyCl	Psychopathology/Clinical
M	Methodology
Ap	Applied

Subject Area Chart

Use this chart to determine the subject matter covered by each question in Test 4.

1.	SnP	21.	LM	41.	SnP	61.	CHL	81.	D
2.	SnP	22.	SnP	42.	PC	62.	LM	82.	CHL
3.	SnP	23.	SnP	43.	PC	63.	D	83.	LM
4.	SnP	24.	SnP	44.	PC	64.	LM	84.	PC
5.	SnP	25.	PC	45.	LM	65.	LM	85.	LM
6.	LM	26.	PC	46.	LM	66.	M	86.	CHL
7.	LM	27.	SnP	47.	PC	67.	CHL	87.	D
8.	SnP	28.	SnP	48.	PC	68.	CHL	88.	CHL
9.	SnP	29.	SnP	49.	PC	69.	LM	89.	D
10.	LM	30.	PC	50.	LM	70.	M	90.	CHL
11.	PC	31.	SnP	51.	LM	71.	D	91.	LM
12.	PC	32.	LM	52.	PC	72.	CHL	92.	CHL
13.	PC	33.	PC	53.	SnP	73.	D	93.	LM
14.	SnP	34.	LM	54.	SnP	74.	CHL	94.	D
15.	SnP	35.	LM	55.	SnP	75.	D	95.	D
16.	SnP	36.	PC	56.	PC	76.	D	96.	D
17.	SnP	37.	PC	57.	PC	77.	PC	97.	D
18.	SnP	38.	SnP	58.	PC	78.	D	98.	D
19.	LM	39.	SnP	59.	PC	79.	CHL	99.	D
20.	LM	40.	PC	60.	LM	80.	D	100.	LM

101.	CHL	121.	PrS	141.	PrS	161.	PyCl	181.	Ap
102.	D	122.	Ap	142.	PrS	162.	PyCl	182.	M
103.	LM	123.	Ap	143.	PrS	163.	PyCl	183.	M
104.	CHL	124.	PrS	144.	PrS	164.	PyCl	184.	M
105.	D	125.	PrS	145.	PrS	165.	M	185.	M
106.	CHL	126.	PrS	146.	PrS	166.	PyCl	186.	M
107.	D	127.	PrS	147.	PyCl	167.	M	187.	Ap
108.	LM	128.	PrS	148.	PyCl	168.	PyCl	188.	Ap
109.	CHL	129.	PrS	149.	PyCl	169.	PyCl	189.	Ap
110.	CHL	130.	PrS	150.	PyCl	170.	PyCl	190.	Ap
111.	CHL	131.	Ap	151.	M	171.	PyCl	191.	M
112.	M	132.	PrS	152.	PyCl	172.	PyCl	192.	Ap
113.	D	133.	PrS	153.	PyCl	173.	PyCl	193.	Ap
114.	LM	134.	PrS	154.	PrS	174.	PyCl	194.	Ap
115.	CHL	135.	PrS	155.	PyCl	175.	CHL	195.	Ap
116.	M	136.	PrS	156.	PyCl	176.	Ap	196.	M
117.	M	137.	M	157.	PyCl	177.	Ap	197.	Ap
118.	CHL	138.	M	158.	PyCl	178.	M	198.	Ap
119.	PrS	139.	M	159.	M	179.	M	199.	M
120.	PrS	140.	PrS	160.	PyCl	180.	M	200.	Ap

Record the number of questions you missed in each subject area.

PC —   CHL —   PyCl —
SnP —   D   —   M   —
LM —   PrS —   Ap   —

Test Score Scale

The first number given is the number of questions in the test in that subject area. The number in parentheses indicates the 75th percentile score. To determine how well you score in each subject area, subtract the number of questions you missed in a certain area from the total number of questions in that area. Compare the result with the 75th percentile number. If it is lower than 75%, you probably need more review.

PC —23(18)   CHL —20(15)   PyCl —23(18)
SnP —25(19)   D   —20(15)   M   —23(18)
LM —26(20)   PrS —23(18)   Ap   —17(13)

Test Five

Time 170 minutes

Directions Each of the following questions contains five possible responses. Read the question carefully and select the response that you feel is most appropriate. Then completely darken the space on your answer grid that corresponds with your choice.

1. Hysterical anesthesias
   (A) correlate closely with body areas covered by specific articles of clothing
   (B) correlate closely with body neural patterns
   (C) never include the feet
   (D) never include any portion of the main torso
   (E) never include the head area

2. Current trends in mental health do *not* include
   (A) construction of larger state hospitals
   (B) stepped up emphasis on outpatient care
   (C) greater emphasis on community mental health centers
   (D) prominent use of behavior modification
   (E) group therapy

3. "It treats symptom rather than cause!" This is a criticism commonly leveled at
   (A) psychoanalysis   (B) implosive psychotherapy   (C) insight-oriented therapy   (D) behavior therapy   (E) transactional analysis

4. Among first admissions to public mental hospitals, which one of the following diagnoses is most prevalent?
   (A) schizophrenic reaction
   (B) psychoneurotic disorder
   (C) alcoholic addiction
   (D) involutional psychotic reaction
   (E) cerebral arteriosclerosis

5. The view that neurosis is essentially synonymous with personal immaturity is held by
   (A) Fromm   (B) Mowrer   (C) Jung   (D) Skinner
   (E) Watson

6. Body metabolism is a key function of the
   (A) pituitary gland   (B) adrenal gland   (C) thyroid gland
   (D) pineal gland   (E) lymph gland

7. Which one of the following would be considered an operational definition in GSR lie detection?
   (A) Changes in emotionality result in measurable physiological changes.
   (B) Changes in emotionality result in observable behavioral change.
   (C) Changes in emotionality result in changes of thought.
   (D) Changes in emotionality result in brain-wave changes.
   (E) Changes in emotionality result in attitude changes.

8. Studies of emotions in twins suggest that the intensity and manner in which emotion is expressed is
   (A) at least partially hereditary
   (B) wholly learned
   (C) dependent entirely upon intrauterine environment
   (D) a matter of sibling modeling
   (E) dependent entirely upon "expected value of response"

Questions 9–12 are based on the following experiment.

Each subject was given serial presentation of a twelve-item list of nonsense syllables. Following the presentation, the subject was dismissed from the laboratory with instructions to return the following day at the same time. Upon returning, the subject was asked to recall the items on the list presented the preceding day. The number of items correctly recalled was recorded, and the subject then received serial presentation of a second list of nonsense syllables with instructions to return the following day for similar procedures and a new list. The subjects each received a total of nine lists, and the recall data (in percentages) is presented in the following table.

List	Percentage Recall
1	75
2	67
3	56
4	50
5	42
6	33
7	25
8	17
9	8

9. A phenomenon that appears to be operating within this learning procedure is
   (A) retroactive inhibition   (B) proactive inhibition   (C) retroactive facilitation   (D) proactive facilitation   (E) von Restorff effect

10. Which one of the following correctly expresses the dependent variable within this experiment?
    (A) nonsense syllable   (B) percentage recall   (C) number of lists
    (D) number of items per list   (E) serial presentation

11. The results suggest that
    (A) the more lists a person learns, the better he remembers them
    (B) serial anticipation is the best method for use in recall-type studies
    (C) time delay between learning and recall is the single most important factor in forgetting
    (D) longer exposure to individual items within a list enhances recall
    (E) there is a negative correlation between the number of lists learned and the percentage recall

12. In analyzing a study of this type, the statistical design most likely to be used is the
    (A) treatments-by-subjects, repeated-measures design
    (B) Latin Square design
    (C) Kendall Rank-Order Correlation
    (D) Pearson Product-Moment Correlation
    (E) *t*-test for unrelated measures

13. The fact that a person can awaken at a specific hour without alarm clock assistance is

attributable to
- (A) correlation of bodily processes with predictable time passage
- (B) predisposed stimulus in the form of external noises heard regularly at a given hour
- (C) predisposed response generalization
- (D) convergence
- (E) configuration

14. On the basis of McClelland's findings, in which one of the following groups could a person expect to find the lowest achievement need?
    - (A) male college graduates with bachelor's degrees
    - (B) female college graduates with bachelor's degrees
    - (C) male professional students with Ph.D.s
    - (D) female professional students with Ph.D.s
    - (E) male high-school graduates with vocational training

15. In probability and decision-making settings, EV signifies
    - (A) Edwards's valence (B) energizing variable (C) enervating variable (D) expected value (E) experimental variable

16. *Not* reduced during sleep is the level of
    - (A) respiration (B) blood pressure (C) body temperature
    - (D) heart rate (E) gastric contractions

17. Which one of the following is an *incorrect* statement?
    - (A) The brains of no two persons are structurally identical.
    - (B) Brain lesions sustained in infancy have less incapacitating effect on sensory-motor functions than similar lesions sustained in adulthood.
    - (C) Brain lesions sustained in infancy have greater incapacitating effects on intellectual-learning functions than similar lesions sustained in adulthood.
    - (D) The cerebral hemisphere dominant in speech is, without exception, the cerebral hemisphere dominant in handedness.
    - (E) The right cerebral hemisphere is most often dominant in nonverbal intellectual functions.

18. The concept of equipotentiality refers to
    - (A) the visual learning of synonyms
    - (B) bipolar adjectives
    - (C) recovery of function within the brain
    - (D) performance impairment as a function of phenobarbital
    - (E) electroconvulsive shock effects on long-term memory

19. In a well-known study by Barker, Dembo, and Lewin, frustrated children
    - (A) engaged in aggression toward their toys
    - (B) engaged in aggression toward each other
    - (C) regressed to behaviors they had performed at an earlier age
    - (D) engaged in cooperative play
    - (E) engaged in parallel play

20. Which one of the following bodily patterns does *not* accompany dreaming activity?
    - (A) a distinctive EEG pattern
    - (B) rapid eye movement
    - (C) high level of cerebral blood flow
    - (D) higher brain temperature
    - (E) higher level of general muscle activity

21. Which one of the following best describes the central nervous system?
    (A) autonomic system
    (B) efferent fibers
    (C) the brain and the spinal cord
    (D) the spinal cord and the glandular system
    (E) afferent fibers

22. Dember believes figure reversibility is evidence of the fact that
    (A) the eyes are highly adaptable
    (B) cone vision predominates during bright intensity viewing
    (C) change is essential to the maintenance of perception
    (D) figure-ground is an essentially useless perceptual concept
    (E) texture gradient is not functioning properly

23. Which person's work and writing triggered the "psychocivilization versus electroligarchy" debate and discussions?
    (A) Magoun   (B) Mowrer   (C) Sperry   (D) Fisher
    (E) Delgado

24. Restle's adaptation-level theory
    (A) confirms the existing apparent-distance theory
    (B) seeks to explain the phi phenomenon
    (C) seeks to explain the horizontal-vertical illusion
    (D) seeks to explain the "moon illusion"
    (E) seeks to explain the trapezoidal window phenomenon

25. As a person views a picture one way, he sees craters. When he turns it 180 degrees, the craters become bumps. The perceptual phenomena are due to
    (A) linear perspective   (B) convergence   (C) texture
    (D) relative position   (E) light and shadow

26. In work with schizophrenics and normal male subjects, McGinnies found that, for taboo words, recognition threshold was
    (A) higher only within the normal group
    (B) higher only within the schizophrenic group
    (C) lower in both groups
    (D) higher in both groups
    (E) lower only within the schizophrenic group

27. When a pilot pulling out of a dive undergoes "3 g's," one could expect reaction-time capacity at that moment to be
    (A) shorter than normal
    (B) longer than normal
    (C) shorter in auditory modality, longer in visual modality
    (D) shorter in visual modality, longer in auditory modality
    (E) generally unchanged in all modalities

28. The phrase that "the bodily changes follow directly the perception of the exciting fact, and . . . our feeling of the same changes as they occur *is* the emotion" expresses a central aspect of the
    (A) Cannon-Bard theory   (B) Yerkes-Dodson law   (C) Cannon-Washburn theory   (D) Freudian theory   (E) James-Lange theory

29. Which one of the following terms is most aptly defined by the words "how behavior gets started, is energized, is sustained, is directed"?
    (A) emotion (B) motivation (C) achievement need
    (D) aspiration (E) osculation

30. Which one of the following sayings would social-attraction research find most generally acceptable?
    (A) "Birds of a feather flock together."
    (B) "Likes repel, opposites attract."
    (C) "Familiarity breeds contempt."
    (D) "Misery loves company."
    (E) "Friends till the end."

31. You could expect Maslow's self-actualized person to be
    (A) id-dominated
    (B) ego-dominated
    (C) relatively independent of his culture and environment
    (D) thanatos-oriented
    (E) highly aggressive

32. Prominent among the persons associated with ego analysis is
    (A) Sullivan (B) Horney (C) Fromm (D) Erikson
    (E) Rank

33. For many of their perceptual differentiations, the phenomenologists are indebted to the
    (A) Gestaltists (B) psychoanalysts (C) behaviorists
    (D) trait theorists (E) ego analysts

34. In the classic Asch experiment
    (A) five individual booths were utilized
    (B) the "critical" subject was less likely to conform to group opinion if one other subject dissented from the group
    (C) the "critical" subject under no circumstances conformed to group opinion
    (D) the "critical" subject was the middle subject in the group
    (E) five individuals at a time were given an attitude test

35. Which one of the following name combinations contains two Gestalt psychologists?
    (A) Koffka, Kohler, Kelman
    (B) Kohler, Cohen, Kelman
    (C) Wertheimer, Wundt, Kelman
    (D) James, Jensen, Kelman
    (E) Wundt, James, Wertheimer

36. In some neurons, the axon is insulated by the
    (A) Sylvian sheath (B) Pacinian sheath (C) nerve fiber
    (D) ganglion (E) myelin sheath

37. Which one of the following most accurately defines the function of the middle ear?
    (A) synaptic transmission (B) formation of neural impulse (C) sound collection (D) sound-wave amplification (E) transmission to the brain

38. Comparatively speaking, which one of the following animals has the most prominent cerebral cortex?
    (A) salmon (B) alligator (C) pigeon (D) rabbit (E) dog

39. What Hull referred to as reaction potential, Spence referred to as
    (A) habit potential (B) drive potential (C) incentive
    (D) excitatory potential (E) summation potential

40. The fact that hues at the short-wave end of the color/spectrum appear bright at nightfall is a function of
    (A) light adaptation (B) Purkinje effect (C) Zeigarnik effect
    (D) Young-Helmholtz effect (E) Rutherford effect

41. Among animals or humans, which one of the following is *not* a cycle affecting the degree or prominence of sexual behavior?
    (A) life (B) estrous (C) androgenous (D) menstrual
    (E) breeding, seasonal

42. The S-O-R terminology was developed initially by
    (A) Woodworth (B) Pavlov (C) McDougall (D) Tolman
    (E) Lewin

43. Which of the following is *not* an entry in a sensory grouping based on locus of stimulus source?
    (A) exteroceptors (B) proprioceptors (C) interoceptors
    (D) nociceptors (E) peripheroceptors

44. The sympathetic nervous system
    (A) is a subdivision of the somatic nervous system
    (B) is a subdivision of the autonomic nervous system
    (C) parallels the effects of the parasympathetic nervous system
    (D) preserves the homeostatic model
    (E) promotes syntonic functioning

45. Which one of the following would have a central role in developing bodily immunity?
    (A) gonads (B) Islets of Langerhans (C) adrenal cortex
    (D) thymus (E) pineal gland

46. McGinnies's experiments pioneered in the field of
    (A) ESP (B) phi phenomenon (C) autokinesis (D) GSR
    (E) perceptual defense

47. For the experience of taste to occur, a substance must be
    (A) at least slightly soluble in water
    (B) highly soluble in butric acid
    (C) in contact with receptors located in the center of the tongue
    (D) insoluble in butric acid
    (E) slightly above 7 on the pH scale

48. Which of the following terms is *least* likely to appear in the formulations of Lewin?
    (A) force field (B) valence (C) life space (D) tension
    (E) interference

Questions 49–50 are based on the following statements.

(1) The animal eats because it needs certain nutrients.
(2) The animal eats because it knows it needs food.
(3) The animal eats because it feels hungry.
(4) The animal eats because it is aware of its need for nutrition.
(5) The animal eats because of a change in blood-sugar level.

49. Which one of the preceding would comparative psychologists consider the most purely teleonomic statement?
 (A) 1   (B) 2   (C) 3   (D) 4   (E) 5

50. Which one of the preceding would comparative psychologists consider the most purely mechanistic statement?
 (A) 1   (B) 2   (C) 3   (D) 4   (E) 5

51. Which one of the following perceptual charts contains several rows of letters of decreasing size?
 (A) Landolt chart   (B) Vernier chart   (C) Snellen chart   (D) Ricco chart   (E) Talbot chart

52. The perception of distance as one views a two-dimensional picture of a railroad track is due primarily to
 (A) the phi phenomenon   (B) motion parallax   (C) texture gradient
 (D) linear perspective   (E) closure

53. Jastrow illusion involves
 (A) parallel straight lines
 (B) straight lines at right angles
 (C) geometrical curvatures positioned one above the other
 (D) geometrical curvatures positioned at right angles to each other
 (E) straight lines emanating from a center point at 45-degree angles

54. The "piano" theory holds that
 (A) all nerve fibers fire in all frequency ranges
 (B) specific nerve fibers respond to specific sound frequencies
 (C) specific nerve fibers respond to specific decibel ranges
 (D) all nerve fibers fire in all decibel ranges
 (E) Rutherford's theory was essentially correct but needed elaboration

55. Body maintenance of a state of internal physiological balance is described by the term
 (A) innervation   (B) ionization   (C) reflex   (D) homeostasis
 (E) piloerection

56. The corpus callosum of an individual has been sectioned as part of a treatment for epilepsy. On which of the following WAIS subtests could the person be expected to encounter the most postoperative difficulty?
 (A) information   (B) arithmetic   (C) similarities
 (D) vocabulary   (E) block design

57. The cells that respond to changes in their environment and signal these changes to the nervous system are known as
 (A) receptors   (B) effectors   (C) striated   (D) myelin
 (E) affectors

Questions 58-62 are based on the following diagram. Using the drawing below, mark the number corresponding to the primary area for the following functions.

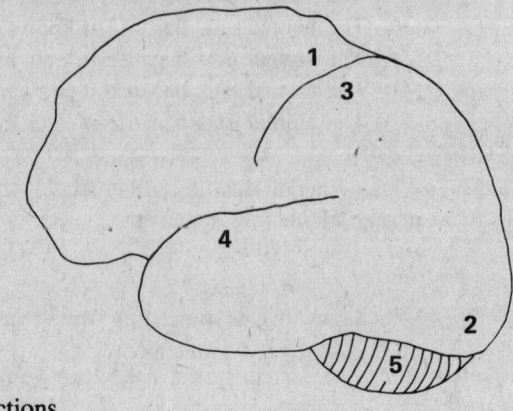

58. Motor functions
    (A) 1   (B) 2   (C) 3   (D) 4   (E) 5

59. Visual functions
    (A) 1   (B) 2   (C) 3   (D) 4   (E) 5

60. Auditory functions
    (A) 1   (B) 2   (C) 3   (D) 4   (E) 5

61. Somatosensory functions
    (A) 1   (B) 2   (C) 3   (D) 4   (E) 5

62. Maintenance of balance and posture
    (A) 1   (B) 2   (C) 3   (D) 4   (E) 5

63. Which one of the following pairs does *not* contain synonyms?
    (A) classical conditioning–type S
    (B) operant conditioning–instrumental conditioning
    (C) instrumental conditioning–type R
    (D) discriminative stimulus–S(Delta)
    (E) reinforcement–increased likelihood of response repetition

64. During dating, which one of the following relationships takes on critical importance for the adolescent?
    (A) same-sex parent
    (B) opposite-sex parent
    (C) both same- and opposite-sex parent relationships
    (D) neither same- nor opposite-sex parent relationship
    (E) grandparent confidant

65. Which one of the following word combinations is completely compatible with the phrase *knowledge of results*?
    (A) feedback, potential for improved performance
    (B) proactive inhibition, feedback
    (C) positive transfer, feedback
    (D) feedback, punishment
    (E) feedback, reward

66. According to the tenets of the Zeigarnik effect
    (A) a completed task is more likely to be remembered than an interrupted one
    (B) an interrupted task is more likely to be remembered than a completed one

(C) a task at the beginning of a sequence is more likely to be remembered than a task in the middle of the sequence
(D) a task in the middle of a sequence is more likely to be remembered than a task at the beginning of the sequence
(E) a digit is more likely to be remembered when it is part of a word list than when it is part of a list of digits

67. Which one of the following is *not* true of a normal distribution?
    (A) Approximately 68 percent of the scores are within one standard deviation of the mean.
    (B) Approximately 68 percent of the scores are within one standard deviation of the median.
    (C) Approximately 68 percent of the scores are within one standard deviation of the mode.
    (D) Negative skew is equivalent to positive skew.
    (E) Approximately 34 percent of the scores occur between a z-score of $+1$ and the mean.

68. A correlation coefficient of 0.0 means
    (A) a negative relationship
    (B) the absence of any systematic linear relationship
    (C) a positive relationship
    (D) that predictability is 25 percent better than chance
    (E) the absence of intervening variables

69. The point in a learning curve during which no increase in performance is evident but physiological limit has not yet been reached is called
    (A) asymptote   (B) reminiscence   (C) latency   (D) extinction
    (E) plateau

70. A single-goal object has both desirable and undesirable features in
    (A) approach-approach conflict
    (B) approach-avoidance conflict
    (C) avoidance-avoidance conflict
    (D) double approach-avoidance conflict
    (E) double avoidance-avoidance conflict

71. Identical twins raised separately and found to have similar IQ's are cited as examples of the contribution made to intelligence by
    (A) environment   (B) infant stimulation   (C) heredity
    (D) learning   (E) parental interaction

72. High correlation with premature birth has been found in cases where the mother's behavior included
    (A) depression   (B) exposure to radiation   (C) smoking
    (D) thalidomide   (E) alcoholic beverages

73. In the early work of Hartshorne and May, designed to assess children's moral behavior, it was found that
    (A) moral children always adhere to generally recognized moral standards
    (B) children seem to apply situational morality, acting differently in separate situations involving the same moral principle
    (C) moral children never cheat
    (D) a basic distinction can be made between cheaters and noncheaters and that, invariably, the noncheaters were from religious home environments
    (E) boys generally have stronger consciences than girls

74. Responding to a conditioned stimulus in order to avoid electric shock is an example of
    (A) punishment (B) shaping (C) avoidance conditioning
    (D) escape conditioning (E) successive approximation

75. In Guilford's approach to intelligence, the ability to generate a variety of hypotheses in a given problem situation is known as
    (A) cognitive memory (B) convergent production (C) divergent production (D) mediational memory (E) intuitive production

76. Hungry rats that do not find food reinforcement at the end of a T-maze learn very slowly in comparison with another group of rats that find such reinforcement. Immediately after the rats in the first group are given food reinforcement, their performance parallels that of the rats in the second group. This is an example of
    (A) behavior chaining (B) law of effect (C) law of exercise
    (D) latent learning (E) intrinsic learning

77. Preparation for a test causes a student to forget much of what he studied earlier for another upcoming test — a case of
    (A) reminiscence (B) retroactive inhibition (C) retroactive facilitation (D) proactive inhibition (E) von Restorff effect

78. In a corporate hierarchy, a person could expect communications to be initiated most frequently in which of the following patterns?
    (A) lower to higher echelon (B) higher to lower echelon (C) women to women (D) men to men (E) women to men

79. A primary function of human engineering is
    (A) vocational testing
    (B) personnel screening
    (C) to modify aspects of a specific job to promote efficiency
    (D) to modify aspects of an employee's behavior to fit a job requirement
    (E) consumer research

80. Industrial psychologists and human engineering personnel employ the term ET, which means
    (A) evaluative technique (B) effective temperature (C) efficiency test
    (D) evaluation and training (E) evaluation and testing

81. The National Training Laboratory at Bethel, Maine, is involved in which type of managerial training method?
    (A) role playing (B) incident (C) case (D) sensitivity
    (E) free association

82. With a month to go before an English test, a student would be well advised to engage in
    (A) massed practice
    (B) distributed practice
    (C) massed-distributed-massed practice pattern
    (D) distributed-massed-distributed practice pattern
    (E) massed-distributed-distributed practice pattern

83. An expectant mother in her eighth month of pregnancy decides to initiate a sequence involving banging loudly on the side of the bathtub followed by application of a vibrator to her abdomen. The developing fetus

(A) probably will not be classically conditioned by such a procedure
(B) very likely can be classically conditioned by such a procedure
(C) will be operantly conditioned by such a procedure
(D) will be unable to detect either the vibration or the sound
(E) will be permanently damaged by such a procedure

84. Among the following, the *incorrect* pairing is
    (A) fetal period—eighth week until birth
    (B) germinal period—first two weeks
    (C) embryonic period—second week until eighth week
    (D) embryonic period—rapid neural development
    (E) germinal period—onset of initial heartbeat

85. DNA refers to the
    (A) molecular configuration making up chromosomes
    (B) germ-cell configurations in genes
    (C) atom structure in genes
    (D) neural structure in cell bodies
    (E) dinitroacetic structures

86. Experiments demonstrate that infants register strongest preference for which one of the following visual stimuli?
    (A) plain, solid colors   (B) bright colors   (C) patterned triangles
    (D) likenesses of the human face   (E) likenesses of animals and pets

87. The prenatal period during which X-rays and specific drugs can have the most detrimental effect upon development is
    (A) the first eight weeks
    (B) the second to fourth months
    (C) the sixth to eighth months
    (D) just prior to birth
    (E) the fifth to seventh months

88. Toilet training is most effective
    (A) between the ages of one and two years
    (B) when successes are immediately rewarded, and accidents are punished
    (C) midway or late in the second year
    (D) between six months and one year of age
    (E) very shortly after weaning

89. How many stages of cognitive development are associated with Piaget?
    (A) seven major stages   (B) three major stages   (C) two major stages
    (D) five major stages   (E) one major stage

90. Which one of the following is *not* true of the WAIS?
    (A) used with adults
    (B) separate verbal and performance IQ scores
    (C) block design
    (D) $MA/CA \times 100$
    (E) digit span

91. Which one of the following combinations would *not* be possible in a set of triplets?
    (A) three fraternal   (B) three identical   (C) three mongoloid
    (D) two identical, one fraternal   (E) two fraternal, one identical

92. Which one of the following expressions could act as a substitution for "nature-nurture controversy" without changing the basic meaning?
    (A) heredity-maturation controversy
    (B) environment-learning controversy
    (C) achievement-acquisition controversy
    (D) heredity-environment controversy
    (E) evolution-mutation controversy

93. Retrograde amnesia is a phenomenon in which a person suffering brain injury in an accident loses memory of
    (A) early childhood experiences
    (B) events immediately after the injury
    (C) events immediately prior to the injury, with earlier memory being unimpaired
    (D) middle childhood events, then forgets early childhood events
    (E) early childhood events, then forgets middle childhood events

94. Which one of the following types of acceptance is most critical and pervasive to the long-range emotional health of a child?
    (A) peer (B) sibling (C) self (D) vocational
    (E) educational

95. The play pattern most prevalent among three-year-old children is
    (A) solitary play (B) associative play (C) cooperative play
    (D) parallel play (E) covariant play

96. Sex differences in the area of perception and personality are
    (A) apparent before age five
    (B) initially detectable at age seven
    (C) indistinguishable prior to age eight
    (D) essentially mythical
    (E) not as apparent as those in the area of cognition

97. The Ebbinghaus curve
    (A) shows a gradual drop in retention followed by a steep decline
    (B) shows a steep initial drop in retention followed by a gradual decline
    (C) shows an S-shaped pattern
    (D) shows higher retention for rote learning than for concept learning
    (E) shows a steady, gradual decline throughout its span

98. Phonemes are
    (A) measurements
    (B) the smallest units of meaningful sound
    (C) syllables
    (D) a series of morphemes
    (E) the smallest units of sound

99. When a child modifies an existing cognitive schema to make it compatible with the cognitive aspects of an incoming stimulus, the process is called
    (A) assimilation (B) adaptation (C) conservation
    (D) accommodation (E) mediational clustering

100. Which one of the following accurately describes an aspect of prenatal development?
    (A) Heartbeat begins during the second week.

(B) Wastes are absorbed through the placental walls into the mother's blood.
(C) The developing child and the mother have completely intermixing, constantly interchanging blood supplies.
(D) The fetus has immunity to syphilis.
(E) It encompasses a 250-day gestation period.

101. Under which one of the following reinforcement schedules is it most important for an organism to learn to estimate time accurately?
(A) fixed interval
(B) fixed ratio
(C) variable interval
(D) variable ratio
(E) a combination of fixed and variable ratio

102. That language patterns play a dominant role in shaping a person's thoughts and subsequent behavior is a view advanced in the hypothesis developed by
(A) Gardner   (B) Whorf   (C) Brown   (D) Miller
(E) Dollard

103. The earliest studies of verbal learning and rote memory were conducted by
(A) Thorndike   (B) Pavlov   (C) Miller   (D) Mowrer
(E) Ebbinghaus

104. Which one of the following statements appears to be true of punishment?
(A) It is effective in behavior control without undesirable side effects.
(B) It has a long-range inhibitory effect upon behavior.
(C) Its inhibitory effect is only short-range, and the general behavior tendency remains essentially unchanged.
(D) It is effective as a means of extinction.
(E) It is effective specifically in cases of retroactive inhibition.

105. Which one of the following would be of primary importance in determining the accuracy of inferences being made about a population?
(A) size of the population
(B) sample variance
(C) sample representativeness
(D) sample mean
(E) sample standard deviation

106. On a certain scattergram, the pattern extends from the lower left-hand corner to the upper right-hand corner. From this knowledge it can be determined that the scattergram exhibits
(A) positive correlation   (B) negative correlation   (C) no correlation
(D) negative skew   (E) positive skew

107. Which one of the following is central to a frequency polygon?
(A) scattergram
(B) bar graph
(C) histogram
(D) flow chart
(E) points connected by lines

108. If a mother must be separated from her child for three months during the child's first year, an absence during which one of the following age periods would be *least* detrimental to the child's development?
    (A) two to five months
    (B) three to six months
    (C) one to four months
    (D) seven to ten months
    (E) birth to three months

109. Which one of the following statements is true of embryonic development?
    (A) The development of organs and organ systems varies among embryos in both timing and sequence.
    (B) Only on sequence — heart development during the fourth week — is consistent among embryos.
    (C) All organ systems essentially develop together.
    (D) Universally consistent sequences and sequential timing characterize organ systems development.
    (E) Fetal growth can compensate for any deficiencies occurring during the embryonic period.

110. Down's syndrome is
    (A) synonymous with hydrocephaly
    (B) synonymous with Klinefelter's syndrome
    (C) caused by the presence of an extra chromosome number 21
    (D) caused only by infectious hepatitis during pregnancy
    (E) caused only by X-ray treatment during pregnancy

111. Which one of the following terms would *not* be part of computer-assisted instruction?
    (A) flow chart   (B) decision step   (C) loop   (D) action step
    (E) reaction phase

112. The pursuit rotor is used in many studies involving
    (A) intelligence   (B) memory   (C) motor learning   (D) mechanical aptitude   (E) pilot training

113. *Not* included in a Bauer or Shannon diagram of communication is
    (A) source   (B) transmitter   (C) channel   (D) receiver
    (E) translator

114. The S-shaped curve indicates
    (A) prior familiarity with the task
    (B) greatest amount of improvement during the last few trials
    (C) the representation of the entire learning process
    (D) greatest amount of improvement in the first few trials
    (E) improvement not dependent on practice

115. Babies allowed to select their own food for a six-month period would
    (A) eat too many sweets
    (B) eat too many carbohydrates
    (C) develop anemia
    (D) overeat consistently
    (E) maintain a generally balanced diet over the long range

116. Which one of the following is true of memory span?
    (A) It is slightly less for letters than for digits.
    (B) It has the capacity for fifteen-item repetition after a single presentation.

(C) It is unaffected by the type of material being learned.
(D) It is unaffected by the meaningfulness of the material.
(E) It is unaffected by intelligence.

117. As a person fills in a number series such as 3, 6, 9, _, _, 18, he is engaging in the thinking process known as
(A) extrapolation (B) interpolation (C) structuring
(D) modeling (E) decision making

118. Bruner sees cognitive growth as
(A) unaffected by the mastery of techniques and skills
(B) strongly affected by the mastery of techniques and skills
(C) occurring at essentially the same speed and level in all human infants
(D) faster for girls than for boys
(E) faster for rural children than for urban ones

119. One of the earliest papers developing a theory of human problem solving was that of
(A) Newell, Shaw, and Simon
(B) Dollard and Miller
(C) Newell and Cortlander
(D) Mowrer and Newell
(E) Miller and Cortlander

120. Among the following, the group test is
(A) WISC (B) WAIS (C) AGCT (D) Stanford-Binet
(E) TAT

121. Partial reinforcement
(A) enhances classical conditioning speed and efficiency
(B) interferes with classical conditioning
(C) interferes with the maintenance of an operantly conditioned response
(D) is never used in operant conditioning
(E) is never used in type R conditioning

122. Alternate forms of a test have which one of the following advantages?
(A) prevention of practice effect in subsequent administration
(B) uniform standard deviation throughout all age ranges
(C) allowance for comparison of test scores of persons differing in age
(D) uniform standard deviation between verbal and performance sections
(E) elimination of the reminiscence phenomenon

123. In Piaget's views on cognitive development, the preoperational child will
(A) consider all spatial possibilities
(B) focus on end products of events rather than on the process itself
(C) engage in both assimilation and accommodation
(D) comprehend only volume conservation
(E) comprehend only number conservation

124. The Law of Effect suggests that
(A) practice alone produces learning
(B) in addition to practice there must be reinforcement
(C) in addition to reinforcement there must be reward
(D) neither practice nor reward is important to learning
(E) Skinner's view has been superseded by Hull's

125. The concept of family constellation is most evident in the works of which one of the following?
 (A) Jung (B) Freud (C) Rogers (D) Adler (E) Horney

126. Which one of the following schools constitutes the Lockean view of personality?
 (A) ego analysis (B) behaviorism (C) psychoanalysis
 (D) archetypal analysis (E) trait analysis

127. In the Jungian view of personality, key functions include
 (A) anima, animus, shadow
 (B) sensing, feeling, intuiting
 (C) prototaxic, parataxic, syntaxic
 (D) extroversion, introversion, interposition
 (E) belongingness, love, safety

128. Absolute freedom of individual choice is evident in the conceptual views associated with
 (A) psychoanalysis (B) individual psychology (C) behaviorism
 (D) trait theory (E) existentialism

129. Most basic among Freudian defense mechanisms is
 (A) rationalism (B) reaction formation (C) identification
 (D) repression (E) denial

130. The field theorist view is compatible with which one of the following statements?
 (A) Learning is based on specific responses to specific stimuli.
 (B) The phenomenal world and the objective world are in agreement.
 (C) Total experience is "greater than the sum of its parts."
 (D) Reward preserves learning.
 (E) The phenomenal world is, in effect, more accurate than the objective world.

131. ". . . Make up as dramatic a story as you can. . . . Tell what has led up to the event shown in the picture, describe what is happening at the moment, what the characters are feeling and thinking; and then give the outcome." This constitutes part of the procedure for
 (A) psychoanalytic free association (B) TAT (C) MMPI
 (D) Rorschach (E) Blacky

132. The foot-in-the-door technique suggests that a person is most likely to gain consumer cooperation on a sizable purchase or a large favor if he or she
 (A) is open about the large purchase or favor in initial contact
 (B) is the first salesman to come to the consumer's door
 (C) represents a reputable company
 (D) can successfully make a small sale or first gain the consumer's cooperation on a small favor
 (E) can associate his company with a famous person familiar to the consumer

133. Among monocular cues for depth perception is
 (A) convergence (B) retinal disparity (C) assimilation
 (D) accommodation (E) interposition

134. The Robber's Cave study underscored the belief that
 (A) intense competition can lead to hostility

(B) intense cooperation can lead to hostility
(C) cooperation leads to more hostility than competition
(D) the presence of threat potential reduces hostility
(E) intense competition actually leads to the breakdown of hostility

135. In the "experimental dormitory" situation with preassigned roommates
    (A) those with similar attitudes were likely to be attracted to one another
    (B) those with dissimilar attitudes were likely to be attracted to one another
    (C) complete roommate rearrangement occurred within the first two months
    (D) proximity proved to be a more significant factor than similarity
    (E) sex proved to be a more important factor than proximity

136. If Adorno informed persons that they had just attained high scores on the F-scale, they could accurately conclude that
    (A) their scores were significant beyond the .05 level
    (B) they had scored high on authoritarianism
    (C) there was strong likelihood that they were not very superstitious
    (D) there was strong likelihood that they had below-average concern in areas involving sex
    (E) they had high flexibility and openness in their attitude formation and change

137. The condition under which a person experiences the perceptual phenomenon of closure involves
    (A) a circle with approximately one-eighth of its line omitted
    (B) parallel lines
    (C) intersecting lines
    (D) a triangle with a dot in the middle
    (E) a square with diagonal lines going to opposite corners

138. Which one of the following is true of afferent neurons?
    (A) located in the dorsal column of the spinal cord
    (B) located in the ventral column of the spinal cord
    (C) not located in the spinal cord
    (D) equivalent in function to the efferent neurons
    (E) found only in the striated muscles

139. Harlow's experiments demonstrate that female infant monkeys raised in isolation with a cloth mother
    (A) develop normally in all respects
    (B) develop normally, but are totally inadequate as mothers
    (C) have unresolved Oedipal conflicts
    (D) die at an earlier age than monkeys raised normally
    (E) are better adjusted than normally raised monkeys

140. Which one of the following is an *incorrect* statement?
    (A) Ethology attained its peak with the work of Lorenz and Tinbergen.
    (B) Lashley helped revitalize comparative psychology in the post-World War II period.
    (C) Tinbergen's work has relied heavily on the experimental laboratory method.
    (D) Darwin's work had far-reaching effects and influence upon comparative psychology.
    (E) Romanes's work utilized the anecdotal method.

141. The phi phenomenon
  (A) is an integral part of telekinesis
  (B) relates to electrical stimulation of the brain
  (C) deals with experience common to the state of alpha-wave relaxation
  (D) occurs in response to sequentially flashing lights
  (E) occurs in response to a spot of light in a darkened room

142. Conservation mastery in which one of the following dimensions indicates the most advanced level of child cognitive development?
  (A) number   (B) length of a line   (C) volume displacement
  (D) "lemonade stand" demonstration   (E) weight of an object

143. Proximity as a factor in social attraction
  (A) proves least important in apartment-building settings
  (B) is generally unimportant
  (C) proves to be of primary importance
  (D) is less important than occupation
  (E) is less important than family background

144. A black and a white in a group have supported the experimental subject's position on several issues; another black and another white have taken positions differing from those of the subject. According to Rokeach the people whose company the experimental subject would later prefer would be
  (A) same-race persons, regardless of their beliefs
  (B) those persons whose views closely paralleled the subject's, regardless of race
  (C) those same-race persons whose views closely paralleled the subject's
  (D) persons who were of both the same race and the same sex as the subject
  (E) persons who were of the same race, same sex, and same beliefs as the subject

145. Zajonc found that familiarity leads to
  (A) positive reaction   (B) negative reaction   (C) contempt
  (D) fear   (E) failure

146. Lewinson-Zubin scales are associated with
  (A) phrenology   (B) philology   (C) syntonomy
  (D) graphology   (E) physiognomy

147. *Not* among the factors associated with the Crutchfield technique is
  (A) individual booths
  (B) critical subjects
  (C) signal-light panels
  (D) false feedback
  (E) each person involved is a subject

148. In the Acme-Bolt Trucking Game research, it was found that
  (A) cooperation is greatest in the presence of potential threat
  (B) cooperation is greatest when the two parties have direct communication
  (C) cooperation is greatest in the absence of threat
  (D) women are more likely to utilize threat than men
  (E) cooperation reaches its peak when both threat and direct communication are present

149. Modern psychological views most readily reject which one of the following theoretical tenets?
  (A) Fromm's relatedness principle
  (B) Erikson's eight stages

(C) Jung's collective unconscious
(D) Dollard and Miller's four types of conflict situations
(E) Horney's three modes of relating

150. In Allen's study of helping behavior, under which one of the following circumstances would passenger B on a subway be most likely to correct erroneous information given to a stranger by passenger A?
(A) if the stranger had asked passenger B directly and A had butted in with the wrong answer
(B) if the stranger had directed his question to both A and B
(C) if the stranger had asked only passenger A with B overhearing
(D) if the stranger were a woman
(E) if the stranger were elderly

151. In relation to communications, "all men are created equal" within which one of the following systems?
(A) chain   (B) Y   (C) circle   (D) wheel   (E) T-design

152. In which one of the following techniques would an emotionally disturbed person be asked to describe and imagine anxiety-producing scenes and situations?
(A) implosive therapy   (B) insight therapy   (C) ego analysis
(D) logotherapy   (E) client-centered therapy

153. Which form of schizophrenia contains delusions of grandeur or persecution?
(A) simple   (B) complex   (C) catatonic   (D) paranoid
(E) hebephrenic

154. Which of the following could lead to psychopathology?
(A) fear of failure
(B) self-actualization
(C) self-confidence
(D) little gap between real and ideal self
(E) self-direction

Questions 155–156 are based on the following passage.

Every profession has its own jargon, and we psychiatrists have ours. But while the strange terms a lawyer or an archaeologist uses are harmless enough — the worst they do is mystify outsiders — the terms psychiatrists use can hurt people and sometimes do. Instead of helping to comfort and counsel and heal people — which is the goal of psychiatry — the terms often cause despair. Words like *schizophrenia, manic-depressive,* and *psychotic,* for example, frighten patients and worry their anxious relatives and friends. The use of these alarming terms also affects psychiatrists. They lead us back into the pessimism and helplessness of the days when mental illness was thought to be made up of many specific "diseases," and when each "disease" bore a formidable label and a gloomy prognosis. (From Karl Menninger, "Psychiatrists Use Dangerous Words," *Saturday Evening Post,* April 25, 1964.)

155. From reading this well-known position statement, one would expect Menninger to draw which one of the following conclusions?
(A) The diagnostic, medical model should be used in emotional disturbances.
(B) Emotional disturbance is an illness in the same sense as any physiological disease.
(C) Psychiatry should dispense with labels for emotional disturbances.
(D) Labels, though frightening to patients and their relatives, have a definite role in emotional rehabilitation.
(E) The nomothetic approach to personality is the only viable approach.

156. Which one of the following persons would you expect to be in most agreement with this stated view of Menninger?
    (A) Szasz   (B) Freud   (C) Sullivan   (D) Templeton
    (E) Hathaway

157. Which one of the following abbreviations is common to discussions of synaptic potential?
    (A) ENSP   (B) APSP   (C) INSP   (D) EPSP   (E) ANSP

158. Ordinary dreaming is
    (A) probably identical to daydreaming
    (B) always in black and white
    (C) selective in the perception and incorporation of the external world into the dreams
    (D) most prevalent in Stage II sleep
    (E) most prevalent in Stage I sleep

159. Functional autonomy of motives is associated with the work of
    (A) Allport   (B) McClelland   (C) Atkinson   (D) McDougall
    (E) Allen

160. The fact that a pinpoint down the railroad track is perceived by a person as a diesel engine is an example of
    (A) continuity   (B) closure   (C) size constancy
    (D) motion parallax   (E) accommodation

161. One of the earliest and most important color vision theories was formulated by
    (A) Rutherford and Hayes   (B) Young and Helson   (C) Meissner and Middleton   (D) Rutherford and Young   (E) Young and Helmholz

162. The detective was in constant danger. One day his head was slightly creased by a bullet, and he indicated immediately afterward that he was blind. Hospital observation indicated no physiological cause for the blindness. This is a case of
    (A) paranoid schizophrenia   (B) obsessive compulsion
    (C) neurasthenia   (D) psychosomatic disorder   (E) conversion reaction

163. A seventeen-year-old girl sits in a corner, weeping continually. This behavior could be
    (A) hypochondria   (B) nomadism   (C) repression
    (D) regression   (E) dyssocial personality

164. Enuresis
    (A) is most common among adults
    (B) has a poor prognosis
    (C) is more common among women than men
    (D) can result from faulty parental discipline
    (E) is contagious and highly communicable

165. A man walking to work counts the cracks in the sidewalk. Although he is almost to his office, he fears the he has miscounted and so returns to the subway terminal to begin counting again. This behavior is known as
    (A) hypochondriacal reaction   (B) conversion reaction   (C) obsessive-compulsive reaction   (D) sociopathic disorder   (E) schizophrenic reaction

166. In reference to alcoholism, the expression "hit bottom" refers to
  (A) memory blackouts
  (B) the commencement of surreptitious drinking
  (C) the crucial phase
  (D) the chronic phase, when complete defeat is admitted
  (E) the occasional drinking phase

167. Using the dynamic model of psychopathology, the theoretical cause of emotional disturbance would be
  (A) faulty learning   (B) lack of responsibility   (C) faulty morality
  (D) unconscious conflicts   (E) faulty perception

168. *Not* a major criterion upon which to define mental illness is
  (A) statistical deviation   (B) cultural deviation   (C) criminal deviation   (D) behavioral deviation   (E) clinical deviation

169. Insulin shock therapy
  (A) has a fatality rate of approximately 5 percent
  (B) has been considered most valuable with depressed patients
  (C) was considered most useful with paranoid schizophrenics but is rarely used today
  (D) involves the creation of a dazed state without loss of consciousness
  (E) has had its greatest success in the treatment of problems associated with alcoholism

170. The term most closely associated with the name Eysenck is
  (A) autonomic reactivity   (B) parapraxes   (C) reintegration
  (D) shadow   (E) functional fictionalism

171. The primary problem encountered in treating drug addicts, alcoholics, and sociopaths is
  (A) their preference for their present life style
  (B) the expense of therapy
  (C) the fact that more want help than can be treated
  (D) the side effects of aversive conditioning
  (E) the exclusive posture of Synanon

172. Which one of the following is within the psychotomimetic drug classification?
  (A) aspirin   (B) chlorpromazine   (C) d-tubocurarine
  (D) LSD   (E) mescaline

173. Researchers have found correlations between juvenile delinquency and such background aspects as
  (A) broken homes and parental absenteeism
  (B) neurotic, dependent fathers
  (C) father acceptance and mother submissiveness
  (D) strong religious background
  (E) warm, permissive family setting

Questions 174–177 are based on the following answer choices.
  (1) z
  (2) t
  (3) F
  (4) chi-square
  (5) r

174. This statistic and its corresponding analysis determines whether there is systematic relationship between two sets of variables.
 (A) 1   (B) 2   (C) 3   (D) 4   (E) 5

175. This statistic assumes direct knowledge of a population mean and standard deviation.
 (A) 1   (B) 2   (C) 3   (D) 4   (E) 5

176. This statistic reflects an unknown population mean and inference based on data obtained from a sample. It is assumed that the terms in the population from which the sample is drawn are normally distributed or, at least, do not depart dramatically from normality.
 (A) 1   (B) 2   (C) 3   (D) 4   (E) 5

177. This statistic deals with differences between the terms *expected value* and *obtained value*.
 (A) 1   (B) 2   (C) 3   (D) 4   (E) 5

178. Because of the rate of a child's physiological development, parents should
 (A) initiate toilet training when the child begins to walk
 (B) initiate toilet training when the child begins to talk
 (C) wait until at least age two for toilet training
 (D) toilet train at the same time as the child is weaned
 (E) begin a form of toilet training almost immediately after birth

179. The setting in which an experimental subject acts as his own control is
 (A) Pearson Product Moment correlation
 (B) point biserial correlation
 (C) *t*-test
 (D) chi-square
 (E) repeated measures

180. To determine representative income level in a neighborhood having mostly lower-middle-class families and a few very rich people, the recommended measure is
 (A) mode   (B) median   (C) mean   (D) *z*-score   (E) *t*-score

Questions 181–184 are based on the following statistical information.

Interval	Frequency
67–69	10
64–66	24
61–63	28
58–60	20
55–57	12
52–54	4
49–51	2

181. The median of the score distribution is
 (A) 55.7   (B) 65.2   (C) 61.8   (D) 60   (E) 57.9

182. The mode of the distribution is
 (A) 60   (B) 64   (C) 65   (D) 62   (E) 59

183. The 40th percentile of this distribution would most closely approximate
 (A) 59   (B) 61   (C) 62   (D) 64   (E) 65

184. The mean of this distribution most closely approximates
(A) 60 (B) 61 (C) 63 (D) 65 (E) 66

185. Within the human embryo, activity related to the development of hair and nails is centered in the
(A) mesoderm (B) endoderm (C) exoderm (D) ectoderm (E) ochloderm

186. A young child's disobedience generally signifies
(A) creativity (B) intelligence (C) unhappiness (D) need for punishment (E) reinforcement

187. Anoxia is
(A) a disease of the blood cells
(B) interruption of the oxygen supply to the brain
(C) an oversupply of oxygen to the brain
(D) hyperventilation
(E) never fatal but a primary cause of retardation

188. The term *circadian* refers to
(A) the cyclic daily body rhythms of activity and repose
(B) the circles around the eyes noted in newborns
(C) the cycle accompanying toilet training
(D) the babbling between identical twins
(E) the childhood ability to distinguish circles from squares

189. Strong evidence suggests that the newborn
(A) sees only blurred shadows
(B) has visual capacity for pattern discrimination
(C) sees clearly but not in color
(D) visually tracks successfully
(E) smiles in response to the human voice

190. In screening for a specific position, the best aptitude test measures
(A) creativity
(B) intelligence
(C) sociability
(D) capacity for position-related tasks
(E) mechanical aptitude

191. From a perceptual standpoint, the most dangerous point for commercial pilots during night flight is
(A) the take off (B) mid-flight (C) a right bank (D) a left bank
(E) the runway approach

192. Human engineers have found that the airplane cockpit is a setting in which
(A) color coding on the dials is extremely important
(B) shape coding is extremely important
(C) the phi phenomenon must be carefully counterbalanced
(D) techniques must be utilized to control autokinetic effect
(E) the Zeigarnik effect poses a perpetual engineering problem

Questions 193–196 are based on the following information for five persons who took different IQ tests. (M = Mean, SD = Standard Deviation)

(1)	(2)	(3)	(4)	(5)
IQ = 110	IQ = 115	IQ = 120	IQ = 130	IQ = 110
M = 100	M = 100	M = 100	M = 100	M = 100
SD = 10	SD = 20	SD = 30	SD = 40	SD = 20

193. Comparing them according to percentile rank, which person has the highest IQ?
 (A) 1 (B) 2 (C) 3 (D) 4 (E) 5

194. Using the same comparative framework, which person has the lowest IQ?
 (A) 1 (B) 2 (C) 3 (D) 4 (E) 5

195. Which person would have a z-score of +.50?
 (A) 1 (B) 2 (C) 3 (D) 4 (E) 5

196. In which distribution is there evidence of greatest score variability?
 (A) 1 (B) 2 (C) 3 (D) 4 (E) 5

197. A type of validity is
 (A) test-retest (B) split-half (C) alternate-form (D) content
 (E) performance

198. Which one of the following was developed by the Army as the first group-administered test of intelligence?
 (A) Otis (B) Bender Gestalt (C) Pintner Patterson
 (D) Alpha (E) Beta

199. To increase the possibility of behavior change, a person would be well advised to create
 (A) only slight cognitive dissonance
 (B) no cognitive dissonance
 (C) a large amount of cognitive dissonance
 (D) a moderate amount of cognitive dissonance
 (E) a large amount of cognitive irrelevance

200. Among human engineering principles relating to man-machine systems, a control principle states that the direction of movement on any control should be
 (A) to the right
 (B) to the left
 (C) compatible with the effects produced
 (D) the reverse of the effects produced
 (E) clockwise

Test 5: Answer Comments

1. (A) Hysterical anesthesias are body-surface-area losses of sensation correlating closely with areas covered by specific articles of clothing.

2. (A) Current mental health trends include emphases on outpatient care, community mental health centers, behavior modification and group therapy — not on construction of large, institution-style buildings.

3. (D) Behavior therapy has been criticized on the grounds that it treats the observable behavior rather than the underlying problem.

4. (A) Schizophrenic reaction is the most prevalent diagnosis among first admissions to public mental health facilities — evidence of the category's breadth and "stretchability."

5. (B) Mowrer has advanced the view that neurosis is a product of personal immaturity.

6. (C) Body metabolism is a key function of the thyroid gland.

7. (A) Operational definitions deal with specific details relating to the measurement of a behavioral phenomenon. In the case of GSR, measurable physiological changes (here meaning electrical conductance of the skin) would satisfy such operational definition requirements.

8. (A) There is convincing evidence of hereditary elements in emotionality, particularly in studies of twins, where heredity can be viewed as a constant.

9. (B) The fact that earlier list learning was interfering with recall of subsequent lists is indicative of proactive inhibition.

10. (B) Percentage recall was the dependent variable, number of lists was the independent variable.

11. (E) Results would suggest a negative correlation between the number of lists learned and the percentage of recall. As the number of lists increased, percentage recall decreased.

12. (A) The measure being taken with these subjects is the percentage of recall after each given list is learned. In effect, there are several treatments (recall measures) on each subject, a factor suggesting the treatments-by-subjects, repeated-measures design.

13. (A) Cycles in bodily processes are related to this awake-at-a-specific-time phenomenon.

14. (E) McClelland finds achievement need positively correlated with amount of formal education.

15. (D) An expression common to motivational studies, the letters stand for expected value.

16. (E) Although heart rate, blood pressure, respiration, and body temperature are lowered during sleep, gastric contractions are not affected.

17. (D) Though the cerebral hemisphere dominant in speech is generally the cerebral hemisphere dominant in handedness, there are notable exceptions.

18. (C) Lashley's concept of equipotentiality refers to a cortical system's capacity to assume functions previously assumed within another portion of the system. The concept has critical importance in cases of brain damage.

19. (C) The Barker-Dembo-Lewin study demonstrated vividly the child response of regression following frustration.

20. (E) Dream activity is accompanied by distinctive EEG patterns, rapid eye movement, high-level cerebral blood flow, and higher brain temperature, but it is not characterized by a higher level of general muscle activity.

21. (C) Basic to the central nervous system are the brain and the spinal cord.

22. (C) Dember sees figure reversibility as evidence that change is essential to the maintenance of perception.

23. (E) Delgado's *Physical Control of the Mind: Toward a Psychocivilized Society* triggered much debate and fear of electroligarchy.

24. (D) Restle's adaptation-level theory relates to the "moon illusion" — the tendency to see the moon as larger when it is on the horizon than when it is overhead.

25. (E) Light and shadow differentiations create such perceptual phenomena as bumps and craters.

26. (D) McGinnies found higher recognition thresholds for taboo words than for other words among both normal and schizophrenic male subjects.

27. (B) A pilot's reaction-time capacity is longer than normal when the pilot is undergoing the experience of "3 g's."

28. (E) This excerpt comes from the James-Lange theory of emotion — that emotion results from behavior rather than vice versa.

29. (B) An apt definition of motivation, and one that Atkinson has used, is how behavior gets started, is energized, is sustained, is directed.

30. (A) The saying "Birds of a feather flock together!" reflects the social attraction notion of attitude similarity — a dominant characteristic confirmed by research.

31. (C) Maslow's self-actualized person is relatively independent of his culture and environment.

32. (D) Erikson and Hartmann are the two most prominent names in ego-analytic personality theory (a contemporary extension of Freud's theorizing).

33. (A) Phenomenology's perceptual formulations are borrowed mainly from the Gestaltists.

34. (B) In the Asch experimental pattern, the critical (naive) subject was less likely to conform to group opinion if one other subject dissented from group opinion.

35. (A) The principal names in Gestalt psychology were Wertheimer, Koffka, and Kohler.

36. (E) The myelin sheath carries the function of insulating an axon.

37. (D) The middle ear provides amplification via a kind of increased "thrust."

38. (E) Among the entries given, the dog would have the most prominent cerebral cortex, and therefore the most advanced brain.

39. (D) Hull's reaction potential was conceptualized by Spence as excitatory potential.

40. (B) The Purkinje effect deals with visual phenomena associated with the transition between cone and rod activation. Such effects as a short-wavelength hue appearing bright, occur prominently at dusk.

41. (C) The life, estrous, menstrual, and breeding cycles affect degree or prominence of sexual behavior, but there is no cycle known as the androgenous.

42. (A) S-O-R (recognition of the organism as an important consideration in the stimulus-response sequence) is a contribution to learning theory by Woodworth.

43. (E) Peripheroceptors is a meaningless term not common to any discussion of sensory groupings.

44. (B) The sympathetic and the parasympathetic form the two subdivisions of the autonomic nervous system. The sympathetic nervous system relates to emotion.

45. (D) Located below the thyroid gland, the thymus has an important role in body immunities.

46. (E) McGinnies pioneered research in the area of perceptual defense.

47. (A) Taste is a chemical sense strongly dependent upon liquid (solubility in water) for its sensitivity.

48. (E) The terms *force field*, *valence*, *life span*, and *tension* are integral to Lewin's field theory; *interference* is not.

49. (A) In relation to the Tinbergen areas for study in animal behavior — development, mechanisms, function, evolution — teleonomic questions deal with function, in this case, the animals *need* for certain nutrients.

50. (E) Mechanistic questions deal with the relationship between behavior and physiological systems.

51. (C) The Snellen chart is the familiar rows-of-letters eye chart used in many eye examinations.

52. (D) Distance perception in a two-dimensional representation of a railroad track is primarily a function of linear perspective — the track lines converging as they "move into the distance."

53. (C) The Jastrow illusion contains two geometric curves (ends downward) placed one above the other. The illusion involves seeing the upper curve as smaller than the lower, though they are identical in size.

54. (B) The "piano" theory of hearing (also called place theory) suggests that specific nerve fibers, in the same manner as piano wires, respond to specific sound frequencies.

55. (D) Homeostasis refers to the body's tendency to maintain a state of internal physiological balance.

56. (E) Persons having had corpus callosum sectioning demonstrate severe problems on the block-design task — the hands, in effect, fighting with each other (one hand "knowing how" and the other hand "ignorant").

57. (A) Receptors are the cells that respond to changes in their environment and signal these changes to the nervous system. Subsequent muscle response would occur as a result of the functioning of effectors.

58. (A) The primary motor area of the cortex is just in front of the fissure of Rolando.

59. (B) The visual area of the cortex is the occipital lobe, located in the back between the parietal lobe and the cerebellum.

60. (D) Audition centers in the temporal lobe of the left cerebral hemisphere, just below the fissure of Sylvius.

61. (C) The somatosensory (sensation from knees, wrists, hands, fingers, face, etc.) center is located just behind the fissure of Rolando.

62. (E) Maintenance of balance and posture is a function of the cerebellum, which adjoins the brain stem and the occipital lobe.

63. (D) S(Delta) refers to the absence of a discriminative stimulus.

64. (A) At dating age, an adolescent's relationship to the same-sex parent becomes critically important.

65. (A) Knowledge of results is synonymous with feedback and houses the potential for improved performance.

66. (B) The Zeigarnik effect suggests that an interrupted task is more likely to be remembered than a completed one.

67. (D) A normal distribution is symmetrical, being completely free of either positive or negative skew.

68. (B) A correlation coefficient of 0.0 means the complete absence of any systematic linear relationship.

69. (E) When no performance increment is occurring but physiological limit has not been reached, the learning-curve expression that covers the situation is plateau.

70. (B) A combination of desirable and undesirable aspects attached to the same goal object is central to approach-avoidance conflict.

71. (C) An identical-twin study involving separate environments for one member of each twin pair would seek to study the effects of heredity.

72. (C) Significant positive correlation has been found between maternal smoking and the incidence of premature birth of offspring.

73. (B) The Hartshorne and May studies found that children seem to apply a situational morality, even in cases where different situations involve the same moral principle. It was impossible for the experimenters to divide the children into groups labeled *cheaters* and *noncheaters*.

74. (C) In avoidance conditioning, as in this description, UCS is not received.

75. (C) Guilford's model describes divergent production as the ability to generate a variety of hypotheses in a given problem situation. This is a central aspect within creativity.

76. (D) The rats that do not receive reinforcement have been learning nonetheless, which is evident when reinforcement is introduced. Central to Tolman, the concept is known as latent learning.

77. (B) More recent learning interfered with earlier learning — retroactive inhibition.

78. (B) Corporate communication is initiated most frequently in a higher-to-lower-echelon direction.

79. (C) Human engineering seeks to promote efficiency in a specific job setting.

80. (B) In human engineering usage ET refers to effective temperature.

81. (D) The National Training Laboratory has been central to the sensitivity-training movement.

82. (B) Given sufficient time to utilize it, the distributed-practice approach will prove most effective in examination preparation.

83. (B) Experiments identical to the one described have resulted in classical conditioning of the fetus.

84. (E) The germinal period refers to the first two weeks after conception.

85. (A) DNA (deoxyribonucleic acid) is a molecular configuration making up chromosomes.

86. (D) Experiments show that newborns demonstrate a distinct preference for stimuli that contain a likeness of the human face.

87. (A) The prenatal period during which X rays and specific drugs could be most detrimental to development is the first eight weeks, when basic structures are being formed.

88. (C) Toilet training is most effective and least stressful when the child has well-developed physiological capacities for its mastery. Such readiness would occur late in the second year.

89. (B) Piaget speaks of three major stages of cognitive development — sensorimotor, concrete operations, formal operations.

90. (D) The WAIS standardizes for each age level and does not utilize the *MA/CA* × 100 formula.

91. (E) There is no such thing as "one identical" member of any group.

92. (D) The nature-nurture controversy deals with the respective influences of heredity and environment upon human development.

93. (C) In retrograde amnesia resulting from an accident-caused brain injury, a person loses memory of events immediately prior to the injury.

94. (C) Self-acceptance has the most critical, long-range effect upon the emotional health of an individual.

95. (D) Three-year-old children normally conduct individual activities side-by-side and close to one another without any evidence of cooperative or associative interaction.

96. (A) Sex differences in personality and perception become well established during the first few years of a child's life.

97. (B) The Ebbinghaus curve's steep initial drop followed by a gradual decline is evidence that most forgetting occurs shortly after learning.

98. (E) Phonemes are the smallest units of sound. Morphemes are the smallest units of *meaningful* sound.

99. (D) *Accommodation* is Piaget's term describing a child's modification of an existing cognitive schema to make it compatible with the cognitive aspects of an incoming stimulus.

100. (B) In prenatal development, fetal wastes are absorbed through the placental walls into the mother's blood.

101. (A) Time estimation is most critical to a fixed-interval reinforcement schedule.

102. (B) Whorf's well-known position advances the belief that language patterns play a dominant role in shaping a person's thoughts and subsequent behavior.

103. (E) The earliest studies of verbal learning and rote memory were the nonsense-syllable studies of Ebbinghaus.

104. (C) The inhibitory effects of punishment appear to be only immediate and short-range.

105. (C) To make accurate inferences about a population, a representative sample is essential.

106. (A) Such a scattergram pattern — lower left to upper right — indicates positive correlation.

107. (E) A frequency polygon consists of points connected by lines.

108. (D) The critical social-development period for the infant is the period between six weeks and six months of age.

109. (D) During embryonic development, both a universally consistent sequence and timing characterize organ systems development. Therefore, one embryo could not undergo brain development before heart development while another embryo developed in the reverse order.

110. (C) Down's syndrome — Mongolism — has been associated with an extra chromosome number 21.

111. (E) The reaction phase relates to the general-adaptation syndrome and has no relevance to computer-assisted instruction.

112. (C) The pursuit rotor is a turntable-style apparatus designed to measure effectiveness in motor tracking.

113. (E) Source, transmitter, channel, receiver, and audience are Bauer-Shannon entries in communications diagramming.

114. (C) The span of a normal learning process is depicted by the S-shaped curve.

115. (E) Research suggests that a child has a tendency to maintain a generally balanced diet, long-range, if placed in a self-selection food situation (the balance not being apparent in any given meal).

116. (A) Memory span is slightly less for letters than for digits.

117. (B) Establishing a principle on the basis of existing information and then filling in missing information on the basis of the principle is an example of interpolation.

118. (B) Bruner sees a strong relationship between a child's mastery of techniques and skills and his cognitive growth.

119. (A) One of the earliest influential papers on human problem-solving theory was written by Newell, Shaw, and Simon.

120. (C) The group test is the AGCT (Army General Classification Test), which contains sections testing vocabulary, arithmetic reasoning, and block counting. It was a follow-up to Army Alpha in the mid-1940s.

121. (B) Classical conditioning relies upon consistency in CS-UCS pairing — a consistency not maintained by partial reinforcement.

122. (A) Alternate forms avoid the possibility of practice effect, which might occur if a person took the same test at two different times.

123. (B) In Piaget's theoretical framework, the preoperational child's conceptual focus is upon end products of events rather than on the processes themselves.

124. (B) Thorndike's Law of Effect points to the central role of reinforcement in learning.

125. (D) Adler initiated the personality concept of family constellation, suggesting specific personality characteristics for family members on the basis of their position in the family birth order.

126. (B) The Lockean view underscores the importance of environment in personality, a view held strongly be proponents of behaviorism.

127. (B) Jung's key functions are sensing, feeling, thinking, and intuiting.

128. (E) That the individual is virtually the master of his fate and actions is a basic view of existentialism.

129. (D) Freud considered repression the grandfather of all other defense mechanisms — in effect, the key to and most basic of all such mechanisms.

130. (C) Field theory and the Gestalt influence suggest that total experience is "greater than the sum of its parts."

131. (B) Instructions to make up a story about a specific picture, describe current events and the thoughts and feelings of the main characters, and conclude with a description of how the situation turns out would be characteristic of the Thematic Apperception Test (TAT).

132. (D) The foot-in-the-door technique suggests that a person who has agreed to a small favor is more likely to agree later to a larger favor than a person not approached about the initial small favor.

133. (E) Interposition refers to objects viewed as standing in front of other objects — a monocular cue to depth perception.

134. (A) Sherif's experiment with boys' camp groups demonstrated the strength of hostility resulting from intense competition.

135. (A) In Newcomb's "experimental dormitory" research, proximity functioned in early associations, but attitude similarity proved to be the more dominant long-range factor.

136. (B) The F-scale (Fascism scale) was developed by Adorno to measure authoritarian tendencies.

137. (A) Closure is the perceptual tendency to complete a circle or a square where a gap in the needed stimulus line currently exists.

138. (A) Afferent neurons are located in the dorsal column of the spinal cord.

139. (B) Harlow found apparent normal development in the cloth-mother-reared females, but they proved woefully inadequate as mothers — sitting on their young, etc. The opportunity to interact with peers during early development resolved this problem.

140. (C) Tinbergen's work used the method of naturalistic observation, not the laboratory method.

141. (D) Lights blinking in sequence (as in many neon signs) and perceived as movement are an example of the phi phenomenon.

142. (C) In the Piaget framework, the concept of volume-displacement conservation would be the most advanced and the last to occur developmentally.

143. (C) Proximity holds prominence and importance in social attraction (e.g., It is important to be a neighbor or friend to the person living next door rather than to the person living "three doors down").

144. (B) Rokeach and Mezei's work underscored the importance of attitude similarity in social attraction (a much more critical element than racial similarity).

145. (A) Zajonc has found that familiarity leads to positive reactions and liking (rather than to contempt).

146. (D) The Lewinson-Zubin scales are associated with graphology interpretations relating to personality.

147. (B) Critical subjects are present in the Asch, but not in the Crutchfield, technique of conformity research.

148. (C) Deutsch has found that threat is totally ineffective as an incentive for cooperation. Cooperation is most likely in the absence of threat.

149. (C) Jung's collective unconscious and archetypal concepts have been most heavily criticized and rejected by personality theorists.

150. (A) Allen found that a passenger was most likely to correct erroneous information being given a stranger if the passenger had been directly addressed by the stranger.

151. (C) The circle pattern is a democratic, equal-opportunity pattern of communication.

152. (A) The implosive-therapy technique of Stampfl involves imagining high anxiety-producing scenes and situations. It utilizes the two-factor learning tenets of Mowrer.

153. (D) Paranoid schizophrenia involves delusions of grandeur or persecution.

154. (A) Fear of failure is one of the main bases for emotional disturbance. Such fear becomes intricately interwoven with a poor self-concept.

155. (C) Menninger concludes that psychiatry should dispense with labels for emotional disturbances, relying more on a way of behaving than on a disease concept.

156. (A) Szasz — well known for *The Myth of Mental Illness* and *The Age of Madness* — would be in agreement with Menninger.

157. (D) EPSP means excitatory postsynaptic potentials. Its often-seen counterpart is IPSP (inhibitory postsynaptic potentials).

158. (C) In ordinary dreaming, the external world gets incorporated selectively. Frequently, a dream contains aspects of the preceding day's activity.

159. (A) Allport speaks of functional autonomy whereby an activity that initially satisfied a basic need (e.g., hunting) now becomes rewarding simply as an activity itself.

160. (C) Size constancy is functioning in any setting where a large object far in the distance is perceived as that large object rather than as a tiny speck on the retina.

161. (E) The Young-Helmholz Trichromatic Theory of color vision was one of the earliest and most important.

162. (E) The lack of a physiological basis for the blindness is evidence of conversion reaction.

163. (D) The continual weeping could be indicative of regression to a behavior characteristic of an earlier period in her life.

164. (D) Enuresis (bedwetting) has a close relationship to parentally instilled fears.

165. (C) Such behavior as compulsive counting and recounting on grounds of having miscounted indicates a strong obsessive-compulsive reaction.

166. (D) "Hitting bottom" for the alcoholic means entering the chronic phase and admitting complete defeat. At this point, the alcoholic may have sufficient motivation to be helped.

167. (D) The dynamic model of psychopathology spotlights unconscious conflict as the basis of emotional disturbance.

168. (C) Statistical, cultural, behavioral, and clinical deviation are four basic models on which to define mental illness. Criminal deviation is not a similar definitional model.

169. (C) When used, insulin shock therapy centered upon the diagnosis of paranoid schizophrenia.

170. (A) Within his mathematical approach to personality theory, Eysenck utilizes the term *autonomic reactivity*.

171. (A) The fact that these people prefer their present life style is a continuing and nagging problem in the treatment of drug addicts, alcoholics, and sociopaths. A sincere desire to be helped is critically important to effective treatment.

172. (D) Psychotomimetic drugs (hallucinogens) produce symptoms in normal subjects resembling those found in psychotic patients — distortions of body image, disorganized thinking, and hallucinations. LSD is a major drug in this category.

173. (A) Significant correlation has been found between juvenile delinquency and the background of a broken home and parental absence.

174. (E) An *r* indicates correlation — a systematic relationship between two sets of variables.

175. (A) A *z*-score assumes direct knowledge of a population mean and standard deviation.

176. (B) A *t*-score reflects an unknown population mean and inference based on data obtained through sampling procedures.

177. (D) The extent to which obtained value differs from expected value is a central concern of the chi-square statistic.

178. (C) Because of the pace of a child's physiological development — particularly the development of his sphincter muscles — it is recommended that parents wait until the child is at least two years old before attempting toilet training.

179. (E) In the repeated-measures (test-retest) experimental design, a subject acts as his own control.

180. (B) Because the mean is extremely sensitive to divergent scores, the median is a more representative measure in the situation described.

181. (C) The median, or 50th percentile, of the score distribution is 61.8 (in effect, 12/28 of the way into the middle interval of 61-63).

182. (D) The mode is the midpoint of the most frequently occurring interval, in this case 62.

183. (B) The 40th-percentile — the point in the distribution where 40 percent of the scores are less than or equal to that point — is approximately 61.

184. (B) The mean (average score) most closely approximates 61.

185. (D) The ectoderm is the center of activity for development of the hair and nails.

186. (C) Developmental psychology views disobedience of the young child in the context of frustration and unhappiness.

187. (B) Anoxia refers to interruption of the oxygen supply to the brain — a cause of death among newborns.

188. (A) *Circadian* refers to the cyclic daily body rhythms of activity and repose — a special problem for air travelers crossing several different time zones in close succession.

189. (B) Experiments with newborns suggest the presence of pattern discrimination.

190. (D) An aptitude test is best and most timely if it measures the person's capabilities on position-related tasks.

191. (E) From the standpoint of dependence on perceptual cues, the most dangerous point for commercial pilots during night flight is the moment of runway approach.

192. (B) Human engineers have found that shape coding is extremely important in airplane cockpit design. A common shape for different function knobs could cause confusion and possibly fatal accidents.

193. (A) This person has scored one standard deviation above the mean — at approximately the 84th percentile. None of the others has scored at the one-standard-deviation-above-mean level.

194. (E) This person has scored only a half standard deviation above the mean, while all the other persons have scored at least a two-thirds standard deviation above the mean.

195. (E) This score of a half standard deviation above the mean would be expressed by a z-score of +.50.

196. (D) The size of the standard deviation is indicative of score variability. The largest standard deviation is 40.

197. (D) Content validity relates to a test's capacity to measure the type of information mastery it was designed to measure.

198. (D) The Army Alpha was the first group-administered test of intelligence developed by the Army. It was developed by Yerkes in 1921.

199. (C) There is strong positive correlation between likelihood of behavioral change and amount of cognitive dissonance.

200. (C) In human engineering, one of the control principles states that the direction of movement on any control should be compatible with the effects produced. Therefore, turning a steering wheel counterclockwise to achieve a right turn would be a case of incompatibility.

Test 5: Evaluating Your Score

Abbreviation Guide

PC	Physiological/Comparative
SnP	Sensation/Perception
LM	Learning/Motivation/Emotion
CHL	Cognition/Complex Human Learning
D	Developmental
PrS	Personality/Social
PyCl	Psychopathology/Clinical
M	Methodology
Ap	Applied

Subject Area Chart

Use this chart to determine the subject matter covered by each question in Test 5.

1.	PyCl	16.	PC	31.	PrS	46.	SnP	61.	PC
2.	PyCl	17.	SnP	32.	PrS	47.	SnP	62.	PC
3.	PyCl	18.	LM	33.	PrS	48.	LM	63.	LM
4.	PyCl	19.	LM	34.	PrS	49.	PC	64.	D
5.	PyCl	20.	PC	35.	SnP	50.	PC	65.	CHL
6.	PC	21.	PC	36.	PC	51.	SnP	66.	CHL
7.	LM	22.	SnP	37.	SnP	52.	SnP	67.	M
8.	LM	23.	PC	38.	PC	53.	SnP	68.	M
9.	M	24.	SnP	39.	LM	54.	SnP	69.	LM
10.	M	25.	SnP	40.	SnP	55.	PC	70.	LM
11.	M	26.	SnP	41.	PC	56.	PC	71.	D
12.	M	27.	SnP	42.	LM	57.	PC	72.	D
13.	SnP	28.	LM	43.	PC	58.	PC	73.	D
14.	LM	29.	LM	44.	PC	59.	PC	74.	LM
15.	LM	30.	PrS	45.	PC	60.	PC	75.	CHL

76.	LM	101.	LM	126.	PrS	151.	PrS	176.	M
77.	CHL	102.	CHL	127.	PrS	152.	PyCl	177.	M
78.	Ap	103.	CHL	128.	PrS	153.	PyCl	178.	Ap
79.	Ap	104.	LM	129.	PrS	154.	PyCl	179.	Ap
80.	Ap	105.	M	130.	PrS	155.	PyCl	180.	Ap
81.	Ap	106.	M	131.	PrS	156.	PyCl	181.	M
82.	Ap	107.	M	132.	Ap	157.	PC	182.	M
83.	D	108.	D	133.	SnP	158.	PC	183.	M
84.	D	109.	D	134.	PrS	159.	LM	184.	M
85.	D	110.	D	135.	PrS	160.	SnP	185.	D
86.	D	111.	CHL	136.	PrS	161.	SnP	186.	D
87.	D	112.	LM	137.	SnP	162.	PyCl	187.	D
88.	D	113.	Ap	138.	PC	163.	PyCl	188.	D
89.	CHL	114.	LM	139.	LM	164.	PyCl	189.	D
90.	CHL	115.	D	140.	SnP	165.	PyCl	190.	Ap
91.	D	116.	CHL	141.	SnP	166.	PyCl	191.	Ap
92.	D	117.	CHL	142.	Ap	167.	PyCl	192.	Ap
93.	CHL	118.	CHL	143.	Ap	168.	PyCl	193.	M
94.	D	119.	CHL	144.	PrS	169.	PyCl	194.	M
95.	D	120.	CHL	145.	PrS	170.	PyCl	195.	M
96.	D	121.	LM	146.	PrS	171.	PyCl	196.	M
97.	CHL	122.	CHL	147.	PrS	172.	PyCl	197.	M
98.	CHL	123.	CHL	148.	PrS	173.	PyCl	198.	Ap
99.	CHL	124.	LM	149.	PrS	174.	M	199.	Ap
100.	D	125.	PrS	150.	PrS	175.	M	200.	Ap

Record the number of questions you missed in each subject area.

PC —   CHL —   PyCl —
SnP—   D   —   M   —
LM —   PrS —   Ap   —

Test Score Scale

The first number given is the number of questions in the test in that subject area. The number in parentheses indicates the 75th percentile score. To determine how well you scored in each subject area, subtract the number of questions you missed in a certain area from the total number of questions in that area. Compare the result with the 75th percentile number. If it is lower than 75%, you probably need more review.

PC —24(19)   CHL —20(15)   PyCl —22(18)
SnP —22(18)   D   —25(20)   M   —22(18)
LM —24(19)   PrS —23(18)   Ap   —18(14)

Writing The Psychology Paper

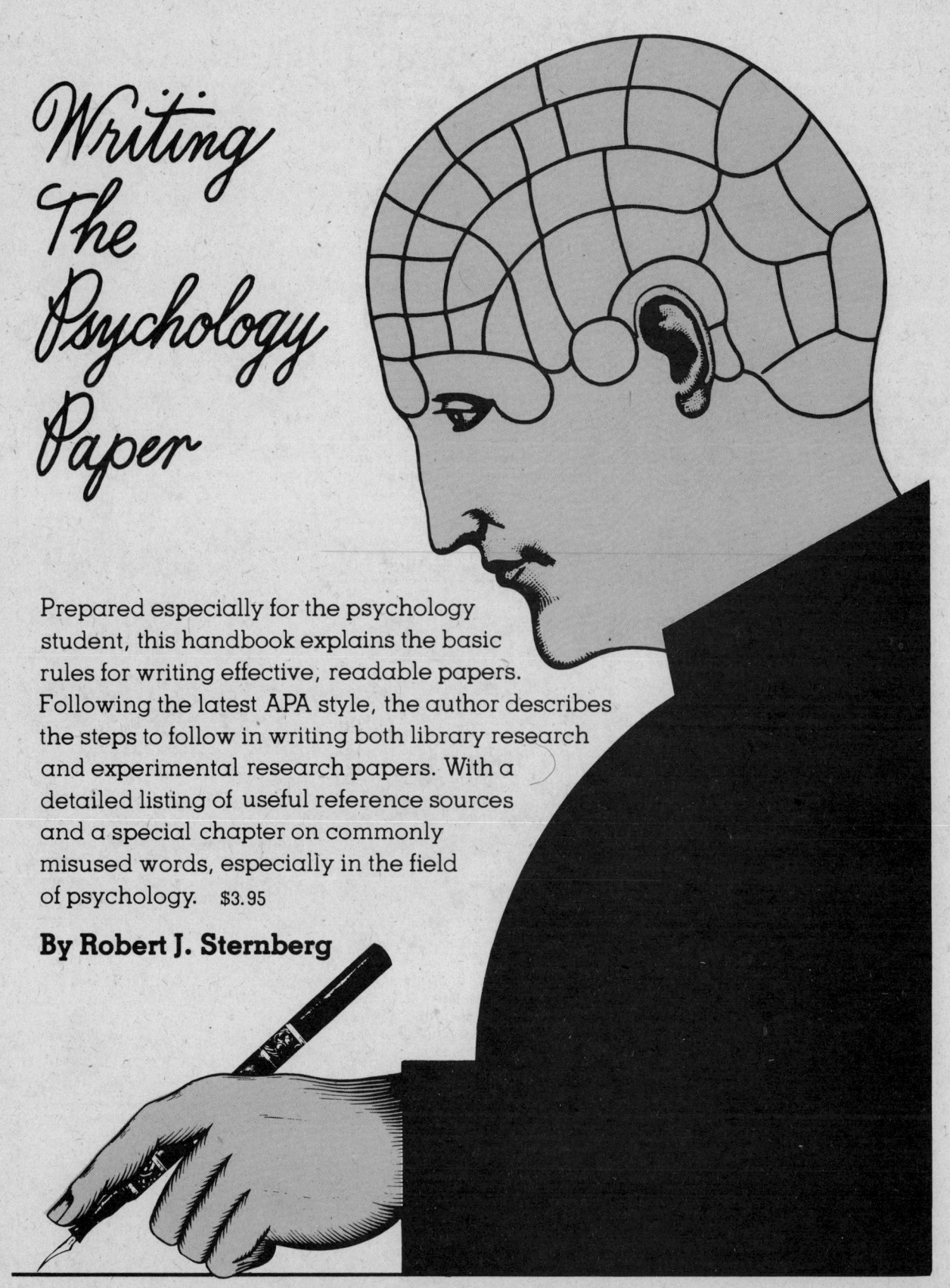

Prepared especially for the psychology student, this handbook explains the basic rules for writing effective, readable papers. Following the latest APA style, the author describes the steps to follow in writing both library research and experimental research papers. With a detailed listing of useful reference sources and a special chapter on commonly misused words, especially in the field of psychology. $3.95

By Robert J. Sternberg

Barron's Educational Series, Inc.
At your local bookseller or use order form on next page.

Descriptions of master's and doctoral programs. Data provides department enrollment, faculty make-up, publications, admissions and degree requirements, financial aid provisions, and other pertinent information. $6.95

A concise look at Freud's discoveries, theories, methods, and innovations; current applications in psychotherapy. An effective study guide and supplementary college text. $2.50

Covers the history, philosophy, and literature of the existentialist movement; with selections from Sartre, Camus, Pinter, Albee, Beckett, and others. $3.75

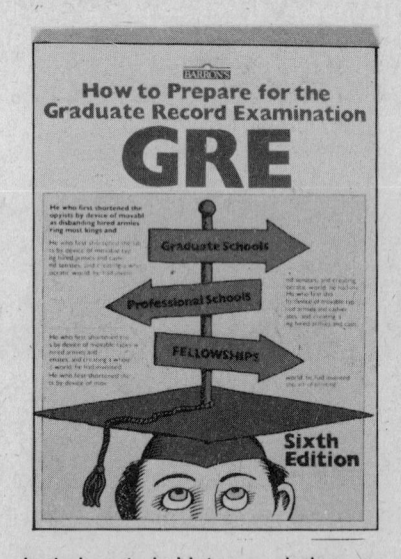

Includes study hints; vocabulary review, word relationships, sentence completion and reading comprehension, and a thorough study of mathematics with emphasis on interpretation of data. $7.95

BARRON'S EDUCATIONAL SERIES, INC. 113 Crossways Park Drive, Woodbury, N.Y. 11797

_____ Writing the Psychology Paper, $3.95
_____ Guide to Graduate Schools, Social Sciences/Psychology, $6.95
_____ Freud and Modern Psychoanalysis, $2.50
_____ Existentialism, $3.75
_____ How to Prepare for the Graduate Record Examination, $7.95
_____ How to Prepare for the Miller Analogies Test, $4.50

I am enclosing a check for $_____ which includes applicable sales tax plus 10% transportation charges. Prices subject to change without notice.

Name _____
Address _____
City _____
State _____ Zip _____

Barron's How to Prepare for the
MAT
Miller Analogies Test · Third Edition
The Only MAT Study Guide with 10 Practice Tests Plus a Diagnostic Pretest

Build confidence through practice on the 10 model tests
Use the Diagnostic Pretest to assess your strengths and weaknesses
Work with more than 1100 sample MAT analogies
Reinforce your skill by studying the detailed answer explanations

NEW FEATURE: A chapter on the Doppelt Mathematical Reasoning Test (DMRT), with current information, a practice test modeled after the actual exam, and explained answers.

$4.50

At your local bookseller or order direct adding 10% postage plus applicable sales tax.

NOTES

NOTES

NOTES

NOTES